CW00952062

A History of Ship Launches and Their Ceremonies

To Sarah

A History of Ship Launches and Their Ceremonies

with thanks and best wishes

Gene

George Hodgkinson

PEN & SWORD
TRANSPORT
AN IMPRINT OF PEN & SWORD BOOKS LTD.
YORKSHIRE – PHILADELPHIA

First published in Great Britain in 2023 by
Pen and Sword Transport
An imprint of
Pen & Sword Books Ltd.
Yorkshire - Philadelphia

Copyright © George Hodgkinson, 2023

ISBN 9781399049450

The right of George Hodgkinson to be identified as author of this work has been
asserted by him in accordance with the Copyright, Designs and Patents Act 1988.

A CIP catalogue record for this book is available from the British Library.

All rights reserved. No part of this book may be reproduced or transmitted in
any form or by any means, electronic or mechanical including photocopying,
recording or by any information storage and retrieval system,
without permission from the Publisher in writing.

Typeset in INDIA by IMPEC eSolutions
Printed and bound in England by CPI Group (UK) Ltd, Croydon CR0 4YY.

Pen & Sword Books Ltd incorporates the imprints of Pen & Sword Books
Archaeology, Atlas, Aviation, Battleground, Discovery, Family History, History,
Maritime, Military, Naval, Politics, Railways, Select, Transport, True Crime,
Fiction, Frontline Books, Leo Cooper, Praetorian Press, Seaforth Publishing,
Wharncliffe and White Owl.

For a complete list of Pen & Sword titles please contact

PEN & SWORD BOOKS LIMITED
47 Church Street, Barnsley, South Yorkshire, S70 2AS, England
E-mail: enquiries@pen-and-sword.co.uk
Website: www.pen-and-sword.co.uk

or

PEN AND SWORD BOOKS
1950 Lawrence Rd, Havertown, PA 19083, USA
E-mail: Uspen-and-sword@casematepublishers.com
Website: www.penandswordbooks.com

This book is dedicated to my darling wife, Sarah, who sadly passed away before it was published, but without whose constant encouragement and support it would never have happened.

Disclaimer

Every effort has been made by the author to contact copyright holders but in some cases this has not been possible. If any of these parties contact Pen and Sword Books Limited, they will be happy to correct omissions in future editions.

Contents

Introduction

This book has been inspired by the author's great privilege to have attended some fifty ship launches or ship-naming ceremonies in different countries. His thirst to learn more about the origin of the rituals performed on such occasions resulted in extensive research, which is shared in this book. The evolution of different launching methods down the ages and incidents when the launch did not go to plan are recalled but a main theme of the book is launch rituals. Down history man has been performing rituals at the launch of a new ship to seek supernatural or divine protection for his new ship and those who will sail in her. The form varies from one country to another, according to local custom or religion, but the sentiment that lies behind all launching rituals is fear. At the moment of launching, a new seafarer is anxious and alert to any sign that his ship is not sound. He is superstitious and seeks reassurance that his ship and those who will sail in her will be protected. This book seeks to throw greater light on these rituals and to examine the evolution of the now universally practised custom of inviting a lady, the ship's sponsor or godmother, to break a bottle of wine against the bow of a new ship at its launch.

List of Illustrations

1. Bow first launch, Arsenal of Toulon, using capstan and pulley system, Album de Colbert 1670
2. Buckler's Hard, private shipyard on Beaulieu river, site of eighteenth century launching slip
3. Bow first launch of polytherme cargo ship *Ivondro*, CAF, Dunkirk, 27 September 1968
4. Side launch of SS *Lake Fernando*, Buffalo Dry Dock Company, Lake Erie 1919
5. Side launch of liner *Homeric*, Papenburg, seen from opposite bank, 28 September 1985
6. Side launch of liner *Homeric*, Papenburg, aerial photo, 28 September 1985
7. Launch over rollers consisting of vulcanised rubber airbags, Shandong, China 2012
8. Launch of RMS *Titanic*, Harland & Wolff, Belfast, 31 May 1911
9. Launch of HMS *Formidable* 17 August 1939 – collapse of forepoppet (seen from stand)
10. Launch of HMS *Formidable* 17 August 1939 – collapse of forepoppet (towards stand)
11. Tragic capsize at launch of SS *Daphne*, river Clyde, 3 July 1883
12. SS *Principessa Jolanda* heeling to port after launch, Italy, 22 September 1907
13. Launch of SS *Great Eastern* 1857 I.K. Brunel and three assistants on launching platform
14. Launch of SS *Great Eastern*, 5 December 1857 at Milwall, sideways to the river Thames
15. Launch of RMS *Mauretania*, river Tyne, 20 September 1906
16. Damage to SY *Turbinia*, following unchecked launch of MV *Crosby*, river Tyne, 11 January 1907

Chapter 1

A Ship is Born

A typical launch

All eyes were on the vast bow towering above them on the launch way. The palpable excitement had begun a second or two before. Below the bow on the launching platform stood a lady, the ship's 'godmother' – a title adopted from the Christian religious ceremony for the baptism of infants. As befitted this important occasion, she was dressed elegantly and sporting a broad-brimmed festive hat. Without revealing the nervousness she was feeling, she proclaimed in a clear voice: 'I name this ship … success to her and all who sail in her!'; and immediately thereafter she pulled a lever that caused a bottle of champagne, tied in multi-coloured ribbon, to smash against the bow.

She had rehearsed this moment a thousand times in her mind since she had unexpectedly received the invitation that she was to have the honour of naming this ship. The sound of splintering glass, as the bottle smashed against the metal hull, was joy to her ears. Loud applause and praise from all the spectators greeted her successful breaking of the bottle – at the first attempt too – a good omen! The order had simultaneously been given to knock away the last blocks holding the hull in place on the launch way.

All eyes now took in the full length of the gigantic hull from the bow at the top of the launch way down to the stern by the water's edge. The hull was dressed overall with multicoloured flags, which fluttered gently in the breeze. What majesty! Here was the hull in all its glory, waiting to be launched!

This was the critical moment. In a few seconds the hull, the product of man's science and endeavour, was about to be put to the test in water for the first time. On the launching platform, decorated with flowers, standing next to the godmother, was the managing director of the shipyard. He whispered: 'We have been planning for this moment since the order was placed; but when it comes to launch no rehearsal is possible.' Even for a professional naval architect who has put hours of forethought, care and his great experience into the construction of the ship and the meticulous planning of the launch, there is still that small moment of anxiety. Everything must go right first time. Once the launch is commenced it is too late to make any corrections. At that moment the hull is beyond the shipbuilder's control. The same anxious moment is felt by every shipbuilder as his creation moves down the launch way. The responsibility for a safe launch is his. In the short interval between the end of the naming ceremony and the entry of the hull in the water, all that the shipbuilder can do is to await events and pray that the launch will go well.

The hammers thudded on the blocks. It seemed she would never move. All waited and watched, intently. Then a cry: 'She's off!'

Yes! The hull was moving! Slowly but now gathering pace. As the drag chains – which would slow the velocity once the hull was in the water – rattled with the movement, dust rose into the air and there were a few sparks from the friction; and, with the hull grating on the launch way, the noise, first a low growl and now a loud roar, reached a crescendo – and the human tumult witnessing the event joined the cacophony of sounds – as with an ever increasing speed that brought the heart to the mouth, the hull moved down the launch way.

'She's in!' 'She's in!'

The stern entered the water with a huge splash. Great clapping; some hats were waved in the air amidst ringing cheers; and a sustained blast from the sirens and horns on the other ships in the harbour greeted the new arrival and celebrated the successful launch. As soon as the hull was waterborne, the drag chains attached to the shore pulled tight and slowed down the speed of the hull across the dock. Two tugs bustled around the bow and flanks to nose the hull alongside the fitting out berth.

A new ship had been born! The builder's house flag fluttered proudly on the flagstaff above the launching platform! For the men who built her the moment when the hull ceases to be just a hull number and is floating on the waves with a name is a moment of special satisfaction.

A perfect launch! The managing director of the shipyard allowed himself a quiet smile of satisfaction. It had gone well. Congratulations all round on the launching platform: to the godmother for successfully naming the ship in such a distinguished manner and bringing her good luck, to the managing director of the shipyard for a smooth and successful launch, and to the proud owner on the latest addition to his fleet.

'I had never realised the intense excitement of the actual moment of the launching,' gasped a lady spectator, suddenly feeling quite breathless.

'An unforgettable experience!' cried another.

What a spectacle! Even for those who had witnessed a ship launch before, this was a profoundly moving moment. The thrill of seeing a ship go down the ways loses little of its interest by repetition. Nothing had been left to chance, nothing could have been done better. The crowd buzzed with animated approval; and more cheering and clapping – an event not to have been missed.

From the time of the release of the blocks to the hull being stopped in the water barely a minute had passed, but the potential for damage in that short journey from land into water is greater than at any time during the ship's life at sea.

This account of a ship launch is fictionalised but reflects a typical stern-first launch down a launch way. The other accounts of ship launches in this book are, unless stated otherwise, factual with the source annotated in the end notes.

'She' or 'it'

Prior to launch the hull on the launch way simply had the builder's hull number. It was an 'it'. Now the godmother had given the hull a name. On entering the water the hull had become a ship with a name and in most countries, ship being a feminine noun, it had become a 'her'.[1]

Launch is not simply the transfer of an object from land to water, it also symbolically marks the moment the inanimate object acquires many of the properties of a living thing, feminine in gender and with a name. The ancient Greeks gave ships feminine names[2] – a tradition that has continued in many countries. She now had her own personality, her own name, and character. 'This [launch] ceremony is unique in our society ... in that it symbolically brings to life an artefact! ... It is the role of the sponsor,' usually, but not invariably, known as the godmother for merchant ships, to 'exercise her mystical powers to imbue the ship with luck and life by naming her in strict adherence to the ritual detail: the bottle must move, the ship begin to move, the name (the generator of the luck and life) pronounced – all at the same moment. Anything else augurs bad luck for the ship.'[3] For this to happen the launching arrangements of the shipyard and the actions of the godmother must be carefully co-ordinated. This does not always happen.

Into this already complex mix of physical transit of the hull from land to water and metamorphosis from inanimate object to fictive female person, there must be added two further elements – superstition and, in some countries, religion. It is well known that sailors of whatever nationality are superstitious. The ever present dangers of life at sea and the self-evident fact that the ship represents for the sailors who sail in her their security increases their sensitivity that this should be a lucky ship. Anything which at launch might indicate otherwise is of concern.

In Catholic countries a blessing by a priest of the ship and those who are to sail in her, often including secular features from the christening of infants, has been part of the launch ceremony for many centuries. In protestant England, however, it was not until 1875 that a religious service formed part of the launching ceremony of naval ships. In other countries the ceremonies vary according to local religion and tradition but at the heart of all launching ceremonies is fear – fear of the force of nature, fear of the unknown and an invocation to a deity or the supernatural for the safety of the ship and the welfare of those who will entrust their lives to her. Even in today's highly technological age, sailors are conscious that man and his ship are at the mercy of the elements. They are superstitious, too.

Despite all the planning that goes into launching arrangements, there remains anxiety at the moment just before the launch, and not just for the shipbuilder. This is described by Mr J. Barker in a sermon given in Deptford in 1810 shortly after the launch of the 110-gun first rate HMS *Queen Charlotte*:

She moves; and all the hearts of the spectators are moved with her. What solemnity; what concern; what solicitude is depicted on the countenances of the gazing thousands! But she enters the watery element; enters slowly but safely and majestically.

The acclamations are attended however with no small degree of anxiety, in some, respecting her future destiny. And have not some parents felt an anxiety somewhat similar, though superior, at the birth of a child ...[4]

There are some obvious parallels between the 'birth' of a ship at launch and the birth of a child. The dangers, the risks, the anxiety, the impossibility of a dress rehearsal, the excitement and the final drama at launch or at birth are in common. That is where the similarities end. A child is christened after birth; a ship is sometimes given its name before launch, sometimes after launch. The giving of a name to a ship is often referred to as its 'christening', but this is in reality a misnomer. The baptism of a child in the Christian world involves the giving of a sign that the child belongs to Christ and from this is derived 'christening' of children, the ceremony associated with infant baptism. However, for a ship, although it is often blessed there can be no baptism in the sense of the giving of a sign that the ship belongs to Christ. Nonetheless the expression 'christening of ships' has endured as meaning the ceremony at which a ship is given its name. The last significant difference is this: a ship launch is frequently a public spectacle; the birth of a child, unless it is a royal birth, rather more private!

In some jurisdictions, as from launch, a ship acquires a separate legal personality. This is so in the United States of America [USA]:

A ship is born when she is launched, and lives so long as her identity is preserved. Prior to her launching she is a mere congeries of wood and iron-an ordinary piece of personal property ... In the baptism of launching she receives her name, and from the moment her keel touches the water she is transformed, and becomes a subject of admiralty jurisdiction. She acquires a personality of her own; becomes competent to contract, and is individually liable for obligations, upon which she may sue in the name of her owner and be sued in her own name ... she is capable too of committing a tort and is responsible for damages therefor ...[5]

'Launch' defined

'Launching' a ship is 'To cause a (vessel) to move or slide from the land, or the stocks, into the water; to set afloat; to lower a (boat) into the water'.[6] This definition encompasses the very first float up by Noah's Ark as well as the more traditional movement down a slipway into the water. The essence of 'launch' is that a ship built on land is set afloat by one means or another. Adopting this definition in this book, float off or up of a hull or the floating up and out of a newly constructed ship from a tidal dock or a covered construction dock is as much a 'launch' as its movement down a slipway into the water, whether it be bow first or stern first or sideways from a ramp.

This book is not a technical manual on how to calculate the required declivity of the launch ways, or the speed of launch, or what weight of drag chains will be needed to slow down the launched hull after it enters the water. These are matters for a naval architect. That said, a few technical terms have unavoidably been used and, for a better understanding of these, a Glossary is included.

Rather, this book is an account of some of the rich rituals and traditions which have accompanied ship launches and naming ceremonies down the ages.

Chapter 2

A Ship's Shortest Trip[1] – Launching methods

Whe Noah constructed his Ark all those centuries ago he faced
a problem that continues to challenge builders of ships in
more modern times: how to find a practical but safe method
of transferring a large ship, built on land, into water.

Noah's float up

In Noah's case he just waited for the rains to fall and, as the flood waters
rose, his Ark became buoyant of its own accord. It was the first float up!
This simple but effective method of launch used by Noah has ironically
now become the most popular method for launching ships built in the
covered construction halls of the modern shipyard; the entrance to the
construction hall is opened and the dock of the covered yard is flooded,
enabling a hull or even a completed ship to be floated up and out. To leave
it there, however, would be to skip over centuries of shipbuilding history
during which different launch methods have been tried, not always with
the same degree of success.

Before passing on from Noah and his float up of the Ark, mention
should be made of a spectacular recent example of the float up method
used to launch the new 65,000-ton aircraft carrier HMS *Queen Elizabeth*,
christened by Queen Elizabeth II on 4 July 2014. The new carrier was
assembled in a dry dock at Rosyth Dockyard in Fife, Scotland, from
components constructed by shipyards across the United Kingdom.
She and her sister ship HMS *Prince of Wales* are currently the largest
warships ever constructed in the UK. HMS *Queen Elizabeth* was named
in the dockyard at Rosyth with no water in the dock, but a bottle of Islay
malt whisky was smashed against her hull. It was some thirteen days after
the spectacular naming ceremony that the cavernous dock was flooded.
This operation took a mere two days, unlike the forty days and nights

of rain experienced by Noah in the Biblical story, but the result was the same: a successful launch.

Runway of wooden poles

If Noah's Ark was the first float up, one of the first launches to be mentioned in literature must be the one described in the Epic of Gilgamesh. In this narrative poem, thought to be from 2100 BC from ancient Mesopotamia, there is described in Tablet XI the building and launch of a ship: 'When the boat was finished, the launching was very difficult. A runway of poles was used to slide the boat into the water.'[2]

Of significance is the fact that the launch was effected, as some translators of the ancient tablet suggest, over a runway of poles used to slide the hull into the water, a method that was to be followed centuries later in ancient Greece with the use of wooden rollers and by the Vikings after them.

Seafaring was an important part of life in ancient Greece and Rome, but there are surprisingly rather few passages in ancient Greek and Latin literature that describe shipbuilding and ship launches. However, the apparent lack of literary sources is compensated by the exciting underwater archaeological discoveries made recently by, for example, the Danish Institute at Athens. These have added considerably to our knowledge of the shipsheds and of slipways generally in Piraeus in the fifth century BC:[3] but before we come to that period we should not forget earlier launching methods.

By manpower down the beach

In the books of Homer there are references to boats being launched; the ancient Greek word *kateruo*[4] used to effect a 'launch' having the technical meaning of drawing or hauling down to water or 'the glorious sea', as Homer colourfully describes it; and, as such, is descriptive of the principal launching method used. Boats were literally dragged by manpower up and down the beach between voyages; but trenches or runways were evidently also dug to receive their keels and facilitate the process. Heaps of stones were built up on either side of the boat to act as shores and these needed to be cleared before a launch.

Rollers

The use of poles in effecting a launch that, as noted, may have been used as early as 2100 BC in Babylonia was reflected in the use of rollers, which are clearly mentioned by Apollonius writing in the third century BC. A Greek epic poet from Rhodes, he gives a colourful description of the launch of the Argonauts' ship in the Argonautica – the story of Jason and the Argonauts and their quest for the golden fleece:

> They dug a downward slope in front of the stem and set smooth rollers in place in the trench. They tipped the boat down on the first rollers so that she might slip and be carried along by them. Above, they reversed their oars on either side and bound them projecting a cubit's length to the thole pins. The heroes stood on both sides in a line and pushed with hands and chest together, and ... bending to it with all their strength they moved the ship from its stocks and, straining with their feet, forced her onward ... they cried from either side as they rushed along. The rollers groaned with the friction beneath the strong keel, and around them thick smoke arose because of the weight, but she slipped down into the sea.[5]

Although Apollonius was a Homeric scholar, we cannot be certain as to what period the launch method he describes should properly be attributed. What we can deduce is that in ancient Greece rollers were used and also sometimes oars to lever a ship into the water; and there is ongoing debate among scholars as to when wooden sleepers started to be used to facilitate launching. This is where the exciting archaeological evidence from the recent underwater surveys in Piraeus comes in.

Slipways with wooden sleepers

In 483–482 BC, with Persia's army and navy gathering, Themistocles persuaded his fellow Athenians to use a rich strike of silver from the mines at Lourion to finance the building of a large fleet of triremes. This decision was the foundation of Athens' naval power. The wisdom of this policy was soon put to the test when the Persian and Greek allied fleets met at the battle of Salamis in 480 BC, resulting in a famous victory for the Athenians and their allies. These ships, in order to be swift, were of light wooden construction but were vulnerable to deterioration from sun and rain. In addition, if left in salt water, the timbers would be susceptible to damage by the aggressive ship worm, the Teredo Navalis. The delicacy of the construction of the trireme and the large investment in this fleet made it necessary that the ships, when not in use, should be protected carefully. This led to the construction of the so called 'shipsheds' where the triremes could be hauled up, stored and repaired but be ready to be deployed again at short notice. They became as necessary to the maintenance of Athens' sea power as the triremes themselves. The general appearance of the shipsheds would have been of a continuous line of narrow hangars sloping down into the water.

The triremes, after being deployed, would be retrieved and returned to store in these sheds. Archaeological surveys have found these sheds had tiled roofs and ramps dug into the rock as a base for transverse wooden sleepers along which the ships slid during launching and retrieval. The ships were hauled up the slipway stern first until they were completely out of the water and under the cover of the sheds. The bow at the lower end pointing to the water meant that relaunching would be easier. 'No remains of hauling gear have yet been found at the top of the slipways … so we must assume that the ships were manhandled up the slipways …'[6] Since the triremes were state property and only in the temporary custody of individual trierarchs,[7] it is understandable that every care should be taken of them when being hauled in and out of the water. They were essential to the security of Athens. The dimensions of the shipsheds give guidance as to the likely dimensions of the triremes, which are thought to have been 35m long and 5m wide, so as not to fit too tightly into the sheds.

The life of a trireme is estimated to have been about twenty years, so there must have been shipbuilding facilities to renew the fleet, but there is at present a lack of archaeological evidence. The discovery by the Danish Institute at Athens of inclined slipways or ramps using transverse timber sleepers to support keels – so as to facilitate hauling and slipping operations – is a remarkable statement about the advanced technology for ship handling being practised by the Athenians in the fifth century BC. The same slipway method used for retrieval and relaunching of triremes out of the shipsheds would presumably have been available for the launch of a newly constructed ship.

Pulleys and Archimedes' invention of the windlass

The invention of a windlass and its use in assisting with a ship launch is widely attributed to Archimedes.[8] The story runs that in the third century BC Archimedes demonstrated to King Hieron II of Syracuse the use of a fulcrum pulley system to launch a 55m ship that had proved impossible to launch by the combined efforts of many men. Archimedes, who had been examining the properties of pulleys and levers, is said to have built a machine which, with a complex system of pulleys, single-handedly allowed him to move back into the water a three-masted ship that had been dragged ashore with immense effort and labour. It was this system which, it is said, enabled Archimedes to launch in about 240 BC the 55m-long *Syracusia*,[9] reputed to be the largest transport ship of antiquity. Whether the story is fact or legend, it does suggest that by this period mathematical thinking in Greece had progressed to a point where pulleys and other mechanical devices were being considered which could assist a launch. Some seventeen hundred years later the same fulcrum pulley system was being used in the naval shipyards of Louis XIV, who had ambitions to build a powerful French navy. The Album of Colbert, written by an unknown author in 1670, has fifty detailed illustrations to describe the various stages of construction in the arsenal at Toulon of an 80-gun man-of – war, including its launch. Illustration No. 1 shows a fulcrum pulley system, which could easily have been employed by Archimedes himself, with gangs of workers hauling on ropes with a fulcrum to gradually pull the immense hull down a slipway into the water, bow first.

In Roman times, again there is little in the literature but Horace, the lyrical poet of the Augustan era, writes that in spring 'the machines drag the dry hulls'.[10] The reference to 'dry hulls' suggests that, as in Athenian times, the ships were, in similar fashion to the Athenian triremes, stored in shipsheds. Scholars think that by this period: 'Ships were manoeuvred onto a sled and kept upright with blocks. The sleds were either fitted with wheels or laid above rollers or boards, and were moved sometimes by a compound pulley, sometimes by a winch.'[11]

Moving north, there is archaeological evidence that the Vikings used wooden rollers to assist with ship launches. Rollers were also used elsewhere on the Continent.

Launching channel

Some ships in the fourteenth century in England were built above water level and launched by pulling them down to the water. In other cases a launching channel was dug from the place of construction to the water's edge and the vessel was pulled down on rollers.

In the reign of Henry V there is evidence that ships were being built in specially dug out building docks. The Accounts and Inventories of William Soper, Keeper of the King's Ships 1422–27,[12] refer, for example, to a royal barge specially commissioned by the King to be built at Southampton as having been launched on 22 October 1416 'from a digging called a dook where she was built onto the water to flute after her making …' This suggests float up and out as the chosen launch method. A much larger ship, perhaps the largest in Europe at that time, was Henry V's *Grace Dieu* of 1,400 tons built by John Hoggekyn, also constructed in a specially built dock in Southampton. These ships were constructed using oak from the King's trees in the New Forest.

Even by Tudor times there were few permanent slipways or dockyards; the places for launch appear to have been chosen fairly randomly and were often dug for a one-off launch and on completion the ships were floated out. There was no permanent workforce of shipwrights, with many workmen being 'pressed in'. Upon his accession to the throne in 1509, King Henry VIII immediately embarked on an expansion of his navy. *Mary Rose* was constructed, most probably in Portsmouth in 1511 but was then sailed round to London for fitting out with her guns. However, during Henry VIII's reign Woolwich and Deptford became important places for shipbuilding on the River Thames, which had the advantage that they were not far from the royal palace at Greenwich, so the King could keep an eye on progress. An example of the fairly random choice of places for launching is the construction of Henry's special ship, the 100-ton *Katherine Pleasaunce* built to carry the King and Queen Catherine of Aragon to the Field of the Cloth of Gold in France in 1520. She was laid down in 1514 and launched in Deptford in the autumn of 1519 or early part of 1520 down a special channel; the creation of this channel apparently involved the partial demolition of a stable to make way for the ship launch! We know this from a statement of account of John Hopton for 2,000 tiles, lathe, lime and nails bought from John Webster of Peckham Rye and stated to be spent 'upon the stabull that was brokyn to make way for the lanchinge of the schipp'.[12] Seven labourers were employed for 27 days 'that laboryd & dygged abowght the seid schip', presumably a channel to launch the ship.[13]

Float out from tidal dock

From the beginning of the sixteenth century Noah's 'float up', or rather a 'float up and out' method of launching, was the method employed in England. Ships were built in excavated tidal docks constructed alongside tidal waters with a wall or dam in place during construction, the tide being used to float off the completed hull at high water. On the Continent, especially in the Mediterranean, where the tide is not so strong, this method was not readily available. However, the 'float up' method had its limitations since the launch of the ship was entirely dependent on the timing and level of the tide. Phineas Pett, Master Shipwright and First Resident Commissioner of Chatham Dockyard, in his autobiography refers to the difficulty of launching a new ship at Deptford in 1610: 'the tide was so bad that the great ship could not be launched out of the dock.'[14] Conversely, if the tide arrives early and is higher than expected, it can cause the ship to launch itself. This occurred on 3 April 1884 with the launch of HMS *Boscawen* at Woolwich Dockyard, when 'an unexpected overflow of the tide ... took the vessel out of their hands and carried her off the slips'.[15]

Tidal docks were the predecessors of the dry dock. As early as 1495 Henry VII constructed a dry dock at Portsmouth for the maintenance of his ships. The dry dock was a great advance since it meant that water could now be emptied from a dock without having to rely upon a suitable tide. By the middle to end of the seventeenth century there were several privately owned dry docks in London.

Invention of the 'cradle'

On the Continent generally, ships were at first laboriously dragged afloat, using manpower but sometimes with the assistance of capstans, tackle and rollers, which sounds like a variation of the Archimedes fulcrum system. However, with the use of a slipway becoming more common, it was appreciated that where a ship was being launched down a slipway the hull needed to be supported and held upright in a so called 'cradle'. The following account written by an Englishman in 1636 is of a cradle being used to launch ships by the Portuguese in Goa, their enclave in India:

> She was launched in a device wherein she was built, called a cradle, which is a world of timber made up and fastened on either side to keep her upright, and so with cables, capstans and a multitude of people they forced her into the water.[16]

It appears that the concept of a 'cradle' was not an invention of the seventeenth century but was known to shipbuilders many centuries earlier in the Hellenistic period. It was mentioned by Athenaeus in his book *Deipnosophistae*, 'The Learned Banqueters'. This book, written in Greek at the end of the second century AD, takes the form of an imaginary erudite dialogue between guests at an extravagant dinner and is of great interest to scholars for the multitude of its literary and historical references. The ship whose launch is described by Athenaeus was a huge showpiece catamaran constructed by King Ptolemy IV, the Macedonian ruler of Egypt, who reigned between 221 and 204 BC. The ship is said to have been 420ft long with a double bow and a double stern, propelled by oars: 'At the beginning it was launched from a kind of a cradle which, they say, was put together from the timbers of fifty-five bank ships and it was pulled to the water by a crowd to the accompaniment of shouts and trumpets.'[17]

Whether the immense ship described by Athenaeus was fact or fiction, what is remarkable is that the concept of using a wooden 'cradle' as a launching device was clearly known in the third century BC. Many centuries later, in the seventeenth and subsequent centuries, the size of the cradle used was gradually reduced and increased in efficiency.

The fore poppet

When a ship is launched stern first down a slipway, there comes a point when the stern starts to lift long before the ship is fully afloat. When the buoyancy of the stern is sufficient it transfers the weight to the extreme fore-end of the hull. This led to the development of the 'fore poppet', a temporary structure, usually made of wood, which supports the bottom of the bow during the slide down the launch ways.

In the period from the Middle Ages up to the nineteenth century launching bow first appears to have been traditional in the Mediterranean, the Low Countries and in Scandinavia, as is evidenced by many paintings and etchings showing vessels under construction head down on the building slip.

In England, where, as noted, shipwrights used the tides to build ships in excavated docks, they let in the water when construction was completed to float them out at high water; and they presumably came out bow first. Such an excavated dock system was not possible in Holland, where the land was already below sea level; and in Mediterranean countries there was not sufficient rise and fall of tide.

Slipways

By the middle of the eighteenth century in the numerous shipyards along the river Thames, it is evident from contemporary paintings and etchings, many of them to be found in the National Maritime Museum, that ship construction was by then conducted not only in tidal dry docks but down slipways. By 1820 onwards many slips were covered, the reason being to protect the timbers of the ship under construction from the weather. Slipways were not always positioned at right angles to the river but sometimes at finer angles across a corner in the river, which had the advantage of providing a longer space in which to stop the launched hull before it reached the far bank, this being particularly beneficial for longer or heavier ships. See Illustration No. 2, which shows the site of a former launching slip at Buckler's Hard on the River Beaulieu where ships for Nelson's navy were constructed.

Bow first or stern first

If a ship had to be hauled ashore for repair this would more easily have been done bow first and after repair it would be relaunched stern first. This may have assisted in the realisation that the initial launch could also be done stern first. Until the advent of the propeller it was mostly a matter of habit or local tradition for the individual shipbuilder whether to launch bow first or stern first. After the introduction of the screw propeller in the middle of the nineteenth century it became expedient to launch stern first in order to avoid undue stress on the foot of the propeller frame in the last second before the weight of the hull becomes fully waterborne. There is the further point that if launched bow first there is a risk of damage to the screw from flotsam from the launching cradle.

Recent example of bow-first launch

These days a bow-first launch is rare, unless there are compelling technical or other reasons that require it. At Ateliers et Chantiers de Dunkerque (CAF) in 1968–69, a lack of construction space was the reason for some unusual bow-first launches. CAF had received an order for a series of eight medium-sized refrigerated ships of similar specification for six different owners. At that time CAF only had two building slips in use and, in order to speed up delivery of the eight ships in the series, it was decided to construct two hulls at the same time on the same slip. The hull on the bottom end of the slip nearest the water was constructed in its full length with its bow facing down to the water. The hull on the upper end of the slip was a half-length stern section only at this stage with its stern facing down the slip, back to back with the stern of the lower hull, which, as explained, had its bow facing down the slip. This was by reason of the fact that the stern section took longer to construct and was, therefore, built first. In the case of the first pair of ships, the *Narval* and the *Fribourg*, the official stand for the launch (without ceremony), bow first, of the lower hull, *Narval*, on 11 April 1969 was set up on the stern of *Fribourg* above it on the slip.[18] A similar procedure was followed for the next three pairs of ships in the series. This resulted in the hull at the bottom end of the slip in each pair being launched bow first. See launch of *Ivondro* in Illustration No. 3.

In the case of a bow-first launch there is the intriguing issue of where the christening bottle is to be broken. This may answer the question why the ships launched bow first were often launched without ceremony, as was the case with *Ivondro* on 27 September 1968.[19]

Covered slips for Russian winter

Further launching challenges occurred in countries such as Russia, where in the nineteenth century the rivers adjoining the shipyards were frequently frozen solid during the winter months and the climate was such that construction of a large battleship in the open air at that time of year was virtually impossible. Fred Jane, who visited the New Admiralty Yard at St Petersburg on the banks of the River Neva, writing in 1899, describes how this problem was overcome:

> A slip in Russia is a much more important thing than in England. It is not possible there to construct a battleship in the open air, as is often done in England. Here not only are the slips enclosed by solidly built stone walls but both end walls are solidly built in also. When the ship is ready for launching the river end is pulled down, to be rebuilt immediately thereafter.[20]

Even this arrangement meant that, while ships could successfully be built under cover in 'cathedral-like' covered slips during the winter months in Russia (see Illustration No. 29), they still could not be launched until the ice melted. This meant that, unlike England where ships after launch were moved to a separate fitting out berth or dock for completion, in Russia ships were frequently launched in an advanced state of construction.

Sideways launch

There is little available evidence on the origin of sideways launching or 'beam-ways' or 'broadside-on' as it is also sometimes called. There are some shipyards where the basin, river or canal next to the shipyard that is used for launching is confined or the water is relatively shallow so that the side-launching method must be used. An interesting early example of sideways launching is to be found at Mangalore in south India, where in 1775 two frigates were launched that way into the river with the assistance of elephants.[21]

A sideways launch subjects the hull to less stress than a stern-first launch but on occasion causes extra stress to the shipwright organising this more technically demanding operation! This is because in a side launch the vessel is required to slide sideways with sufficient velocity to carry it free of the launch ramp into an adjacent body of water. It is important for the shipwright to avoid an uneven launch resulting from either the fore or aft end of the hull moving uncontrolled in advance of the hull's opposite end. If this occurs the hull will move down the launch way in transverse position with the risk of considerable damage being caused by one end of the hull dropping off the launch ramp with the other end still secured in position. A series of heavy drag chains attached to the hull and secured to the launch ramp then restrain the velocity of the hull after it hits the water, so as to prevent it colliding with the opposite side of the basin or river.

The art of side-launching was practised at Collingwood Shipyards, Ontario, from 1901, when the MV *Huronic* was the first steel-hulled ship to be constructed there and the first vessel to be side launched, continuing until closure of the yard in 1986. There the basin was small so that the side-launching method had to be used. The shipwright at Collingwood responsible for cutting the ship loose on the launch day was known as the 'launchmaster'. More than 200 ships constructed at Collingwood were successfully side-launched during the history of the shipyard, with only one serious accident occurring in 1969 when the hull of *Tadoussac* 'broke loose prematurely from her secured position atop the launch ramp and roared down the launchways while the 350-man launch crew scrambled in all directions'.[22] Two lives were lost and more than forty workers injured. 'Officials observing the tell-tale marker at the hull's bow realized that that a serious situation was developing when they detected the vessel's bow moving up the launchways as a result of the stern sliding down toward the launching basin. But there was no time to sound an alarm; disaster was already in progress.'[23] After 1969 the record was flawless. A system was established that in the event of danger to the launch crew the launchmaster activated three portable alarm horns. This was 'a specific signal for the entire launch crew to evacuate the launch site by running in between and parallel to the drag chains'.[24]

Side launches are dramatic; and the launch of SS *Lake Fernando* at Buffalo Dry Dock Co. in 1919 was even more exciting than most (see Illustration No. 4):

> Yesterday afternoon in the presence of a large crowd of spectators the steamer 'LAKE FERNANDO' the last of nine which the Buffalo Dry Dock Co. had a contract to build in the last year was launched successfully. It was the most thrilling launch ever seen at this end of Lake Erie. In fact it was sensational for the launch was from a drop of ten feet five inches.
>
> Every person held her breath as she struck the water on her beam end. She remained on her side for fourteen seconds and that brief interval seemed to the spectators an hour, so tense was the situation. Many thought that the boat would not right herself and it was with a feeling of extreme relief that the new steamer was seen gradually to pick herself up with the back wash and come onto an even keel. For an instant the spectators stood still, and then a tremendous cheer rent the air.[25]

The president of the yard, Edward N. Smith, said:

> It was the highest drop ever launched and she went over further on her side than any boat we ever launched here. There is a question now whether she stuck at an angle of 90 or 100 degrees. It was a launching well worth looking at and we were all well satisfied with the result even if it did give some of our friends a scare.[26]

Side launching was such an exciting spectacle for members of the public in Ontario that a society under the name of The Great Lakes Society for the Preservation of Side Ship Launching[27] was formed. It recognised that the Collingwood Shipyards was the only remaining side-launch location in

Canada and the society actively encouraged the continuance of the practice. The members of the society were issued with certificates recording which side launches they had witnessed. Today, sadly, the buildings at the site of the shipyard at Collingwood have been redeveloped and all that is left to remind us of its great shipbuilding past and the excitement of its side launches is that the road by the harbour has been aptly named Side Launch Way.

Another dramatic sideways launch (see Illustrations 5 and 6) was that of the passenger liner *Homeric* on 28 September 1985, the first luxury liner to be constructed at Meyer Werft at Papenburg in north Germany. As the shipyard reported on its website:

> ... the construction of such a large cruise ship was primarily a technical master stroke ... Up to the construction of the ... roofed building dock, ships in Papenburg were launched sideways. No shipyard in the whole world did ever try to launch a passenger ship the size of the *Homeric* sideways.
>
> On the day of the launching the new construction with yard number 610 was still about 40 metres away from the edge of the harbour basin. By means of a cleverly devised system of hydraulic presses the colossus of 16,000 tons was heaved towards the water centimeter by centimeter.
>
> On September 28 1985 there was a great festival mood all around the shipyard. Nobody wanted to miss the event of the century ... At 11.30 o'clock sharp the command was given 'Clip!'. Axe hits rode the air and only a few seconds later the giant ship sided majestically into the water ...[28]

In 1986 Meyer Werft did a spectacular twin sideways launching of two 5,685 gross registered tons (grt) passenger ferries named *Kelimutu* and *Lawit* on the same day for the Republic of Indonesia, one after the other. They had been built on slips.

Since these side launches Meyer Werft has built a large, modern, roofed building dock and ships are no longer launched sideways from a slipway but the dock is simply flooded and the new ship is floated up and out. This has enabled the yard to construct large cruise ships under cover, which are then launched by 'float up' in a very simple and safe method without risk to the hull.

In general, sideways launches are now comparatively rare except where the shipyard has only a confined space in which to put the hull into the water, such as at Barkmeijer Shipyards in Stroobos in the Netherlands, where sideways launches are the norm.

From a spectator's viewpoint, a float up has none of the drama of a sideways launch or even a launch down a slipway.

Vulcanised rubber airbags as rollers

As already noted, the concept of using wooden rollers to assist in a ship launch was well known to the ancient Greeks and the Vikings, but rubber rollers in the form of launching airbags are now the subject of a new and innovative application. They were invented by the Chinese in the 1980s. The bags are manufactured with synthetic cord reinforced layers and then vulcanised. The number of layers are calculated carefully to reach a certain weight bearing, pressure resistant and puncture resistant capacity depending on the different weight and circumstances of the ship being launched; usually more than three layers. Once construction of the hull has been completed on blocks on the slipway, the airbags are inserted uninflated under the keel. Compressed air at the required pressure is then pumped into the air bags, enabling the blocks to be removed and leaving the keel supported on the airbags alone. Usually the slope of the slipway is sufficient to start the launch once the wire ropes holding the hull to the slipway are released, but, if necessary, more air can be put in the airbags under the ship's bow to increase the height of the bow or a push on the hull can be gently applied to commence the roll of the airbags supporting the hull into the water. The key to this launch method is 'careful planning of the forces at play, then gentleness and dexterity'.[29]

These launching airbags have now been tried and tested for several years and are becoming popular with small and medium-sized shipyards in China and South East Asia. See Illustration No. 7. The International Organisation for Standardisation (ISO) has issued guidelines for the methodology for ship launching utilising airbags and these contain a modern definition of 'ship launching', in the context of using airbags to roll the ship into water, as 'conveying a ship from a site to water so that the ship becomes buoyant'.[30]

Using these rubber airbags is a cost-effective launching method and it is believed that the airbags, if properly maintained and cared for, can be used for between seven and fifteen years. The main advantages are seen to be flexibility and the saving in cost for shipyards, which do not need to rebuild launching ways for each new ship. Like the 'float up' method experienced by Noah and now used extensively to launch ships constructed in a modern covered dock, here we have another old launching method – the roller – now having a modern application using vulcanised rubber airbags. *Plus ça change …*

Chapter 3

The Superstition of Sailors

and why a bottle of wine is traditionally smashed against the bow of a ship at its launch.

'These days most people, if asked whether they are superstitious, would probably answer "Not particularly" and do not take superstitions very seriously. At the same time they generally do not flout superstitions unnecessarily and most would walk round a ladder in their path rather than pass under it!'[1]

So what relevance has superstition to ship launches and the tradition of smashing a bottle of wine against the bow of a ship at its launch? The short answer: quite a lot.

The appeasement of the gods – animal sacrifice

In the ancient world, life at sea was inherently dangerous and for a sailor there was no knowing if he would ever return to port. Without any of the modern methods of communication and sophisticated navigational aids, he relied on his own skill and the guidance of the sun, moon and stars but was otherwise at the mercy of wind and weather. In these circumstances, not surprisingly, he looked for and believed in any means that would give him reassurance as to whether it was propitious to set sail and an answer to his fears. For ancient Babylonians, Phoenicians, Greeks – and the Romans after them – fear of the unknown dominated their lives and inspired superstition – and this was particularly so in the minds of sailors. Their interaction with the gods was motivated primarily by fear. They, therefore, developed what they believed were effective ceremonies and rituals to deal with the spirits and assuage their fear. The gods they invoked were different but their fear and their need for reassurance were the same.

A Babylonian narrative dating from the third millennium BC describes the completion of a ship:

Openings to the water I stopped;
I searched for cracks and the wanting parts I fixed;
Three sari of bitumen I poured over the outside;
To the gods I caused oxen to be sacrificed.[2]

On the assumption that the text of this narrative and its date is correct, this is one of the earliest known launching ceremonies. Out of the many gods of the ancient Mesopotamian religion we can imagine that the sailor of Babylon at the launch of his new ship would have wished to propitiate Enlil, the god of wind and weather, Enki the god of seawater, and Utu, later known as Shamash, the god of sun.

The Babylonian seafarers' wish to please the gods through the making of sacrifices before they set out to sea was a rite that was similarly followed by the ancient Phoenicians and Greeks. The Phoenicians, who were a dominant seafaring and trading power in the southern Mediterranean in the period 1200–800 BC, were well known in the ancient world for being superstitious. They imagined themselves being in a world inhabited by supernatural powers and they felt the need to seek protection from the dangers of the deep. Before setting sail and in order to seek a safe passage, they made sacrifices to Baal, the storm god, who controlled the winds – a word that also meant 'master' – and to Melqart, the guardian of Phoenician sailors. The Phoenician ships, which had a horse head image on their prows, were called *hippoi* by the ancient Greeks, meaning horses. This image symbolically placed the ships under the protection of the winged sea horse, which in ancient mythology was the divine companion of several maritime gods pictured riding on such a beast. To appease these deities the Phoenician sailors worshipped their patrons at temples in ports, at isolated shrines on promontories along sea routes as well as on board their ship. The Phoenician ships had sacred areas at the prow or 'poop deck' in the stern for conducting ceremonies and there was a general belief, for the comfort of the fearful sailor, that the ships themselves were imbued with the spirit of a divine guardian to ward off dangers. Similar beliefs and rituals were practised by sailors in the northern Mediterranean in ancient Greece.

The ancient Greeks believed it was necessary to express honour and respect towards the gods and to please them so they would be ready to help them when needed. This was achieved by gifts, hymns and sacrifices.

Before a battle, or before setting sail and committing their ship and themselves to the dangers of the seas, sailors made a blood sacrifice through the ritual slaughter of an animal. The animal was specifically domesticated, most often a sheep, pig or goat. The blood sacrifice was commenced with the participants taking a handful of barley groats from a sacrificial basket and all throwing them forwards towards the altar and the sacrificial animal. After the sacrifice came the pouring of libations, wine being most common but milk, oil or honey were also used. As part of the sacrifice ceremony there was often a 'reading' of the entrails of the sacrificial victim by soothsayers. This was an example of the widely used practice of 'divination' in order to interpret the will of the gods, other methods being observation of birds or so called 'auspices', the oracles and the interpretation of dreams and of omens, being chance or unusual events regarded as significant.

Libations

In ancient Greece no warrior would leave for battle without first offering a libation to the gods. A traditional, but poignant, image painted on many Greek vases is that of the departing warrior depicted in Attic armour extending his *phiale* – a flat and shallow bowl specially used for libations to the gods – to his wife, who lifts her veil and pours from a wine jug called an *oinoche*. So too a sailor, before setting out on a voyage, would invariably offer libations to the gods. In Homer's Odyssey, the mythical figure Telemachus, before he sets sail to Ithaca, is portrayed standing on the shore by the stern of his boat praying and sacrificing to Athene, the goddess of heroic endeavours in Greek mythology, and pouring libations in prayer.[3]

In similar tradition, but without any reference to any animal sacrifice, when the Athenian fleet was ready to sail for Sicily in the year 415 BC, the historian Thucydides records that:

... when the ships were manned and everything had been taken on board which they meant to take with them on the voyage, silence was commanded by the sound of the trumpet, and the customary prayers before putting to sea were offered up, not by each ship separately but by them all together, following the words of the herald. The whole army had wine poured into bowls, and the officers and men made their libations from cups of gold and silver. The crowds on the shore also, the citizens and others who wished well to the expedition, joined together in the prayers. Then when the hymn had been sung and the libations finished, they put to sea ...[4]

A pre-battle ceremony as described, with the enemy just over the horizon, was, of necessity, a much simpler affair.

Although these examples of Telemachus and the Athenian fleet about to set sail to Sicily are not of ship launch ceremonies, they are instructive as to the libations and prayers that it was the common practice for ancient Greek seafarers to perform before setting out on a voyage and are, therefore, indicative of the likely rituals performed at the launch of a new ship in ancient Greece before embarking on its maiden voyage.

A libation was performed by the wine first being mixed with water in large vases, known as *kraters*, poured into *phiale* and then emptied into the sea from the stern of the ship amidst prayers and vows.[5] The making of a libation from the stern of a ship into the sea appears to be the image depicted in a fragment of an Attic vase painting that shows a hand holding a cup used to hold wine for drinking or for ritual use, pouring wine over the stern.[6] Garlands were also thrown into the water from a departing ship in a final act of worship and invocation for the protection of the gods. Then, in Pindar's Fourth Ode about Jason and the Argonauts, written in 466 BC, we find the image of the captain, before he sets sail, standing on the stern of his ship with a golden bowl in his hands calling on the gods for good weather on their voyage and for their homecoming to be fortunate.

Deposition offering

There is also archaeological evidence of the practice of a departing sailor to make a deposition offering into the sea in order to obtain the favour of the powerful sea gods and appease the evil spirits of the deep. At Syracuse at the furthest point of the island of Sicily, when the shield on the temple of Athena was no longer visible from the sea, the sailors had the ritual of throwing a cup into the sea after putting in flowers, honey and lumps of incense and other aromatics.

Virgil, who between 29 and 19 BC wrote the Aeneid – a legendary story of the travels of Aeneas, a Trojan who fled after the fall of Troy – describes the following religious ritual performed by Aeneas before he sets sail, which involves both an animal sacrifice and a deposition offering:

> He orders them to slay three calves to Eryx and a lamb to the Storm – gods, and that the ship's cable be loosed in due order. He himself, with temples bound with the sprig of a cut olive branch as he stands off on the vessel's prow, holds a sacrificial plate and casts entrails upon the briny waves; then he pours out a sacrifice of flowing wine.[7]

The writings of Virgil also tell of garlands being displayed on the stern of a ship at the start of a voyage or on safe return.[8]

Sacrifice by taking human life?

The evidence of blood sacrifice by taking a human life is less substantiated. There are several tales of such actual or threatened sacrifices but little fact. It is told that when a ship was launched by the Vikings it was the custom for victims to be bound to the rollers over which the war galley was run down to the sea,[9] so that the stern was sprinkled with blood. This was called the *hlunn-rod*[10] or 'roller reddening' mentioned in the poetry of the old Northern tongue and remembered in Viking folklore.[11] It is said that such sacrifice took place at a launch of a new canoe or when an important expedition was setting out. Launching of ships across the beach into the sea over rollers is acknowledged as being the normal Viking practice of launching ships but doubts have been expressed over whether this in truth involved human sacrifices.

The gruesome practice of 'roller reddening', if it be fact, is also paralleled in a story from Roman times. Valerius Maximus, in his *Memorable Doings and Sayings*, writes of the Carthaginians launching ships over captured Roman soldiers:

> With the same cruelty they strewed our men who had fallen into their hands in a naval engagement under ships to be crushed by the weight of their keels, satiating their barbarous savagery by the extraordinary manner of their death. With fleets polluted by the foul deed they would violate the very sea.[12]

It is, however, as well to remember that Valerius Maximus was an anecdotalist, not a historian.

Another legend refers to the practice – whether legend or historical fact again we do not know – said to have been employed in the launch of sailing ships in ancient times when a convict equipped only with an axe was instructed to knock down the last block that retained the ship to the land. If he had time to run he was saved; if not, he perished under the keel as it slid down the ways. This legend is recalled in the practice of a ceremonial axe being used in certain countries[13] to symbolically cut the final cord that attaches a newly constructed hull to the land.

Pouring of wine as symbol of blood sacrifice

So the evidence of any rite of human sacrifice at a ship launch in the ancient world appears to be based more on legend than fact; and over time even the Greek and Roman tradition of propitiating the gods through animal blood sacrifice and 'reading of the entrails' was altered in favour of the pouring of red wine over their boats as a symbol of the former rite of blood sacrifice.[14] A libation, a ubiquitous ritual in ancient Greece performed for the sake of the gods to appease them, may be considered as a sufficient act of sacrifice in itself, independent of animal sacrifice.

In the ritual of libation, man pours away something valued by him in an irretrievable act of gift and in recognition of a higher will. It is therefore, reasonable to conclude that it is to the superstitions of the sailors of ancient Greece and Rome and their libations to the gods that, at least indirectly, we owe the origin of the modern ceremony of breaking a bottle of wine over the bows of a ship at its launch.

Standing cup ceremony

The last traces of the ancient rite of consecration of a new ship by blood sacrifice we can find in the 'standing cup' ceremony practised in England from the poop deck of a newly constructed naval ship, most probably since the reign of King Henry VIII[15] and continuing until the seventeenth century. It is described by Phineas Pett, writing in his diary in 1610, as being an 'ancient custom and ceremony performed at such times'.[16] It is to be noted that this ceremony, which was a christening, took place *after* the hull had been launched and the ship had been brought alongside the dock. It was performed by the sovereign or a dignitary appointed by him or her to name the ship ('the personage'). Amidst the sounding of trumpets, part of the wine was drunk by the personage from a ceremonial gilt cup and a toast to the health of the King was drunk. After drinking again from the cup, the personage solemnly announced the name of the new ship, wishing her 'success'.[17] The rest of the wine was thrown forward on the ship's half deck, part to the north, part to the east, part to the south and part to the west, before the gilt cup was thrown overboard. The spilling of the wine can be seen as representing the bloodshed ritual and the throwing of the ceremonial cup into the water recalls the ritualistic deposition in the sea of a cup and other offerings practised by the Phoenicians and the ancient Greeks. One of the editions of the Admiralty Manual of Seamanship suggests that the thinking was that the gilt cup was cast into the sea 'in order to prevent a toast of ill intent being drunk from the same cup',[18] but this interpretation of the ceremony ignores the ancient ritual of sacrifice. The pouring of the wine should be seen as an irretrievable act of renunciation and, therefore, a sacrificial act in its own right.

Commencement of the tradition of breaking a bottle of wine against the bow

With the cup being made of precious metals, with launchings becoming more frequent this 'standing cup' ceremony proved too expensive and disputes inevitably arose over who owned the cup once tossed into the water; and by 1610 the ceremony was altered so that at the end of the ceremony instead of the 'standing cup' being thrown overboard it was formally handed by the sovereign to the Master Shipwright as a gratuity for his service in effecting a successful launch.[19] By the end of the seventeenth century the practice was discontinued and was replaced by the ceremonial breaking of a bottle of wine against the bow before the keel touched the water. Both ceremonies can be seen in some way as symbolic substitutes for blood sacrifice: the pouring out of blood to appease a deity and, finally, the throwing away of the cup as a deposition offering.

The year 1690 is often given as the one in which the 'standing cup' ceremony came to an end and the custom of breaking a bottle against the bow started. Certainly in December 1690 the House of Commons approved expenditure on the construction of twenty-seven new warships, and with so many ships on the slips it is easy to see that the wasted expense of a gilt cup being thrown overboard on each launch would have been called into question. The introduction of the ceremonial bottle-breaking tradition was, therefore, probably in origin a cost-saving measure. It is not certain that the custom of breaking of the bottle started immediately after the 'standing cup' was thrown overboard for the last time. There does not appear to have been any official order for a change and it seems more likely that the two practices co-existed for a period before ceremonial bottle smashing became the norm.

It appears that one of the first records of an English man-of-war being christened over the bow with a bottle of red wine or fortified wine was in a newspaper of 1780 describing the launch of the 64-gun *Magnanime* at the Royal Dockyard in Deptford on 14 October 1780. At much the same time, on 21 October 1797, in Boston there occurred the earliest recorded christening in the United States [US] Navy, when a bottle of Madeira was broken by Captain Sever on the heel of the bowsprit of a frigate, declaring her to be named *Constitution*.[20]

By the beginning of the nineteenth century the custom of breaking a bottle against the bow of a new ship at its launch was evidently well established, being described in one newspaper report of 1802 as 'usual': the East Indiaman *Sir William Bensley* was built at the Stoke Yard at the head of the Orwell estuary by George and Jabez Bayley of Ipswich for the East India Company and the *Suffolk Chronicle* on 27 March 1802 reported that at her launch her prospective commander, Captain Lynch, 'as is usual, broke a bottle of wine over her stem'. That was a launch of a merchantman but the *Naval Chronicle* contains similar reports on the launch of naval ships from that period where a bottle of wine or port was broken against the bow. The report on the launch of HMS *Howe* at Chatham on 28 March 1815 describes the breaking by her sponsor, Lady Torrington, of a bottle of port against the 'cutwater', as being 'agreeable to the ancient mode of christening'.[21]

As we have noted, the 'standing cup' naming ceremony took place after launch with the new ship safely alongside. In the breaking of the bottle ceremony, the breaking of the bottle against the bow was either completed at the instant the keel touched the water or immediately before launch. In the 'standing cup' ceremony wine was drunk from the cup by the sovereign before the rest of the wine was thrown forward across the half deck, with the name of the new ship being solemnly called out and with the cup then being thrown into the sea. There were certain similarities between the 'standing cup' ceremony and the early versions of the bottle-breaking ceremony that suggest that the latter may have evolved from the former. This is illustrated by an account of the launch of HMS *Agamemnon* in 1852:

Mrs Eden, wife of the Commodore Henry Eden, proceeded to the bow of the *Agamemnon*, where a bottle of wine was uncorked and Mrs Eden drank success to the *Agamemnon*. The bottle with the remainder of the wine was then suspended and broken on the bow of the vessel in the usual manner by Mrs Eden, who named her *Agamemnon*. The shipwrights. ... immediately after commenced driving out the blocks ...[22]

It will be observed that Mrs Eden drank wine poured from the ceremonial bottle in much the same way as wine was drunk by the sovereign from the 'standing cup', in each case before the new ship was named by breaking the bottle on the bow 'in the usual manner'. This description supports the theory that the bottle-breaking ceremony evolved from the 'standing cup' ceremony. It has continued to evolve and change. In today's format the sponsor does not get to drink from the ceremonial bottle but the ship is named by the sponsor, followed by a wish or prayer for the new ship and those who will sail in her *before* the bottle is smashed against the bow and the hull is launched.

For sailors living in a dangerous environment in which their ship is their security, it is natural for them to be concerned with any sign that a new ship may be unlucky and will not protect them. Even today it is well known that sailors are superstitious and inclined to trust in magical protection. This is a natural consequence of life at sea. As William Jones has written: 'We should not judge too harshly the credulity of seamen whose isolated occupations and peculiar mode of occupations render them more susceptible of fanciful impressions'.[23] That is why it is so important that the launch and the christening ceremony of a new ship should proceed without any mishap. Of course, in the rare cases where the launch itself demonstrates a physical defect in the ship, this will be self-explanatory; but often the defect is in the performance of the ceremony or the unexpected occurrence of an event during the launch indicating that something is potentially amiss, making it an 'omen', in the sense that would have been readily understood by the Romans. Typically such events include if the ship does not move, or the wine is not spilled, or an accident happens during the launch operation, especially one that results in death or injury.

Death or injury during launch is taken by some as an omen of an unlucky ship

The ill-fated RMS *Titanic* was not christened at her launch by Harland & Wolff. Illustration No. 8 shows her being launched. This was in line with the common practice of White Star Line, which preferred to formally name their ships upon completion rather than at launch.

A popular expression of the shipyard workers in Belfast at that time was 'we just build them and shove them in the water', with no ceremonial bottle being broken on the bow at launch. The launch itself on 31 May 1911 was technically faultless: she took a mere 62 seconds to make her journey down slip No. 2 but the superstitious would point out that she entered the water without being named or having any ceremonial bottle broken against her bow; not a good omen, they would say. In addition, a shipyard worker, James Dobbin, was hit by falling timber during the launch operation. He was dragged clear by his colleagues but sadly died later the same day. A death or injury during launch is taken by some as an omen of an unlucky ship, so a second bad omen. As is well known, on her maiden voyage RMS *Titanic* struck an iceberg in the North Atlantic on 14–15 April 1912 and sank, with more than 1,500 persons tragically losing their lives.

An equally unfortunate incident occurred on the launch of a yacht belonging to Sir Edward Heath, the former British Prime Minister and a very successful ocean racer. In his book *Sailing – A Course of My Life* he describes the launch of his third yacht, *Morning Cloud*:

At the launching on 14 April 1973 an unhappy incident occurred. In the crush of people on the wall alongside the slipway, the wife of one of my crew lost her balance and fell on the concrete below, just as *Morning Cloud* had passed. Suffering badly from concussion, she was rushed off to hospital. 'This will be an unlucky ship', I heard someone nearby mutter.[24]

And unlucky she proved to be. In September 1974, on the way back from Burnham to Cowes, with the owner not at the helm but abroad, two members of the 'movement crew' were swept overboard in rough seas and drowned 'through no fault of the crew' – as the coroner found at the subsequent inquest – and the third *Morning Cloud* itself was wrecked.

'An old sailor once said: "of course there may be nothing in it, but on the other hand when you live in the shadow of death and it costs nothing to take precautions, it is a daring man who breaks taboos and courts disaster"'[25]

A bad omen if the ceremonial bottle does not break

It is said that if the ceremonial bottle fails to break at exactly the right time, the fate of the ship is in doubt. The task of ensuring that the ceremonial bottle smashes the first time is one that has long engaged the attention of shipbuilders. To save embarrassment, filing down or scoring the bottle has been tried but the risk is that the weakened glass will result in the bottle exploding prematurely; if this method is to be used, a reserve bottle should always be on standby. Some shipyards have also used an electric device for breaking the bottle, with the lady sponsor pressing a button to initiate the process. In the case of cargo ships where the bulbous bow, by appropriate ballasting, can be positioned above the waterline for the christening, the ceremonial bottle is frequently attached to an iron rod that at the right moment is released by the godmother to crash down on the bulbous bow, a system that is more or less foolproof. This method is not so readily available for cruise ships, where the bulbous bow is not usually ballasted above the waterline, but a similar system of a christening bottle attached to a rod being brought down against the side of the hull of a cruise ship can often be employed to good effect.

There are many stories from ship launches of the christening bottle not breaking or not breaking first time and of the ship later proving to be unlucky or suffering some misfortune. Here are a few. When you have read them ask yourself the question: can they *all* be brushed aside as mere coincidence?

On 21 June 1898, at the launch of HMS *Albion* at Thames Ironworks, the Duchess of York had three failed attempts to smash the christening bottle against the hull. There were too many spectators standing on a connecting slipway bridge, which had been signposted as dangerous. The ship was launched successfully but a tidal wave created by the ship as it entered the water engulfed the bridge and thirty-four people, mostly women and children, were flung into the water and drowned. The cheers of the crowd celebrating the launch meant that the screams of those in the water were not heard for several minutes, delaying their rescue.

On 27 April 2000 the author was privileged to attend the naming ceremony of P&O's new cruise ship *Aurora* at Southampton. Her Royal

Highness the Princess Royal was the godmother and it was a colourful and memorable occasion. Most unfortunately, the magnum of champagne released by the Princess Royal hit the side of the hull and plunged, still intact, into the water without smashing. On her maiden voyage *Aurora* was forced to limp back to port after breaking down, with a damaged propeller shaft bearing, off the French coast just one day into the cruise. The propeller shaft bearing had overheated.

What is less well known is that on the day after the official naming ceremony, a second unofficial naming of the ship for the ship's company was arranged by the captain. 'All the officers and crew gathered on the dockside as *Aurora* was named again by a cabin stewardess from Romania whose name was fortuitously "Aurora"! This time the bottle broke and everyone gave three cheers for the "Goddess of the Dawn", that is Aurora.[26]. The captain had heard that the failure of the bottle to break the previous day had been of concern to some of his crew, the superstitious among them interpreting it as a sign that the ship would be an unlucky one; and he hastily arranged this second naming ceremony for the ship's company.[27] This suggests that superstition cannot be so readily dismissed as an outmoded phenomenon experienced only by ignorant sailors in the ancient world.

In May 2000 the cruise ship *Costa Concordia* was named by the famous model Eva Herzigova but the bottle of champagne failed to smash. Again, for superstitious nautical types this was a bad augury that unfortunately turned out to be tragically true. On the night of Friday, 13 January 2012 (in itself regarded by some as an unlucky day) the fourteen-deck cruise ship belonging to Costa Cruises rammed into the rocks off Isola del Giglio on the western coast of Italy, gouging a massive tear in her hull. The ship was under the command of Captain Francesco Schettino, who was, allegedly, attempting a 'sail-by' salute. Despite the gradual sinking of the ship, her complete loss of power and her proximity to the shore in calm weather, the order to abandon ship was not given for some time after the initial impact. It was alleged that Captain Schettino himself left the ship while hundreds of passengers struggled to escape. Of the 3,206 passengers and 1,023 crew, thirty-two died. Captain Schettino was prosecuted and sentenced to sixteen years' imprisonment for his role in the incident.

Whether you believe in superstition or not, it is not good news for a company to own a ship that has the reputation of being unlucky. It can make it harder to recruit sailors to serve on her or can damage the reputation of the ship in the eyes of the public and potential charterers. After the failure of the bottle to smash at another christening of a cruise ship in December 2007, this time Cunard's MS *Queen Victoria*, being christened by the then Duchess of Cornwall, Camilla Parker Bowles, P&O decided to take no chances at the naming of its next cruise ship, MV *Ventura*, in April 2008. They recruited a team of Royal Marines to assist. Upon the command of the godmother, Dame Helen Mirren, the Royal Marines abseiled down the side of the ship and successfully smashed, not one, but two christening bottles against the hull![28]

So it is fair to conclude that sailors, even today, are superstitious and reluctant to sail in a ship where it has not been properly christened. The author was present at a naming ceremony in Greece where, once again, the ceremonial bottle did not smash; and a member of the crew immediately seized another bottle and smashed it against the ship's side, so as to ensure that the ship was duly christened before she put to sea. He certainly did not want to serve on an unlucky ship. In Catholic countries it has been frequently said that a ship not blessed by a priest is sure to be an unlucky ship.[29]

It is also supposed to be unlucky for an owner to be on board his ship when it is launched. A tragedy occurred on 5 July 1841 on the sideways launch of the seagoing river boat *John and William* on the River Don at Masbrough. The spectators on board rushed to the river side of the ship as it was launched, curious to get a better view of the boat hitting the water. The boat capsized and sixty-four people, mainly children, drowned. Edwin Cadman, of the buyer, said: 'I was inclined to go aboard but from an impression among the boatmen that it is unlucky for an owner to be on board when a vessel is launched, I was persuaded not to.'[30]

As a result of following that advice Mr Cadman did not flout superstition; and he avoided being caught up in the terrible tragedy at the launch of this boat that was to unfold.

Premature unveiling of name

For others it is believed to be unlucky for the name of the ship to be disclosed before the actual ceremony. For this reason it is quite usual for a shipyard to cover up the name on the bow and the stern with a cloth until the moment when the name is first pronounced by the godmother, whereupon it is simultaneously unveiled.[31]

It is also thought by some to be unlucky to launch a new ship on a Friday, and certainly a Friday the 13th should be avoided.

Change of name

Any delay between naming and launching is thought to bring bad luck for a superstitious builder. A change in the name with which a ship is christened before it enters the water is also a bad omen. Many of these unlucky omens were present in the much-delayed launch of Brunel's SS *Great Eastern*, which is described in some detail in Chapter 6. It is sufficient to note here that there was an accident early in the launch operation that resulted in injury to five workmen, one fatally. Although she was christened *Leviathan*, the name later painted on her bows was *Great Eastern* and she was finally launched eighty-nine days after Brunel first gave the signal to launch. She proved to be an unlucky ship for both Brunel and her owners.

Of course, it is easy to dismiss as pure coincidence any unfortunate incident that occurs to a ship during its launching or christening, or any link between a defect in the performance of the ceremony and a subsequent misfortune after launch. It is equally easy to provide other examples of ships that encountered unlucky omens during launching or naming but which went on to have perfectly successful and uneventful careers. However, what cannot be denied is that for seafarers who work in a dangerous environment, this is not an idle issue. The number and frequency of accidents or other misfortunes suffered by ships during their lives whose launching and christening did not go smoothly adds credence to their beliefs. Why should a seaman venture on board a ship that has been unlucky in its building and launch? Even those of us who are not seafarers, or do not believe in such matters, may at least be prepared to acknowledge that sailors are entitled to take this view.

Chapter 4

Things do not Always go to Plan

Planning the launch

A ship launch has earlier been described as its 'shortest trip', but it is also potentially its most perilous. Launching is an inherently dangerous undertaking. Throughout the construction of a ship no operation is likely to cause the shipbuilder more anxiety or to result in more serious consequences than a major launch failure. The transfer of a heavy ship from land to water involves the serious risk of damage to the hull, of injury to spectators and, if the launch is undertaken in confined waters, of damage to other ships. Almost as soon as the ink has dried on the shipbuilding contract, the shipyard needs to start to plan not just the construction but the launching arrangements. The careful shipbuilder has to consider before construction commences whether the launching slip is sufficiently strong. Any subsequent sagging in the foundation of the slip may cause trouble at the critical moment of launching. Initial stability on launch, the declivity of the launching ways, the balance of the hull on the ways, the material to be used in the ways, the greasing of the ways, the sufficiency of the launching space, the likely velocity down the ways and how the speed of the hull is to be restrained when it enters the water are but a few of the many other vital calculations to be made. As the hull starts to move down the ways, this is the 'moment of truth' when all the calculations and launch arrangements will, in the space of a few seconds, be put to the test. Tank tests of a launch with a model hull are sometimes made to good effect; but on the day of the actual launch there can be no practice-run. Everything must go right first time.

Modern-day ship launches appear to be such a smooth operation that it is easy for the spectator to be unaware of the anxiety that the shipyard and the owner often feel at the moment of launch, even today. Things do go wrong and accidents do unfortunately happen despite all the planning. However, lessons have been learned from the past and most of the incidents mentioned in this chapter are unlikely to occur again today.

Are the dock gates wide enough?

A basic point you may think, but are the gates of the dock where the hull has been constructed wide enough to permit the ship to pass through comfortably and so be launched successfully?

A previously unknown but relevant story relates to the launch of Nelson's famous ship, HMS *Victory*, at Chatham Dockyard in 1765. This was recently uncovered by naval historian Dr Brian Lavery in connection with the 250th anniversary exhibition of the Battle of Trafalgar.

The launch of HMS *Victory* was publicly announced by a 'Launch Notice' in the London *Public Advertiser* on 7 May 1765:

> This day will be launched his Majesty's ship the *Victory*, estimated the largest and finest ship ever built. Several of the Lords of the Admiralty, Commissioners of the Navy and many Persons of Quality and Distinction are expected to be present, for whose receptions great preparations are making through the Town.

Early on the day of the launch, the shipwright in charge of the launch at the Royal Dockyard in Chatham realised to his horror that the hull was too wide to fit through the wooden gates of the dock from which it was to be launched into the River Medway in the presence of many distinguished spectators, including Prime Minister William Pitt. He immediately summoned the help of every available shipwright to chop the frame holding the dock gate to pieces and just cleared enough space for the hull to pass. The launch went ahead.[1]

We can only speculate as to the historical consequences if HMS *Victory* had not been launched successfully that day. However, what the story illustrates very clearly is the importance of getting the basic dimensions right when it comes to launching a ship out of a dock.[2]

To put the story about Nelson's flagship HMS *Victory* and its launch out of the construction dock in Chatham – which nearly wasn't – into a modern context, just imagine what would have happened if Rosyth Dockyard, where the Royal Navy's new aircraft carrier HMS *Queen Elizabeth* was assembled, had suddenly realised that the 932ft long, 240ft wide ship weighing 65,000 tons – of comparable status to HMS *Victory* – was too wide to pass out of the basin into the Firth of Forth. All the measurements were doubtless checked over and over again. The exit was completed with the aid of tugs on 26 June 2017 but there was 'less than 14in clearance on either side of the vessel, and just 20in of water below the keel'.[3] Close enough, one suspects, to have given some anxious moments for the dockyard and those on the bridge of Great Britain's largest warship ever.

Sticking on the launch ways; and the problems of cold weather

Of great importance too is to calculate the correct angle of the launch ways. If the angle is too shallow the risk is that the hull will become stuck on the ways. If the angle is too steep the risk is that the hull will travel too fast, with potential loss of control and the risk of damage to both the hull and the ways and maybe injury to spectators.

There are many examples of ships sticking on the ways. The problem experienced with the launch of HMS *Caesar* in 1853, which became stuck for seventeen days at Pembroke Royal Dockyard, will be recounted in a later chapter.[4] We shall also learn shortly what problems Brunel encountered in 1857 when he took eighty-nine days to complete the sideways launch of his *Great Eastern*.[5]

Cold weather has frequently been a factor in causing a hull to stick on the ways. The launch of one of the Navy's first ironclad warships, HMS *Warrior*, on 29 December 1860 took place in the middle of the coldest winter in England for fifty years. After the ship had been christened it remained immovable despite the action of hydraulic pumps. The *Illustrated London News* reported:[6]

> The grease on the ways was hardened by cold; the ship's cradles were frozen to their timbers and after four or five inches had passed over the ship came to a stand and there were not a few present who feared that there was going to be the same lingering process as that of the *Great Eastern*.

The men on board the ship ran along the deck towards the bow to try to free her and eventually with the aid of three tugs and hydraulic rams the great mass of 5,000 tons of iron was dragged down the slip. The *Illustrated London News* concluded its report: 'As the *Warrior* passed down its "ways", the band played the National Anthem and the spectators cheered lustily.'[7]

Excessive launch weight, not the cold weather, was to blame for the problems in the launch in 1874 of another ironclad ship, ARA *Independencia*, a frigate ordered by the Brazilian navy from J. and W. Dudgeon on the Thames. She had been designed by the naval architect and MP for Pembroke, Edward Reed. We will meet Mr Reed again in connection with his intervention in Parliament in response to the First Lord of the Admiralty's proposal in 1875 to introduce a religious service at the launch of naval ships. No doubt he had the problems encountered with the launch of *Independencia* in mind when in the House of Commons he expressed concern over the suspension during the religious service 'of the important and often critical operations in the launching of heavy ships'.[8] It should be added that, although he had been involved in the design of the ship, Mr Reed had no responsibility for the launch arrangements for *Independencia*. 'As nearly all her armour plates were fixed whilst the ship was on the stocks, her weight is about 6,000 tons, and the operation was one of unusual difficulty.'[9] Her launch was first attempted on 16 July 1874 but she stuck fast and did not move. A second attempt, with the aid of various appliances, was made on 30 July, during which the ship got about one third down the slipway and again stuck, extensively damaging her bottom plating. Some nautical men were worried that her deck was 'hog backed'. She was finally launched on 10 September after the radical step was taken to lighten her by the removal of some of the armour plates at the stern. The incident caused widespread concern in shipbuilding circles as to the problems likely to be encountered when launching heavy ironclad battleships.

Contracts for the construction of ironclad warships undertaken by private shipyards in the 1860s and 1870s, while capable of bringing high returns, proved to be a risky trade for some. Prior to the launch of *Independencia*, on 17 March 1866 another private yard on the Thames, Millwall Ironworks, had the public embarrassment of a launch failure of another ironclad in front of a huge crowd, including the Prince of Wales. At the time of its launch HMS *Northumberland*, an armoured frigate and the last of the Minotaur class built for the Royal Navy, had almost all its armour plating fitted and at 7,000 tons was one of the heaviest ships to be launched down an excavated slipway. At that time the *Great Eastern* was the only heavier vessel and, as we shall learn in Chapter 6, was launched in a different way. *Northumberland*'s sister ships the *Agincourt* and the *Minotaur* had been launched successfully; one was floated out of the dock and the other was launched without the iron plates. *Northumberland*, with its iron plates fitted, was not so fortunate. After it stuck firmly on the slipway and a further attempt to launch with the aid of hydraulic jacks and tugs failed at the next spring tide, the problem could only be solved by four immense camels, 50ft in length, being made at Woolwich Dockyard to lift part of the hull by the stern as the tide rose. After working night and day the ship was launched successfully four weeks later on 17 April 1866.[10] The initial launching failure was very expensive for the yard and this and other factors forced it to close one month later.[11]

In 1929 the bitter cold on the River Tyne was certainly the problem in the launch of a passenger ferry, the SS *Britannia*, for Swedish Lloyd Line at the Neptune yard. On the day fixed for the launch, 26 February, 'it was discovered that the grease on the ways had frozen hard. The *Britannia* refused to move. The ship was frozen to the slipway.' The shipwrights at the yard 'worked tirelessly all night on the slipway. They removed two thirds of the sliding ways, scraped the frozen grease off them, re-greased them and then re-laid them.' Steam was also used to keep the berth as warm as possible and as a result the launch was completed successfully the next day. 'The launch was a triumph for the team of shipwrights in the face of extremely cold and difficult conditions.'[12]

Initial stability

In the chapter on the *Daphne* disaster of 1883,[13] where the same Mr Reed headed the subsequent public inquiry, we will learn of the need for initial stability of the hull in its launched condition. A few years later, in 1907, in Italy a 9,210-ton passenger ship, the SS *Principessa Jolanda*, was launched with its funnels and masts stepped, as was common practice in Italy at that time. She was then the largest passenger ship built in Italy. After travelling down the slipway, dressed overall and in triumphant style, the ship became unstable, listed sharply to port and began to take in water through openings in the upper deck. See Illustration No. 12. After some twenty minutes, during which the captain, crew and guests managed to escape unharmed, the ship capsized on her side and lay in the water like a beached whale with only her funnels just above the surface.

It appears that the reasons for the disaster were that the centre of gravity was too high and that there may have been defective ballasting. In addition, if the openings in the upper deck had been closed it is unlikely that the ship would have capsized and she could have been salvaged. In 1908 her sister ship, SS *Principessa Mafalda*, was launched by the same shipyard without mishap. Photographs show her being launched without funnels or superstructure in place; so lessons about stability at launch had been learnt.

As we have already noted, prior to the tragedy of *Daphne* in 1883 there occurred on 5 July 1841 at Masbrough, in South Yorkshire, on the River Don, another tragic ship launch disaster. It was the custom of the yard to invite people to stand on the boat during the launch to enjoy the rush into the water. On this occasion there were some 150 men and boys on board … 'as the vessel left the stays about half over on the balance, the parties on board (men and boys) rushed to the leeward side of the vessel to see the effect of it dashing into the water. By that means the weight of the men and the boys to the leeward side caused her to overbalance and to overturn before she reached the water …'.[14] Sixty-four lost their lives, the majority being children aged between eleven and sixteen. At the subsequent inquest the Grand Jury found that it had been an accident. One of the many lessons taught by *Daphne* was that only the few workers from the shipyard necessary to help with the launch operation should be on board at the time of the launch. Unfortunately that lesson was learned too late to save the many lives lost at Masbrough.

Collapse of the fore poppet

A critical moment in every stern-first launch is when the stern becomes waterborne and the weight of the forward part of the ship is still carried on the slipway. To relieve this stress the bow is often cradled in a crushable softwood 'fore poppet'. On 17 August 1939, half an hour before the scheduled launch of the 23,000-ton *Illustrious*-class aircraft carrier HMS *Formidable* at Harland & Wolff's yard in Belfast, the fore poppet supporting the bow suddenly collapsed. The cry went up 'she is moving'. The workmen who were removing the shores in preparation for the launch had to dash for safety. The sponsor, Lady Wood, wife of Sir Howard Kingsley Wood, already standing on the launch platform, had the presence of mind to christen the vessel as it slid of its own volition down the ways, leaving behind a trail of bolts, iron bars, nuts, planks of wood and poppets. The huge vessel continued unchecked down the slip. Fortunately, despite some sideways movement, it remained well balanced on the ways. While no damage was done to the hull from its premature launch, tragically the wife of a shipyard worker, a guest at the launch, was killed by a flying bolt; some twenty others were injured. The slipway after the launch looked like the aftermath of an earthquake (See illustrations Nos 9 and 10). HMS *Formidable* was thereafter known as 'The ship that launched herself'.[15]

Speed of the hull down the ways and in the water

The speed of the hull as it slides down the ways into the water is another point of concern for the shipbuilder. Once the hull is released from the daggers or triggers on the launch way, the hull will often travel faster down the ways than she will ever subsequently do in the water. Stopping of the 'way' on the hull in the water is usually achieved by bundles of heavy drag chains attached to the shore, which are gradually brought into play once the hull is clear of the launch ways and exert increasingly greater frictional force as the hull moves away or by the simple method of dropping anchors from the hull, in either case until the speed has slowed sufficiently to enable tugs to take control of the hull and guide it into the fitting out berth.

The launching spaces on each of the rivers Thames, Tyne, Wear and Clyde, all of which have been significant shipbuilding centres in this country, are all limited in breadth and so demand that the shipyards on these rivers include the checking of the velocity of the hull, once launched, as an essential part of the launching arrangements. The risks involved with the launch of a ship in confined waters is well illustrated by an accident that occurred on the Tyne. On the afternoon of Friday, 11 January 1907 the world's first turbine vessel, the prestigious invention of Hon. Charles Parsons, was moored alongside at his works at Wallsend on the North bank of the river. SY *Turbinia*, frequently known as 'the North Sea greyhound', regularly achieved speeds in excess of 30 knots in Parsons' experiments to design a turbine engine that could be replicated in warships and ocean liners. Steam turbine engines, whereby thermal energy stored in steam is converted into propulsion, the direct result of Charles Parsons' invention in *Turbinia*, were incorporated into the famous liners *Mauretania* and *Lusitania*, both of which entered service with Cunard in 1907. Both of these liners went on to have the distinction of holding, at different times, the Blue Riband for the fastest crossing of the Atlantic.[16] So, *Turbinia* was no ordinary vessel.

But back to the accident. The Tyne is some 800ft wide at Wallsend and on the opposite south bank was the yard of Messrs R. Stephenson and Company at Hebburn. There on that afternoon of 11 January the single-deck cargo ship *Crosby* of 6,300 deadweight was launched. There is no detail available as to the launch arrangements other than the fact that a photograph in the Tyne and Wear Archives and Museums collection has a telling manuscript note on the reverse stating that *Crosby* 'carried away her check chains (never properly attached)'.[17] The report in the *Newcastle Evening Chronicle* published the next day simply recorded that the *Crosby* 'ran across the river, and collided with *Turbinia* which was driven onto a slag bank and sustained considerable damage. The *Crosby* was apparently undamaged.'

Illustration No. 16 shows that the *Crosby* hit *Turbinia* immediately aft of the wheelhouse and she was nearly cut in two by the impact; but she survived and was repaired and is now a centrepiece exhibit in the hall of the Discovery Museum at Newcastle upon Tyne.

In the *Newcastle Daily Journal* published the day after the accident there is a general description of the features of the newly launched cargo ship *Crosby* but rather surprisingly no mention of the nearly catastrophic damage that, on launch, it had caused to *Turbinia*, a ship that was already famous outside the Tyne.[18] One is left with the distinct impression that the local press did not wish to give too much oxygen to this unfortunate and embarrassing accident, which might have harmed the reputation of shipbuilding on the Tyne.

If the improper attachment of the check chains was the fault in the case of the launch of the *Crosby*, similar or even more serious consequences from unrestrained velocity are likely to occur if the check chains actually break. This occurred on the River Wear in Sunderland on 6 March 1947 when the check chains attached to merchantman *Lord Glanely*, constructed at Pickersgill's yard, 'appeared to snap' after launch and, instead of pulling up mid-stream, her rudder and propeller crashed into the concrete fitting out quay belonging to Short Brothers on the opposite bank, causing spectators to jump for safety. Fortunately no one was injured, but the incident does illustrate the significant risks of an uncontrolled launch in confined waters.[19]

Uneven sideways launch

In a sideways launch it is essential that both ends of the hull should move evenly down the launch way. Considerable damage occurred to the hull of the steamer *Nevada* at Manitowoc, Wisconsin, in 1915 when the stern end of the hull was launched ahead of the bow 'as a result of the vessel's stern dropping off the launch ramp while the bow was still secured in position'.[20] As we will learn, this was a risk that was very much in Brunel's mind during the side launch of his colossal ship *Great Eastern* in 1857–58.[21]

Safety of spectators

Safe launch of the hull is not the only consideration for a shipyard. It must also consider the number and safety of spectators attending the event.

The launch of HMS *Albion* on 21 June 1898, already mentioned in the context of superstition and the failure of the christening bottle to break,[22] further illustrates the risks that a ship launch can pose for spectators. The ship was constructed at Thames Ironworks, Blackwall, and was launched by the Duchess of York. The shipyard had printed 20,000 tickets for the launch; 8,000 would sit in prepared wooden stages and the remainder would stand in various parts of the shipyard. In addition, the gatekeepers had been instructed to admit people without tickets provided that they were 'respectably dressed', so there were between 25,000 and 30,000 spectators present in a confined area. There was immense interest. HMS *Albion* was the largest ship built at the yard. It appears that many were also attracted by the knowledge that the Duchess of York would be present. Tickets were also issued to the shipyard's workforce to enable them to attend with their families. All wanted to be near the water to obtain a better view.

'The feat of breaking the bottle proved somewhat arduous but she left the ways in perfect style amid great enthusiasm and the distinguished guests did not suspect that the general rejoicing had suddenly become an occasion of mourning ...'[23] There were tumultuous cheers from the assembled crowds as the ship entered the water, causing a huge wave. The cheers of the spectators obscured the cries of those in distress, who within a few seconds had been thrown into the water as a result of the large wave that swept around the dock. At first few noticed the collapse of the wooden staging or gangway between two slips resulting from the large volume of water displaced by the launch. It had been constructed to carry a few workmen rather than a huge crowd. All eyes had up to that moment been focused on the Royal party and the large battleship on the launch way. *The Times* describes how the tragedy occurred, reporting that the wooden staging or gangway:

> was conspicuously marked as dangerous. It was, moreover, well inside of an area also declared to be dangerous on account of the great wave which the launching of the ship would inevitably produce. Policemen did their best to enforce the regulations and to warn people off the bridge and the dangerous area. But they were not in sufficient force ...[24]

The crowd was evidently not in the mood to take notice of warning signs.

Despite many acts of heroism from other spectators diving into the water to assist those in distress, thirty-four people lost their lives, mostly women and children. The obvious lesson for shipyards was to restrict spectators at a ship launch to a number that could be accommodated safely and in such a manner as to provide greater protection from the inevitable dangers – particularly in this case the large displacement of water that would inevitably be caused by 6,000 tons of battleship hitting the surface and causing a *'tsunami'* of a wave in a confined area.

It is of interest to note that the Home Dockyard Regulations 1925, applicable to Royal Dockyards, required the superintendent at each yard to comply with the latest Admiralty instruction as to the erection of booths for visitors, the appropriation of tickets and admission of the public,[25] apparently a stricter regime than that which existed in 1898 for the launch of HMS *Albion* at the Thames Ironworks, a private yard.

These examples, of which there are many more, are sufficiently compelling to confirm the introduction to this chapter that a ship launch is potentially a dangerous operation, which needs to be well planned and every precaution taken.

Chapter 5

The *Daphne* Tragedy 1883

I n 1883 an accident occurred during launch on the River Clyde of a small coaster that was to have a profound and long lasting impact on launch practice and shipbuilding in the UK generally.

How it happened

Just before noon on Tuesday, 3 July 1883 a tragic accident occurred on the Clyde on the launch of the small steam coaster SS *Daphne* at the shipyard of Messrs Alexander Stephen & Sons, Linthouse (Stephen's). This was far more significant than just another example of a mishap during launch. The hull capsized immediately after launch and sank in the middle of the river with the loss of 124 lives. Illustration No. 11 shows the steamer on its side at low water.

The *Daphne* was of iron construction with a length of 177ft (53.9 m) and a beam of 25.3ft (7.7m). The coaster was launched from the Linthouse shipyard of Stephen's on the south bank of the river. She had been ordered by Glasgow and Londonderry Steam Packet Company (later incorporated into the Burns and Laird Lines) for their Irish trade for the carriage of cattle and livestock. She had been constructed by Stephen's to specifications and plans drawn up by the owner's marine superintendent with instructions as to the dimensions and displacement of the ship as well as the power and type of equipment to be used. At this time it was quite usual for shipbuilders to accept the data provided by their owner clients without a detailed examination of the effect on the overall design and stability of the ship they were contracted to build.

By 1883 Stephen's was a successful shipyard with a good reputation and a full order book with contracts from Scotland, England, Italy, Germany and France. In 1881 they built 21,860 gross tons of shipping and 21,470 gross tons in 1882. They were constructing a large volume of ships, so much so that it was said of the firm at that time that 'Messrs Stephens and Sons weave ships'.[1]

The launching arrangements

The launching arrangements for *Daphne* were in accordance with Stephen's normal practice, with drag chains on either side bolted to the hull to slow down the velocity of the hull after she was afloat, which was essential in a narrow river such as the Clyde. The launch ways were new. By July 1883 Stephen's had launched 280 ships without any accident or anybody being injured,[2] so the launch of *Daphne* on 3 July was treated as routine. Nobody had any reason to foresee the tragedy that would unfold that morning. Indeed, launching of ships on the Clyde by 1883 was a matter of everyday life: some 250 ships were launched on the river that year.

200 workmen on board

Stephen's did not have fitting out facilities at Linthouse and the intention was that after launch the hull would, as usual, be towed up the river to a quay at Broomielaw for completion. The two engines were installed prior to launch but the boilers were not, a gap in the deck being left for loading the boilers when the hull reached Broomielaw. The propeller and propeller shaft were also on board. The owners wanted to take delivery of the ship as soon as possible and, with the Glasgow Fair holidays approaching, materials for the completion work were loaded on the deck before launch, as were about 200 workmen, the intention being that they would travel with the hull after launch as it was towed to Broomielaw so as to continue the work and thereby save time. Although Stephen's previous practice had been to launch with workmen on board, it seems likely that the number on *Daphne* that morning may have been larger than was usual.

Joy riders

It also appears to have been the practice that workmen and others took the liberty of inviting their friends on board for a launch; and men in other departments often rushed out and joined a ship immediately before she left the ways. It also emerged later that two young men went down to witness the launch and as a matter of curiosity went on board in order to be able to say that they had been on a ship while it was being launched. So it may be concluded that those on board the ship at the time of launch, increased by non-workmen and joy riders, exceeded by some measure the number of workmen needed to continue the work on the construction of the ship at Broomielaw.

The capsize

When the dog shores were knocked away, the hull started to move at once down the ways and after the hull had cleared the ways the drag chains tightened, first on the starboard side and then on the port, and brought the ship to a standstill. The evidence given at the subsequent inquiry (see below) was that: 'On the vessel leaving the ways she listed slightly over to port, but recovered herself completely when brought up – then inclined to port again – again recovering to upright, and a little over to starboard and then hesitatingly went over entirely to port.'[3] To the horror of all the spectators, the hull then rolled over completely.

The effect of 30 tons of loose equipment and some 200 men sliding to the port side was to accelerate the capsize and as the main deck dipped below the level of the river more water poured through the boiler access hole. Many were trapped inside the hull and drowned. Some escaped by swimming to the shore, or got hold of floating pieces of wood, or were rescued by the two tugs in attendance to tow the hull after launch to Broomielaw. Frantic efforts were made to rescue those in the water and some seventy people were saved, but tragically this still left a total loss of life of 124 men and boys.

'This terrible matter'

Mr Alexander Stephen, a partner in the shipbuilding firm, who was not present at the launch, kept a diary for 1883, which is preserved in the Archives of Glasgow University.[4] There are entries for each day but the entry for 3 July is poignant – it is left entirely blank. In his entry for 4 July he writes of *Daphne* as being 'this terrible matter'. He also records his appointment of Mr Francis Elgar, a member of the Institute of Naval Architects, to examine the launch and stability on behalf of the shipyard. Mr Elgar went on to play an important part in the inquiry into the accident, with which Stephen's co-operated fully. In the days after the accident Mr Alexander Stephen's diary entries reflect his concerns for the victims and their families, the state of the ship and the likely findings of the ongoing inquiry and the extent to which his shipyard would be likely to be found to blame.

The ship was righted in a few days and taken to Salterscroft Graving Dock, and after cleaning and examination was refloated for a carefully monitored inclining experiment to ascertain the full stability particulars of the ship.

Public subscription

Many of the dead left wives and children behind, most of them belonging to Linthouse, Govan or Partick. Mr Alexander Stephen, in his diary entry for 10 July, mentions writing to the Lord Provost (the convener of the Glasgow Council and akin to a mayor) that a public subscription should be started and his intimation to make a contribution of £4,000 (later increased to £5,000). A subscription for the relief of the distressed families was opened in Glasgow. Among the messages of condolences, there was one from Mrs Gladstone, wife of the Prime Minister, who the previous year had been in Glasgow to assist in the launch of another ship. The widespread interest in the tragedy is shown by the fact that the relief fund eventually reached £30,000 and was administered by a committee of Glasgow's leading citizens. In subsequent weeks there was a debate in letters published in local newspapers as to whether bereaved families who instituted legal proceedings against the shipyard could also seek maintenance money from the relief fund; the committee eventually decided that the fund should exclusively benefit those who did not resort to a legal remedy.

Public Inquiry

Edward Reed, by then Sir Edward, the same naval architect and MP who in 1875 in the House of Commons had questioned the practicality of the introduction of a religious service upon the launching of naval ships,[5] was appointed by the then Home Secretary, The Right Honourable

Sir William Vernon Harcourt, to make inquiry and report back on the cause of the disaster. Sir Edward had been Chief Constructor of the Royal Navy from 1863 to 1870, so was well qualified for the task.

Sir Edward inspected the ship, examined the launch ways and drag chains, supervised the inclining experiment and for four to five days took evidence in the Court House in Glasgow from the partners and workmen at Stephen's and other leading Clyde shipyards, as well as a shipbuilder from Le Havre.

The inclining trial was carried out in a wet dock and showed that in the launching condition *Daphne* had a metacentric height of only 4in.

Sir Edward's report was produced very quickly and published on 14 August 1883, only six weeks after the disaster. His conclusions can be summarised as follows:

- no fault was found with the launch arrangements at Linthouse, which he concluded would have been sufficient for a ship much larger than the size and weight of *Daphne*;
- nor was the accident attributable to the drag chains for checking the velocity of the hull in the river after it cleared the launch ways;
- nor was the capsize of the vessel due to the tidal currents in the river other than the tide being a possible small contributor to the inclining forces which were at work on the ship;
- the cause was found to be small initial stability coupled with an excess of loose equipment and men on board;
- the practice of an owner defining so many dimensions and particulars of a ship, leaving the shipbuilder little scope for determining the stability of the ship, was a bad and dangerous one bringing about a division and confusion of responsibility and opening avenues to accidents which neither party can foresee;
- since no shipbuilder had previously estimated the stability of ships before launching, Stephen's were blameless of any negligence. Nonetheless, stability needed to be given much more serious consideration, especially where shipbuilders were ready to build and launch a ship to whatever specifications and dimensions an owner demanded.

Lessons Learned

The *Daphne* disaster was a shock to the general public and a 'wake up' call for the shipbuilding community in the UK. Prior to this date shipbuilders had worked largely by 'rule of thumb' and past experience. The lesson about stability was learned quickly by Laird Lines, the owner who had ordered *Daphne*. It was reported in the *Glasgow Herald* on 23 October 1883 that in specifications for a new ship the company had set out a number of stringent conditions regarding stability, including that the shipbuilder must supply the owner with a curve of stability and incline the ship after completion so as to show the metacentre, centre of gravity and centre of buoyancy.

Stability at launching was very much in everyone's minds after the disaster. At the meeting of the Institution of Engineers and Shipbuilders in Scotland on 24 October 1883 the topic of 'Stability of Ships at Launching' was discussed and there was a call for the experience of other shipbuilders to be shared. Similarly, at the 1884 session of the Institution of Naval Architects, seven of the papers read dealt with stability calculations. The capsizing of *Daphne* at her launch had focused public attention on the need for full stability calculations.

Sir Edward followed up the inquiry and the need for stability to be determined by himself by writing a book titled *A Treatise on the Stability of Ships*,[6] and the whole question of stability was investigated by naval architects and shipbuilders and calculations made to cover the whole lifetime of the ship, not just at launch.

These precautions, of course, have to be far more stringent in the case of a sideways launch, where an initial roll of up to 40 or even 45 degrees must be expected.

The point has also been made that an inquiry of this nature led by a single marine expert – in this case a naval architect – can achieve a much quicker result than a tribunal headed by a lawyer assisted by marine experts.

The immediate lessons were learned quickly: the necessity to secure all loose gear on the deck prior to launch and to limit the number of persons on board at launch to the minimum necessary for the launch operation, to carry out tasks such as handling ropes and releasing check wires.

Shortly after the publication of Sir Edward's report, Mr Alexander Stephen records in his diary for 3 September having a meeting with his lawyer, Dr Robertson, and Mr Napier of Robert Napier & Sons, another Clyde shipbuilder, at which he inquired: 'What should we do as to letting our men on board at future launch.'[7] The clear advice was to preclude anyone being on board unless actually engaged to work the ship at the launch.

This advice was followed. On 19 September 1883 *The Glasgow Herald* reported on the launch of *Gottardo*:

> The vessel was the first that Messrs Stephen have launched since the unfortunate disaster to the *Daphne* on July 3 and not a little interest was in consequence centred on the day's proceedings. It was noticeable as the vessel left the ways that very few workmen were on board.

Similarly, for the launch of *Ella* on 13 December Mr Alexander Stephen records in his diary 'Launched No.282 *Ella* ... I ordered all men ashore except those connected with the launch.'[8] The lesson had been well learnt: only the most essential personnel required in connection with the launch would be permitted to stay on board the ship at the launch; and certainly not strangers or joy riders.

Nowadays just before a launch it is standard shipbuilding practice to secure all loose equipment carefully, limit the number of men remaining on board to those essential to the launch operation and to place lifesaving appliances on board. In addition, since this tragedy shipyards have always estimated the stability of a newly constructed ship, so that taking all these preventative measures together, it made it unlikely that this type of accident at launch would ever happen again.[9]

But there was also a wider and deeper lesson that, while an owner or his superintendent may, and frequently does, make suggestions on the specifications, the ultimate responsibility for the design of the ship and its stability not just at launch but throughout its life must rest with the shipbuilder. The final judgment on the design and the ship's stability is his, not the owner's. This meant an end to the practice of shipbuilders at the end of the nineteenth century adopting, without questioning the effect on stability, the specifications of his owner client for the design of the ship. Since the shipbuilder is ultimately responsible for stability, his judgment in these matters became final.

Control of navigation in the river at time of a launch

One of the side issues to emerge at the inquiry was the absence of any power granted to the Clyde Trustees, as conservator of the River Clyde, to control traffic on the narrow river when a launch is about to take place. Although this issue did not relate to the central question of the inquiry, the lack of any system of controlling navigation on the river at the time of a launch was of sufficient concern to shipbuilders on the Clyde to compel them to ask Sir Edward to mention it in his report.

By 1883 the volume of shipbuilding activity had grown to such an extent that there were some fifty-five shipyards on the Clyde building ships and an estimated 250 ships were launched on the river that year. The evidence given to the inquiry was that launches had become a daily or almost daily occurrence. Indeed, a ship was launched from another yard on the opposite side of the river some 300 yards below the Stephen's yard only a few minutes after *Daphne*. With the volume of ships passing up and down the river at that time there was a real need for regulation to avoid the risk of collision between a ship being launched and passing river traffic. At the same time, detention of traffic up and down the river by reason of a ship launch could not be unlimited. A balance needed to be found.

There must be few other examples in the records of shipbuilding worldwide where the volume of ship launches was as high in a confined stretch of water as it was on the Clyde in 1883. A solution to regulating the traffic on the river was needed urgently and it was not surprising that the inquiry was requested to address this issue.

The by-laws and regulations that were in force at the time of the launch of *Daphne* were those enacted by the Trustees of the Clyde Navigation dated 23 April 1860. These contained no provision whereby the launching of vessels into the river was in any way regulated. An attempt was made in 1868 by the Clyde Navigation Trustees to regulate traffic on the river during launches but it failed to attract sufficient consensus among the shipbuilders to be implemented. It is estimated that in 1860 sixty-nine ships were launched into the Clyde, a number that had almost quadrupled by 1883 with an estimated launch number of 250 ships for that year – an impressive statement on the annual shipbuilding productivity at that time on a narrow river.

In 1878 a further attempt was made by the Clyde Trustees to get a new set of by-laws and regulations passed. A draft regulation for the purpose of dealing with launches read:

> Every master or other person in charge of any vessel passing or being on the river in the vicinity of any ship launch shall observe the signal exhibited to give notice of such launch, which shall be a red flag with the word 'launch' in large white letters thereon, displayed from a boat on the river and shall not pass such signal until the launch has taken place or the signal be withdrawn.[10]

The Trustees also sought to provide that any violation of this law would be attended with a penalty.

The sheriffs of the three counties through whom the jurisdiction of the Clyde extends refused to approve the new by-laws for reasons that had no connection with the ship launching question.

Although by 1883 the new by-laws had not come into force, from the evidence given at the inquiry shipyards along the Clyde appear to have complied in practice with the suggested warning signal requirements. However, it was also alleged at the inquiry that on more than one occasion the danger flags exhibited by shipbuilders from boats up and down the river had been disregarded. Vessels being launched had consequently been in imminent danger of causing accidents that could have been serious. John Elder & Co., a shipbuilder, reported to the inquiry an incident involving the launch of the steamer *Champion* in 1878, which struck a lighter being towed down the river. Two men were sent overboard but were rescued. The person in charge of the launch was summoned to the police court on a charge of culpably, recklessly and negligently directing the launch of the steamer; but was acquitted on evidence that the shipyard had displayed flags from two boats in the river either side of the slipway. The master of the lighter denied seeing the signal.[11]

In 1889 the Clyde Navigation Trust enacted new by-laws; and these contained in a section entitled 'Bye-laws as to Launches' more detailed procedures for regulating launches than those set out in the 1878 draft. The red flag signal 4ft square with the word 'LAUNCH' in large white letters thereon was to be exhibited from two small boats in the river not less than 200 yards from the line of the launch, the one being to the east and the other to the west of the line. It did, however, limit the time that the shipyard could hold up the navigation in the river for a launch to twenty minutes after the flag signal was first displayed, otherwise the shipyard would itself commit an offence for detention of the river traffic enforceable against the shipbuilder.[12] A balance had been struck between the interests of the shipyard for a safe launch and the need for substantially uninterrupted navigation for the traffic in the river. It was also a basic principle for the Clyde Navigation Trustees that the Trust itself should not incur any responsibility in regulating the traffic; this principle was also enshrined in the new by-laws.

The lessons learned from the disaster had a far-reaching effect on launch arrangements and defined a shipbuilder's responsibility to ensure that each ship constructed by it was so designed as to have the necessary stability for safe launching as well as safe navigation. In addition, shipyard workers travelling with the ship down the ways at launch were in future to be limited to those necessary for the launch operation itself and all loose equipment was to be secured prior to launch.

Chapter 6

The Launch of Brunel's Three Great Ships

No book on ship launches would be complete without an account of the unique sideways launch of the SS *Great Eastern* into the Thames in January 1858, then the largest ship the world had ever seen. It took eighty-nine days from the first signal to start her launch until she was afloat. The sheer size of the ship and the extent of the efforts needed to launch her caught the imagination of the public and made her eventual launch into a national event, better recorded than any ship launch before or since.

Most think of Isambard Kingdom Brunel (1806–59) (Brunel) as an inventive engineer in the field of railways and bridges; perhaps less well known is his pioneering work in the construction of iron-hulled and screw-propelled steam ships. As will be described in this chapter, he was the principal engineer for not just the *Great Eastern*, but three 'Great' ships, the SS *Great Western*, the SS *Great Britain* and then the *Great Eastern*, each one larger than the last, all creative in design and all launched in a different manner. He had no formal education in marine engineering and had never built a ship before, so how did Brunel come to play such a key role in the construction and launch of some of the largest and most innovative ships then built?

The short and perhaps surprising answer is that it was the railways that led him to think about ships and it was the railways that played a key part in the design of the hulls of his 'Great' ships.

The Great Western

The story is that at a meeting of the directors of the Great Western Railway in October 1835 when someone objected to the length of the proposed main line from London to Bristol, Brunel is said to have replied, perhaps as a joke: 'Why not make it longer, and have a steamboat go from Bristol to New York, and call it the Great Western?'[1]

Brunel had the vision to link London to New York by combining a steam train journey to Bristol with a crossing of the Atlantic by a steam-powered ship and then the genius to turn his vision into reality.

Joining him in this exciting new maritime venture was Thomas Guppy, a Great Western Railway director who was an engineer and a sugar refiner, and Christopher Claxton, a semi-retired naval officer. Capital from local sources was raised and they set up the Great Western Steamship Company in June 1836. A contract to construct the ship was agreed with the well-respected Bristol shipbuilder William Patterson, who had a shipyard on the Floating Harbour. The Floating Harbour is an artificially created, deep water section of the River Avon in the centre of Bristol created by the water engineer William Jessop in 1803–09 and to which Brunel himself had suggested improvements. The new ship was to be very large, 236ft long overall and of 2,300 displacement tons, constructed of oak with a copper-sheathed hull.

Brunel's contribution was in the overall conception of the project and in the design of the pair of engines that would power twin paddle wheels 28ft in diameter. Brunel's concept was a pair of side-lever engines, each with a cylinder of 70in in diameter placed side by side with their connecting rods linked to a single paddle wheel shaft. They were at that time the largest marine engines that had ever been built. In addition to the engines for the paddle wheels, *Great Western* was rigged as a four-mast schooner.

During 1836–37 the hull was constructed at Patterson's yard and the engines by Maudslay, Sons and Field in Lambeth. Although *Great Western* was a large ship for its day, it was not so large that it could not be launched in the traditional manner down an inclined slipway. Nonetheless, to construct so large a ship in the Floating Harbour was considered by many at that time to be the height of folly due to the tortuous and narrow path of the Avon from Bristol to the sea. There were doubts as to how the ship after launch was to be manoeuvred round the corners in the narrow river; and some joked that it was to be made with a join in the middle, like a collapsing apparatus, so that it could be shortened or lengthened at will.

Others doubted that a steam ship could be constructed so as to have sufficient capacity to carry enough coal to make such a long sea passage as well as to carry cargo and passengers. It was wrongly assumed that if a small ship could not carry enough coal, neither could a large one. The chief proponent of this scepticism was a well-known scientific figure of the day, Dr Dionysius Lardner. In August 1836, Dr Lardner came to Bristol to address the British Association for the Advancement of Science. Dr Lardner argued that the water resistance encountered by a ship was directly proportionate to its displacement, not the surface area of the ship in contact with the water. His prediction was that Brunel's venture would fail since no steamship would be able to carry enough fuel in addition to cargo to make it a commercial success.

This was a direct challenge to Brunel and his *Great Western* then under construction in the Floating Harbour. Brunel had come to a different view; he realised that what is needed to drive a ship through the water depends not so much on the vessel's weight or its displacement as on the weight of the water it has to push against, with the surface area of the hull and its shape being the key factors. His conclusion, which was directly opposite to that of Dr Lardner, was that as the size of a vessel is increased, the space devoted to fuel may be safely reduced. This theory, which was to be proved correct by the performance of *Great Western*, underpinned all future thinking on long-distance passages by steam-powered ships. In this respect Brunel was a leading innovator.

The launch of *Great Western* took place on 19 July 1837:

At five minutes past ten, the dog shores having been struck away, the screw was applied and a general shout arose 'she moves' – which indeed she did in the most majestic and graceful manner. For the moment all was hushed whilst the beautiful and majestic vessel glided into the water; not the least wavering or irregular motion occurred. As she left the shore Lt Claxton performed the usual ceremony of dashing a demi-john of Madeira upon the figure head of Neptune at the bows and she was named by Mrs Miles, who also cracked her bottle against the side, the *Great Western*. At the calculated distance she was checked by a chain cable and brought up within a few feet of the opposite shore without the smallest accident. The launch being concluded, spontaneous and continued cheers took place ...[2]

After launch she departed under her own sail to London to receive her engines from Maudslay's and completed her engine trials in March 1838, achieving an average speed of 11 knots. In April she was ready to return to Bristol for her maiden voyage to New York with passengers and cargo, the first continuous crossing of the Atlantic by steam. By this time it was being realised that Dr Lardner was wrong and Brunel right. In a deliberate bid to challenge *Great Western*, the small steamer *Sirius* was chartered and set off from Cork on 4 April for New York. Unfortunately a fire in the engine room of *Great Western*, in which Brunel was quite badly injured, resulted in *Great Western*'s departure from Bristol being delayed until 7 April. News of the fire discouraged some passengers from embarking and she left with only seven, arriving in New York on 23 April having achieved the crossing in seventeen days. Despite a few days' head start *Sirius* had only arrived the previous evening and had little coal left, whereas *Great Western* had over 200 tons remaining. On the return journey, with more favourable currents, *Great Western* took fourteen days and *Sirius* eighteen. The advantage of steam power over sail was amply demonstrated.

The essence of *Great Western*'s success was the provision of a regular, speedy, two-week passage across the Atlantic. In the seventeen years between 1838 and 1855 when she was in service she completed a total of sixty-five Atlantic crossings.[3] Fast sailing packets could only compete on time with a following wind, so their service was not so reliable and *Great Western* had the further merit of greater stability and ease of passage through the waves. There was only one class of passenger, with no steerage or intermediate class. The fare for a one way passage was '45 guineas plus 1 guinea stewards' fee',[4] which in today's money is the equivalent of about £3,600, so it was a service that only the rich and the distinguished of the day could afford. The Maritime Historian Helen Doe aptly describes *Great Western* as being 'the Concorde of its age, a new, fast and luxurious way to cross the Atlantic'.[5] She would prove to be the most commercially successful of Brunel's three 'Great' ships.

Great Britain

Soon after *Great Western*'s first successful crossing, the company was thinking of a second ship with the same building committee of Brunel, Guppy and Claxton. At first they were planning a larger version of *Great Western* with wooden hull and paddle wheels driven by steam engines. But successful experiments by shipbuilders on the Clyde and the Mersey with ocean-going iron ships led Brunel to recommend an iron hull with six watertight compartments running across the hull and two longitudinal bulkheads giving great strength to the long hull, so as to avoid sagging stress. He had conceived the idea of the hull being like an iron railway bridge and in this sense railway bridge construction contributed to the design of iron hulls for ships. Iron had the added advantage of being stronger and lighter than wood. The hull was also double skinned, another innovative feature.

The new ship of 322ft length, 86ft longer than the *Great Western*, and of 51ft breadth was too large to be constructed on a slip at Patterson's yard and the decision was taken to build her in a specially created excavated dry dock, with a caisson or entrance gate opening onto the Floating Harbour. The bottom of the dry dock was 12ft below the surface of the water in the harbour, which, when the ship was ready to be launched, would be flooded to enable a 'float up' of the hull to take place.

The first design was for paddle wheel propulsion like the *Great Western* until the chance arrival in Bristol in 1840 of the *Archimedes*, the first propeller-driven ship designed by Francis Pettit Smith. After a study of this ship, Brunel realised that propellers, which were fully immersed in water all the time, were a more efficient method of propulsion than paddles, which in rough seas dipped in and out of the water. There were changes in design and interruptions in construction while Brunel and his team considered all the options. Brunel researched the propeller design thoroughly and asked the Navy, who were interested in these propulsion developments, to allow him to conduct experiments on HMS *Ratler*. The result was an innovative design for a single propeller with six blades. Brunel persuaded the Board of the Great Western Steamship Company that the new ship should be solely driven by a single propeller in place of paddle wheels. This necessitated the engine being redesigned to drive a propeller instead of paddle wheels. More delay and greater cost but the end product was a revolutionary ship: the largest and strongest iron ship ever built with a ground-breaking propeller propulsion instead of conventional paddle wheels. Brunel, ever the innovator and perfectionist, was always more concerned about the success of his design than the effect of his ideas on the commercial outcome of the venture.

The launch of the *Great Britain* was on 19 July 1843, the sixth anniversary of the launching of the *Great Western,* and was attended by Prince Albert, the Consort to Queen Victoria. Some 600 guests were invited to a breakfast banquet laid out in a nearby workshop.

The launch of *Great Britain* was totally different from that of *Great Western*. The *Great Britain* was not launched down a slipway but floated out of a dock. Nevertheless, the event caused great excitement and was attended by thousands. After all, when launched, she would be the largest ship afloat. During the banquet the caisson to the dock was opened to let water into the dock. At the end of the banquet it was time to name the great ship. The band struck up 'Rule Britannia' and cannon were fired. Prince Albert had invited Mrs Miles, who had christened *Great Western,* to have the honour again but her throwing of the ceremonial bottle went awry. The Prince was handed a second bottle which he threw and struck the bow, pronouncing her name *'Great Britain'*. She was floated out of the dock into the Floating Harbour in magnificent style, dressed overall with multiple flags.

For the spectators a 'float up' clearly did not have the excitement of the more dramatic launching down a slipway and it is perhaps significant that the heading for this part of the description in the report in the *Illustrated London News* put 'launch' in quotation marks, indicating that the correspondent at least did not regard a 'float up' as a real launch! He added:

With the launch itself some disappointment was expressed by many persons. It was not that the scene was not animating or cheerful – not that the vessel was not as fully stupendous and magnificent as she had been represented to be; but having been built in an excavated dry dock the water had to be let into her, instead of her

dashing from her cradle into the river, according to the usual mode
of launching which, however, could not have been effected in the
confined harbour. Nevertheless the sight was most imposing[6].

When she was launched in 1843 *Great Britain* was the largest and
strongest ship ever built with a steam-powered propeller that was the very
latest invention in maritime technology. Her 1,000hp engine designed
by Brunel himself was the most powerful afloat, and what is more she
could carry enough fuel as well as passengers to power her to America, a
vindication of Brunel in the debate with Dr Lardner over the viability of
steamships for ocean voyages.

It had taken four years to build *Great Britain* but surprisingly it then
took another eighteen months to get her out of Bristol. It was a ridiculous
situation: Brunel had built her too large to fit easily through the gates to
the Floating Harbour and the Bristol Dock Company had assured the
owners that the gates were about to be widened but had not done the
work! The *Bristol Mirror* likened it to 'a weasel in a granary grown too
fat to escape'.[7] Brunel had evidently not learned of, or was probably not
aware of, the similar problem experienced in Chatham in 1765 on the
occasion of the launch of HMS *Victory* recounted in an earlier chapter.
It was not until 12 December 1844 that Brunel was able to move his
huge ship into the River Avon and then only after seeking permission to
remove some of the stone work at the entrance to the dock.

In 1845 *Great Britain* made her maiden transatlantic voyage in just
fourteen days. She was a ship for the wealthy, with early fares between
20 and 28 guineas, equivalent to £3,000 today. She was renowned for
her opulent interior, with gold leaf decorations and mod cons that were
unrivalled by any other ship of her day. She was the world's first grand
ocean liner.

After three successful years on the transatlantic trade she unfortunately
ran aground off Ireland by reason of a navigational error and spent the
winter exposed to storms that would have broken up any other ship. She
survived but the cost of her salvage bankrupted her owners, requiring
the sale of both *Great Western* and *Great Britain*. The latter was sold to
Gibbs Bright and Co. in 1851 and refitted to transport immigrants to

Australia. She subsequently served as a troop ship in the Crimean War. After conversion to a sailing ship in 1886 she was abandoned in Port Stanley in the Falkland Islands.

In 1970 a rescue project was mounted to move *Great Britain* back to Bristol. She was loaded on a pontoon and towed 8,000 miles back across the Atlantic. On 19 July 1970 she was returned to the very dock where she had been constructed, 127 years to the day after she was originally launched by Prince Albert, 19 July also being the anniversary of her keel laying and of the date of the launch of *Great Western*. There in the same dock she can be seen today.

Great Eastern

But back to Brunel's marine engineering experiments in the nineteenth century: despite the closure of the Great Western Steam Steamship Company, Brunel had already made a significant and long-lasting impact on the design of iron-hulled, propeller-driven steamships. And he still had one more 'Great' ship in his locker, his biggest and most ambitious ship project yet: the *Leviathan* as she was officially named, or the *Great Eastern* as she came to be called. The construction of this 'monster' was not as a result of a request from an owner to Brunel for a design followed by the placing of an order for what was to be then the world's largest ship – the normal method of proceeding. It was the other way round. He had the idea and then sought a backer. Unlike Brunel's previous two ships, her launch was to be a sideways launch effected in a controlled fashion and it took eighty-nine days from the first signal to launch until she was afloat. It proved to be a severe test for Brunel and the last great project of his life.

In the 1850s communication to the Far East and Australia was principally by sail; but with the success of the *Great Western* and its ability to carry enough fuel to cross the Atlantic, Brunel began to think whether a ship could be built of sufficient size to carry her own coals, passengers and cargo for a voyage to Australia, and possibly also enough coals for the voyage back. In 1852 he sketched in his notebook a steamship with funnels and masts. It is headed: 'East India Steamship', and beneath it there is scribbled casually the note 'Say 600 feet x 65 feet x 30 feet', dimensions that any contemporary shipwright would have regarded with absolute incredulity.[8]

'By the time the design was finalised … the dimensions had risen to 692 feet long by 83 feet broad weighing 18,915 gross tons and displacing 27,000 tons, with room for 4,000 passengers and 3,000 tons of cargo.'[9] It would be a ship twice the length of *Great Britain*. The majority of the propulsion was to come from a single propeller and the remainder from paddle wheels. Brunel approached the newly created Eastern Steam Navigation Company (ESNC), which had been formed to bid for mail contracts to the Far East but had lost out to The Peninsular and Oriental Steam Navigation Company. There appeared to be a possible opening for Brunel's great ship with this company. Brunel convinced the board of directors of the viability of the project and in 1852 he was appointed their engineer.

By the spring of 1853 Brunel had been authorised to invite tenders. Brunel's initial estimate for cost of the ship was £500,000. John Scott Russell (Russell) of Millwall tendered to build the massive ship for the much lower sum of £377,200, £275,200 for the hull, £42,000 for the paddle engines and boilers and £60,000 for the propeller engines and boilers. Included in Russell's tender price was the expense of 'all the works and machinery necessary for launching the ship or, if it be found preferable, to construct a dock in which to build the ship and there float her out'.[10] Since at the time of making this tender the exact place and method of launching this colossal ship had yet to be determined, the expense of doing so could not be estimated with any degree of accuracy; and this made management of the fixed-price contract difficult for Russell.

Russell was born in Glasgow in 1808 and began his career as an academic in science and mathematics at the University of Glasgow. When it came to applying this knowledge in the field of industry his strong base in science set him apart from his contemporaries in shipbuilding, who largely acquired their knowledge through work experience from being an apprentice. Only Brunel had a similarly strong education in mathematics. Russell made a special study on the theory of waves and hull design. In 1851 he became the sole owner of Millwall Iron Works and Shipbuilding Company on the Thames. He soon obtained an order to construct two large steamers, *Adelaide* and *Victoria*, each of 3,000 tons, for the Australia

Royal Mail Company. This brought him into close contact with Brunel, who was the company's consultant engineer. Russell and Brunel worked closely and harmoniously to produce a successful design. In the summer of 1852 Brunel showed his initial calculations for the new monster ship to Russell. Russell evidently saw this new ship as an extension of the *Adelaide*. He badly needed the work for his yard and put in a low tender.

However, all the figures proved to be gross underestimates. Like Brunel, Russell was a better scientist than a businessman. While Russell expected to design and build the ship in accordance with his usual shipbuilding practice, the detail was left to Brunel. The basis on which the two were to work together was not properly sorted out. Add to this a clash of personalities and it was never going to be an easy project.

On 18 May 1853 the Board of ESNC had accepted Brunel's recommendation to adopt Russell's tender. The shipbuilding contract between ESNC and John Scott Russell dated 22 December 1853 gave Brunel, as the engineer, a great deal of control over all aspects of the construction and launch. As mentioned, at the time of signing the method of launching was left open; it had evidently not yet been decided whether the massive ship was to be launched or floated out of an excavated dock but the final decision rested with Brunel. A report from Brunel to the Board of ESNC dated 7 February 1855[11] helps us to understand the thought process by which the final decision to launch sideways was made. While construction in an excavated dock with float up on completion, the method preferred by Russell, had been the successful method of launch for the *Great Britain*, the size of the dock required for this even larger ship, six times the size, the difficulty of finding a proper site for such a dock and the expense involved as well as the required depth of water in the channel from the dock to the river ruled this option out. The sheer length of the new ship and the narrow width of the Thames at Millwall also made it impossible to contemplate a normal stern launch for a ship of this great length.

Brunel concluded that: 'These considerations led me to consider the practicality of launching or lowering the vessel sideways; and I found that such a mode would be attended with every advantage and, so far as I can see, it involves no counter prevailing disadvantages. This plan has accordingly been determined upon and the ship is building parallel to the river.' Brunel envisaged that 'when launching has to be effected, two cradles will be introduced and the whole will probably be lowered gradually to low-water mark, whence, on the ensuing tide, the vessel will be floated off'.[12]

There appears to have been little experience of sideway launches in the UK at that time and the concept of the hull being lowered gradually in two cradles to the low-water mark prior to float off was certainly untried. Brunel was only able to refer the Board to the experience in launching pontoons or floating piers, one of 300ft that he had launched in Plymouth and another of 400ft launched in the Humber by another contractor, but certainly not a ship of this size and weight. Brunel's report to the directors on the launch options was widely circulated and as a result some comfort was, unexpectedly, given to Brunel by correspondence[13] that he received in March/April 1855 from a Mr G.W. Bull at Buffalo Shipyard on Lake Erie, who had read about Brunel's 'mammoth ship'. In the hope of aiding or strengthening Brunel in the feasibility of his plan, Mr Bull assured Brunel that since 1837 they had launched hundreds of ships sideways without mishap or injury to the hull. Brunel wrote back that: 'The most useful and valuable experience is that derived from failure and not from successes,' and pointing out that the vessel he had to launch sideways was larger and heavier than any that had yet been so launched. Brunel wanted to know what difficulties had been experienced with sideways launches. Brunel, always paying attention to detail, added that: 'I am not at all alarmed at the prospects of the job – yet I shall leave no means unemployed to insure perfect success.' Mr Bull's advice was that to take care that both ends of the hull started down the incline at the same time and that the starting must be 'committed to clear heads'. Brunel evidently felt sufficiently encouraged by this correspondence with Mr Bull to proceed with his concept of a sideways launch.

Another innovative feature of the ship was that it was divided transversely into ten separate watertight compartments by bulkheads up to the upper deck and therefore far above the deepest waterline. The concept was that even if one or two of the compartments flooded this would not endanger the buoyancy of the whole ship. Further protection was provided by the hull being given a double skin so that even if the outer skin was torn on a rock this would not cause the ship to sink.

Construction commenced in May 1854. By February 1855 Brunel was increasingly concerned at what he perceived to be the lack of adequate stock control in the yard at Millwall and felt the need to tighten still further his relationship with Russell. An addendum to the shipbuilding contract was signed on 5 February in which it stipulated that the monthly payments to the yard should only be made after production of a certificate signed by Brunel, as the engineer, that the materials delivered justified the payment. It further required all materials delivered to the yard for the purpose of the contract should be identified as such and become the absolute property of ESNC; and finally that in the event of the yard becoming insolvent it would be lawful for ESNC to take possession of the ship and the materials in, on or about the ship and to complete it using all materials provided by the yard. These stringent additions put into Brunel's hands the ability to slow down the flow of payments to the yard, with potentially serious consequences for its future, if he was not satisfied with the materials and workmanship, over which Brunel's decision was expressed to be final. It was very one-sided and gave Brunel full control. Brunel wrote many letters to Russell, always starting 'My dear Sir', calling into question details of the construction and whether the monthly payments were justified.

Russell had hopelessly underestimated the cost of construction and was further impeded by Brunel's strict control on the cash flow. On 4 February 1856 Russell was compelled to suspend all payments to his creditors and to discharge his workforce. After three months of negotiation with the yard's creditors, work recommenced in May with Brunel now in direct charge of the construction. Brunel found that three quarters of the work had yet to be done and that he had no choice but to re-employ Russell's workforce, who alone had the necessary training and riveting experience to complete the task; but they would only do so at increased rates.

Much has been written on the reasons for the ultimate breakdown of the relationship between Russell and Brunel.[14] It is sufficient to say that Brunel was accustomed from his position as chief engineer in his railway projects to direct the complete engineering project. Russell expected to be given the outline and then be left to build the ship in the traditional shipbuilding manner. Brunel was a perfectionist concerned with every detail and frequently changed his mind to improve his experiment, making it very difficult for Russell to work within the constraints of a fixed-price contract; in brief, they had a different approach, added to which there was a clash of personalities.

By the winter of 1857 the work had progressed and the hull was ready for launching. She lay 330ft from the high-water mark and on an incline of 1 to 12. Brunel's concept was that the ship would not be launched in the ordinary sense of that word – the operation would not offer an 'interesting spectacle' but instead there would be a 'controlled launch', by lowering or drawing her cautiously and gradually down the ways, sideways, to the low-water mark, and then floating her off on the top of a big tide. The lowering was to be achieved by a combination of pushing and pulling. Big hydraulic presses on the landward side would push and chains attached to two launching cradles fore and aft linked to steam-powered winches on barges in the Thames would pull. The two launching cradles were iron plated and in September 1857 Brunel, on behalf of ESNC, had hired 500 tons of iron rails on which he envisaged that the cradles would slide. To act as a restraining force in case the hull moved too quickly two ⅝in chains were attached to the cradles and wound around huge checking drums.

Brunel issued a memorandum asking for 'perfect silence' during the launch operation so that his commands and those of others who would direct operations could be heard. The need to co-ordinate the pushing with the hydraulic presses and the pulling from the barges in the river and to keep both ends of the ship even as the ship eased down the ways made this critical. Although aware of his request for silence, the Board of ESNC had, unknown to Brunel, issued thousands of tickets to the public to witness the launch. The enormous ship had attracted great interest and excitement from the public and the Board saw it as a great opportunity to raise funds to defray the mounting cost.

When Brunel arrived on 3 November 1857 to launch his 'great babe' his first task was to clear away the large crowd from the hauling gear. An estimated 10,000 people had turned up at Millwall to witness the event. It was for Brunel the worst possible start to a tricky launching operation. He needed to keep his head clear and did not need all these distractions. He did not want or like the publicity.

Appropriately perhaps, the naming ceremony was performed by a Miss Hope, the daughter of Henry Thomas Hope, a Conservative MP and the Chairman of ENSC. It was expected that the ship would at once slide into the water but it was in fact nearly four months before she did so. After Miss Hope had broken a bottle of champagne against the hull and named the big ship *Leviathan*, it was time for the launch operation to begin.

Brunel gave the signal from the launching platform (Illustration No. 13). The chains holding the forward and stern launching cradles were slackened off the chain drums. The stern drum started to move rapidly, causing the workmen attending the handles on the drum to be hurled into the air. The result was to cause the stern end of the hull to descend faster than the bow end and Brunel, no doubt recalling the advice of Mr Bull that both ends of the hull should start at the same time, ordered the drums to be braked. 'Five men had been injured – one fatally – and the ship had moved four feet.'[15]

After another attempt was made later that day, the operation was postponed to the next full spring tide on 19 November, when the yard was closed to visitors. This and subsequent attempts only resulted in the ship moving a few feet at a time. Russell had suggested launching down greased wooden planks placed on top of the slipway. There was far more friction on the iron rails beneath the two iron cradles, the method suggested by Brunel, than he had anticipated.

The difficulties of the launch were by this time attracting a great deal of public interest. Illustration No. 14 shows the ship close to the river on 5 December 1857, but not yet afloat. Archived at the Brunel Institute in Bristol are a fascinating series of letters written by members of the public to Brunel between November and December 1857 with various suggestions, some of them fanciful, as to how the launch might best be accomplished. These range from the suggestion of a ten-year-old boy 'to dig a trench all around it [the ship] below the level of the water'[16] to '50 crabs could easily be had and easily secured having a dragging power of from five to ten tons';[17] or 'the weight of the *Leviathan* might be significantly reduced by filling all available spaces with hydrogen gas';[18] or 'You will probably laugh at the suggestion but ... put one or two thousand men on board' to jump up and down to create vibration;[19] or the use of 'gunpowder fired from cannon against strong shields placed behind and in connection with the cradles [to] produce a concussion which might be advantageous in starting her';[20] or, following the Archimedes' invention, the use of a fulcrum 'to accelerate the launching of the monster ship in the channel'.[21] Whether or not Brunel ever read all or any of these inventive suggestions – and there were many more – we do not know but doubtless, if he had, they would have been an irritant to him as he quietly contemplated how best to solve his problem. What the letters do illustrate, however, is the tremendous public interest in the project and the public's great support for Brunel as he tried to put his great ship into the water. No ship launch had ever before or, probably since, received this amount of public attention.

There was criticism too. In the *Mechanics Magazine*[22] we find:

Mr Brunel has not been altogether unfamiliar with failure but no failure of his ever did so much to lower the reputation of English engineers as the launch of the *Leviathan*.

Having first, by the construction of that enormous vessel, concentrated the attention of the world upon him, he has now presented to it the greatest and most costly examples of professional folly that was ever seen ...

It is unlikely that Brunel would have been much concerned with this criticism. As an inventor he was always wanting to experiment. Inevitably, while some of his ideas worked, others did not but, as he had written to Mr Bull at Buffalo Shipyard, 'the most useful experience is that derived from failure'. If the failures led to a solution or a better result, Brunel was content. If there is a valid criticism of Brunel it is that in his single-minded zest for the success of a new invention he often forgot that his experiments were being funded by large sums of other people's money.

During the second week of December, Robert Stephenson, Brunel's friend and fellow engineer, came to Millwall to offer his experience and support. He concurred with Brunel in the conclusion that what was needed was to double the power of the hydraulic presses. Brunel wrote to the directors of ENSC on 17 December, assuring them that no injury to the ship could result from this method of proceeding, although it would be attended 'with some expense and delay, but not considerable'.[23] Brunel scoured the country for additional presses, which after several further attempts moved the hull gradually to a point where the cradles were off the end of the ways. Finally, on Saturday 30 January 1858, on a very high tide, the great monster was afloat, eighty-nine days after Brunel gave the first signal for her launch. Once afloat she was towed across the Thames to her fitting out dock at Deptford amid the pealing of bells and the hooting of sirens.

This must be the longest, or at least one of the longest, ship launch operations on record. What has added to the interest is the volume of photographic and other contemporaneous material on the launch that is available.

The launch itself had cost £120,000 and the total cost had mounted to £732,000 and the ship was still far from complete. The cost to Brunel personally was even greater; not only had he put a great deal of his own funds into the venture but his health was broken.

The cost of completing the great ship was estimated to be £172,000. In order to pay for this, a new company was formed called the Great Ship Company, in which the shareholders of ENSC were offered shares, further capital was raised by public subscription and into which the ship was then transferred for a price of £165,000. Brunel organised tenders for this work but his health continued to deteriorate and he was told by his doctors that he was suffering from Bright's disease, whose severe symptoms may help to explain to some extent the deterioration in his relationship with Russell. On the day that Brunel left with his family for a long period of leave in Egypt the Great Ship Company received two tenders, one from Messrs Wigham and Lucas for £142,000 and the other, perhaps surprisingly, was from Russell (who had revived his shipbuilding business) which was lower; and in Brunel's absence the tender from Russell was accepted. On his return to England, Brunel, although he knew that his health was failing, threw himself back into the task of supervising every detail of the fit out.

By the end of August 1858 the ship had been finished and fitted out in luxurious style and was ready for trials. On 2 September Brunel went on board for a final inspection. It was to be his last visit to his 'great babe'. He was photographed looking pale and ill and moments later collapsed with a stroke and was taken home. On 9 September off Dungeness there was a huge explosion on board the vessel, blowing the forward funnel up into the air. Five stokers were killed and others injured. The cause of the explosion was that the stop cocks on the water heaters feeding the boilers for the paddle engines that should have been opened were left closed. Brunel, at home waiting news of the trials, was told of the tragic news on 10 September. It must have been a cruel blow to him and a few days later he died on 15 September.

For some the death and injuries during launch marked her as an unlucky ship. She was not a commercial success for her owner. After the repairs from the boiler explosion were repaired, again by Russell who again put in another over-optimistic estimate, the vessel was finally able to sail on her maiden voyage to New York in June 1860. Despite being feted on arrival and becoming a local visitor attraction, she was not able to attract a regular full complement of passengers for her transatlantic trade. In September 1861, on a voyage from Liverpool to New York, she ran into a heavy gale and was severely damaged. Her strength and design brought her through the storm but the cost of the repairs of £60,000 wiped out any profit for her owners. In May 1862 she again suffered a serious accident, running aground on an uncharted reef off Milford Haven. There was a severe hole in the outer skin but Brunel's double hull and transverse bulkheads saved her. After a few further unprofitable voyages she was laid up in 1864.

In April 1864 the *Great Eastern* was chartered by the Atlantic Telegraph Company as a cable layer to place a cable across the Atlantic. She was the only ship large enough to take the great length of cable required for this operation. She was refitted by removing the ornate decorations in the grand saloon and converting the saloon into a cable tank. After an initial unsuccessful attempt to lay the cable from Ireland to Newfoundland, the first such was laid across the Atlantic in 1866. At last there was some tangible success for this giant ship. She was never used for the Australian trade for which she had been originally designed by Brunel.

It was not until the launch of *Lusitania* for Cunard Line in 1906, forty-nine years after the launch of Brunel's ship, that any vessel of comparable tonnage to *Great Eastern* was launched. Brunel was an innovator; no ship of the size of *Great Eastern* had ever been built, let alone side launched, before. Brunel had the courage to experiment and in his career as an engineer was not afraid to learn lessons from failure. After *Great Eastern*, which displaced 32,160 tons and was 692ft long overall and of 18,915 grt, it is believed that no ships of comparable size to *Great Eastern* were side launched until the liner *Homeric* by Meyer Werft in Papenburg on the River Elbe on 28 September 1985. *Homeric*, with a length, as built, of 669ft 3in, is thought to be the largest ship ever launched sideways. It was certainly the first cruise ship of this size to be launched sideways.

Homeric was edged centimetre by centimetre towards the water by a series of hydraulic presses;[24] but from the giving of the signal to launch until hitting the water the launch of *Homeric* only took a few seconds, as compared to eighty-nine days for *Great Eastern*. It is, however, noteworthy that hydraulic presses, the ultimately successful method used by Brunel to launch *Great Eastern*, were used again 100 years later to launch *Homeric*. The hull design of *Great Eastern*, with its tremendous longitudinal strength, was a forerunner of much modern shipbuilding. As a commercial venture, except for her service as a cable-laying vessel, she was never a success; but as an engineering experiment she was a triumph. Iron ships with watertight compartments, double skin and screw propulsion were a significant legacy for an engineer whose primary achievement had been in the design of railways and bridges.

Chapter 7

Largest Liner Launched

M uch has been written in this book so far about ship launches that did not go to plan, if for no other reason than that they make for more interesting reading! To redress the balance, there is recalled in this chapter the successful launch of a liner, which when it took to the waters of the Tyne on 20 September 1906, was the largest ship afloat in the world; and which went on to fly the Blue Riband for the fastest Atlantic crossing; an honour that she then held for twenty years between 1909 and 1929. By now the discerning reader will have guessed that the ship is the Cunarder, RMS *Mauretania*. Her successful launch in the confined waters of the Tyne was a triumph for the meticulous foresight and planning of her builder.

The Blue Riband

The Blue Riband of the Atlantic denotes the fastest passage between Europe and America by a merchant ship. It appears to have been invented between 1860–70 as a publicity exercise by passenger shipping companies for their promotion on the increasingly popular and competitive transatlantic route. Whichever ship held the record was entitled to fly the prestigious long blue pennant from its topmast until a rival managed a faster crossing. At the end of the nineteenth century there was intense rivalry for this honour between the German firms, Hamburg America Line and North German Lloyd, and the British firms, Cunard Steamship and White Star Line.

Competition from Germany

Kaiser Wilhelm I, King of Prussia, who in 1871 had become Kaiser of a unified Germany, had the strategic vision that, apart from the obvious prestige of the Blue Riband belonging to Germany, there was potential for these vast liners to be used as wartime armed merchant cruisers. With his encouragement, North German Lloyd in 1897 launched the 14,900-ton *SS Kaiser Wilhelm der Grosse*, which made the run to New York in an impressive five days and twenty hours to claim the Blue Riband. She had four funnels and as such was the first 'four stacker,'[1] a promotional feature that was popular and equated in the public's mind 'with size, speed, luxury and, perhaps above all else, with safety'.[2] The British shipping companies had to respond and in 1899 White Star Line launched *Oceanic*, which became the largest liner in the world; but, from a British point of view, White Star's challenge was complicated by the acquisition of its entire stock in 1902 by the American tycoon J. P. Morgan, who also acquired the stock of five other British passenger shipping companies.

Cunard takes up the challenge with the support of the British Government

These takeovers set alarm bells ringing in the headquarters of Cunard, whose Chairman, Lord Inverclyde, immediately sought the assistance of the British Government. He wanted to ensure that Cunard stayed in British hands and he also requested a loan to construct two steamships to compete with both White Star and the German liners – and thereby seek to regain dominance of the Atlantic passenger trade for Cunard and Great Britain. The British Government agreed to provide a loan of £2.6 million repayable over twenty years with interest at 2.75% and also to make an annual payment of £150,000 to Cunard for carrying mails. Among the conditions of the deal, concluded in 1903, were that Cunard was to remain a British concern and that under no circumstances was the management of the company to be in the hands of, or shares in the Cunard ships to be held by, anyone other than British subjects. The whole of the Cunard fleet was to be at the disposal of the Government for purchase or hire and the two new ships were to be specifically designed for rapid conversion to armed cruisers in the event of war.

British shipyards approached

After an approach to four British shipyards, each of which were unusually for that time given an outline general arrangement plan and specification of the proposed new building prior to making a bid, orders for these two super liners were eventually placed: one with John Brown's yard on the Clyde to be named *Lusitania* and the other with Swan Hunter Wigham Richardson on the Tyne to be named *Mauretania*. Apart from the great size of these ships – each new liner was to be of 31,500 grt and 790ft long overall – which at that time made them the biggest shipbuilding contracts ever signed, the other interesting feature was the revolutionary method of propulsion: steam turbine engines, as mentioned earlier, the invention of the Hon. Charles Parsons. He used steam pressure to drive a series of blades on a revolving shaft connected to a screw propeller. He had earlier built a prototype, the *Turbinia*, which readers may recall was badly damaged in 1907 during the launch of a freighter on the Tyne.[3] Cunard had incorporated a similar steam turbine engine in two of its other vessels and this showed that the steam turbine was faster and also more economic than reciprocating engines.

Tank tests

Cunard wanted to be sure that the new ships with these engines could compete successfully with its rivals. The Cunard design team consulted Sir Philip Watts, Director of Naval Construction for the Admiralty, who put the Admiralty experimental tank at the disposal of the company to test the best hull form. The Admiralty had its own special interest in these ships not only as a high-speed addition to the navy in the event of war but also in the use of steam turbine engines for its ships. The result of the tank tests was that a 'broader hull shape was required' and that in order to obtain the speeds required a vast increase in power was agreed. As a result, the decision was taken to have four screws instead of three. As Wallsend was the birthplace of the Parsons marine steam turbine it was entirely appropriate that it should also be the birthplace of one of these great ships incorporating a turbine engine invented on the same stretch of river. The turbines for *Mauretania* were designed by the Wallsend Slipway Company in conjunction with Parsons Marine Steam Turbine Company.

Launching a large ship in a narrow river

Hull 735, which was to be named *Mauretania*, was constructed inside a huge shed at Wallsend that was more than 130ft high and over 700ft long with a glass roof that enabled work to continue even in bad weather. On completion of construction, Hull 735 had a record launch weight of about 16,500 tons, just above that of her sister vessel *Lusitania*. There were many questions: could such a mammoth ship, which would then be the largest ship in the world, be launched safely down a launch way? If she did reach the water intact, could she be stopped in such a limited space? Would the effect of such a huge mass entering the water cause there to be a giant, and potentially dangerous, backlash of water?

When such a huge mass gets afloat it is important to determine in advance how it is going to be brought to a standstill. At Swan Hunter and Wigham Richardson's yard the Tyne is only ¾ of a mile wide and with the ship's length of 761ft, equating to ⅛ of a mile, there was not much room for error. The *Lusitania* had been launched on 7 June 1906 by Lady Inverclyde, the widow of the Chairman of Cunard who had been the inspiration behind the whole project but had not lived to see it happen. John Brown's yard had the advantage that its slipways were laid at an angle across the Clyde, enabling it to use the entrance to the River Cart on the opposite bank as an additional stretch of water to arrest a hull after launch. Using this extra water, *Lusitania* was launched successfully across the Clyde into the Cart and stopped. Swan Hunter did not have the safety valve equivalent of the Cart. How was the *Mauretania*, the heaviest ship ever launched, to be transferred safely into the water and then stopped? This was the question on the mind of George Hunter, the managing director of the Tyne shipbuilder. As the *Newcastle Daily Journal* wrote on 20 September 1906, the day of the launch: 'The responsibility of securing the safe transfer from the ways to the water of so huge a vessel as the *Mauretania* is no light one.'

The launch spectacle

The Tyne and Wear Archives record that in order to move the hull down the slipway 14.5 tons of tallow, 103 gallons of train oil and a ton of soft soap were used. The chosen method to stop the hull careering across the river was a series of huge chain drags attached to the hull with hawsers, five on each side of the hull, and aggregating more than 1,000 tons, coming gradually into operation as the hull became waterborne.

The launch was scheduled for 4.15pm to coincide with the top of the tide. At 3pm all passing traffic in the river was stopped and the steam tugs required to assist in the launch took up their position on either side of the slipway.

There was great interest in the launch, not just on the Tyne but beyond and large crowds attended, vying for the best vantage points on both sides of the river to view the moment when this great leviathan took to the water. Although it was an overcast day, this did not put off the enthusiasm of the estimated 30,000 spectators. By reason of the size of the new ship and its potential speed, the launch was a subject of interest to ship owners and shipbuilders far beyond the Tyne.

In view of the involvement of the Government and the Admiralty in the whole project Cunard had invited the Duchess of Roxburghe, whose brother-in-law was Lord Tweedmouth, First Lord of the Admiralty, to have the honour of launching the ship. There is a lovely photograph of the official launch party, all smartly dressed, with many of the ladies wearing florally decorated hats and some gentlemen in black top hats standing on the platform just below the bow. The guests included the First Lord of the Admiralty, Lord Tweedmouth, William Watson, Chairman of Cunard and Hon. Charles Parsons, the inventor of the steam turbine engine.

By all accounts, just before the launch, the crowds anticipating the great moment were hushed and all was quiet except for the sound of the band of the First Newcastle Artillery. There was excitement at the imminence of the birth of this large ship; but also some anxiety. Great crowds thronged the surrounding hills in order to have a panoramic view. Among them was a special correspondent of the *Evening Chronicle*, who had climbed the 'Ballast Hills' at Hebburn on the opposite side of the river from the launch way. He describes the scene below and around him: A 'great silence reigned over everything ... everyone was anxiously waiting. Presently in the extreme stillness, the band playing far away on the other side could faintly be heard ...'[4]

At 4.15pm Lady Roxburghe 'pulled the trigger' and smashed a bottle of champagne against the bow, naming the great liner *Mauretania*.[5]

Up on the 'Ballast Hills', the *Evening Chronicle's* special correspondent continued his bird's eye account of the actual moment of launch: 'The motion was seen before the cheering and the screeching of sirens had travelled across the water, and almost at once the hill of silence broke into convulsions of excitement. In contrast with all this wild shouting and cheering the great vessel glided gently and noiselessly into the water ...'[6]

A triumph for meticulous planning

It had taken a mere forty seconds for the hull 'weighing 16,000 tons in launch condition'[7] to move down the ways, during which she reached a speed of '14 knots'.[8] The vessel slowed up with remarkable skill, the huge hawsers and chains doing their work as the five check chains on either side of the hull became taut. 'The river was only 1,130 foot wide and the vessel, it was calculated, would need at least 950 feet to be brought to a stop.'[9] In the event less than three quarters of the river was crossed. When the vast size of the ship and the narrow remaining space in the river is considered, the launch must have been a source of much thought and anxiety to the shipyard. Illustration No. 15 dramatically illustrates the narrow space in which the launch was effected, with the other side of the river clearly visible, and the tension on the ten heavy check chains, five on each side of the hull, coming gradually into operation, which restrained the hull once in the water. There was not only the need to stop the giant hull before it reached the far bank but, as noted already, the fear that the back wash as it entered the water would result in a calamity similar to that which occurred in the Thames some eight years earlier during the launch of HMS *Albion*.[10] Tests on a wooden model 47.5ft long, which was a 1/16th scale replica of the ship's hull, carried out in a dock on the Tyne provided valuable information on how the new ship might perform. The *Newcastle Daily Journal* reported that:

> As the *Mauretania* entered the water, a sheet of water flew up on both sides and a great wave swept across the Tyne on to the opposite bank, wetting many of those standing on the quays. Owing no doubt to the fact that the vessel was launched precisely at high water, the impact with the water did not cause the monster wave that many expected ... The vessel was slowed with remarkable skill, the huge hawsers and chains doing their work in a magnificent fashion.[11]

The fact that it was a triumph, combining safety with success, was due to all the meticulous planning that George Hunter and his team had put into the launching arrangements. The only accident was that one workman was slightly injured when a piece of glass from the shattered ceremonial bottle fell on his head. He was quickly given first aid and was said to be none the worse for his experience.

After the successful launch the guests from the official party were entertained to lunch in traditional fashion. As a memento of the occasion, Lady Roxburghe was presented with a silver casket that was fashioned with the coat of arms of Cunard and a representation of *Mauretania* as it would look when completed with its four magnificent funnels – she would be a 'four stacker' in the best transatlantic tradition. Lord Tweedmouth, in his speech to the guests, said that the Admiralty hoped that it would never be necessary to call upon the *Lusitania* and the *Mauretania* to serve the nation in time of war. His hopes were unfortunately not to be realised.

Regaining the Blue Riband

Lusitania, on her second double crossing of the Atlantic in 1907, regained the Blue Riband, which she held until the honour was passed to *Mauretania*, which was fractionally faster than her sister ship. *Mauretania*'s record of four days and nineteen hours at an average speed of 26.06 knots remained unchallenged for twenty years, to the delight of Cunard and the British. Her record was finally overtaken by German Lloyd's *Bremen* in 1929.

At war

In the interval, the hostilities that Lord Tweedmouth had so feared when speaking on the *Mauretania*'s launch day materialised. At the outset of war in 1914 *Mauretania* was required by the British Government to become an armed merchant cruiser as envisaged in the 1903 agreement. However, due to her size and fuel consumption she proved unsuitable for this role. After a period out of action, during which *Lusitania* was sunk by U-boats in May 1915 with a loss of 1,195 lives, *Mauretania* resumed service as a hospital ship and troopship protected by dazzle camouflage and by her great speed. In the summer of 1915 she made three trips to the Aegean taking troops to the ill-fated Gallipoli campaign and on three occasions transporting wounded soldiers home from the eastern Mediterranean. In September 1919 she resumed her civilian duty and on the transatlantic run became affectionately known as the 'Grand Old Lady of the Atlantic'.

Pride of the Tyne

Mauretania was the pride of the Tyne and a triumph for Tyne shipbuilding and for George Hunter. His reputation, as well as that of Swan Hunter and of the Tyne generally as a centre of shipbuilding excellence, was enhanced. There were those who had questioned whether a ship of this size and weight could be launched successfully in such confined waters. His meticulous planning and expertise ensured that the launch of the world's largest ship in 1906 proceeded safely and successfully. Nothing had been left to chance. The vessel was the largest and most magnificent passenger ship ever launched on the river.

In 1936 President Franklin D. Roosevelt wrote an article extolling her virtues: 'When she was born in 1907, the *Mauretania* was the largest thing put together by man … she always fascinated me with her graceful, yacht-like appearance, her four enormous black topped red funnels, and her appearance of power and good breeding.'[12]

Chapter 8

'Ladies Who Launch'

B y the date of the launch of *Mauretania* in 1906, it was an almost universal custom in England for ladies to be invited to christen ships at their launch, whether naval or merchant. Before the regency of the Prince Regent (1811–20), when a more established pattern can first be discerned, the number of recorded occasions when a lady christened a ship are rather few.

Early examples

Charles II had a great love for the sea. He, with his brother James, was responsible for introducing yachting to the English based on various Dutch-built ships that 'retained a distinctively warlike appearance … with their eight guns and their crews of thirty men'.[1] Charles II had a number of yachts built for him and in 1670 his Portuguese wife Queen Catherine joined the yachting craze that was becoming popular in the royal circle by having a yacht of her own. The 86-ton yacht was designed by surveyor Sir Anthony Deane, constructed in Portsmouth and brought round to Deptford. The Calendar of State Papers (Domestic) 1670–80 briefly reports that on 14 April 1670: 'The Queen was entertained this day by the Duchess of York at Deptford where she went on board her ship, gave it a Portuguese name and fired a gun.' The name given to the yacht was *Saudadoes*, which in the plural signifies good luck or best wishes. However, a more plausible meaning is 'deeply missing someone or something', which it has been suggested was connected to Queen Catherine's feelings towards her home country and family, from whom she had been separated since leaving Lisbon in 1662.[2] In other contemporary papers an eyewitness described that: 'Her Majesty gives life to all by frequent divertisement upon the river in her new vessel *Saudadoes*. They undertake long voyages and, falling short of provisions, victual themselves sometimes at Vauxhall and sometimes at Lambeth'[3] – a colourful picture of yacht cruising on the river Thames in the seventeenth century! However, Queen Catherine's fun on the river was short lived; she only enjoyed the yacht for about three years, after which the yacht was transferred to the navy and in 1673 rebuilt as a 180-ton man-of-war. *Saudadoes*, however, retains the distinction of being one of the earliest known examples of a ship naming by a lady, who was also a member of the Royal family; albeit that this was not a naming at launch but after launch.

Newspaper report

In 1803 we find the record of a christening by a lady in a newspaper. It relates to the launch on the same day, 8 January 1803, at the Randall and Brent's shipyard in Rotherhithe of two merchantmen for The East India Company, the 800-ton *Lady Castlereagh* and the 500-ton *Union*:

> The splendour of the scene received considerable addition from the fineness of the day-and a more impressive sight we have never witnessed on a similar occasion.
>
> At a little after two, Father Thames received into his embrace, the *Lady Castlereagh* christened by Sir Hugh Inglis: the *Union* received her name from the beautiful Daughter of the same Gentleman.[4]

Sir Hugh Inglis was a director and the Chairman of the East India Company but the report (perhaps adhering to the social norms of that time) does not reveal the name of his beautiful daughter, the godmother of the *Union*, nor does it think it worthy of remark that a lady was doing the christening. It goes on to give a detailed account of the other distinguished guests and of the great banquet, the toasts drunk, the decoration of the room using the colours of the East India Company, and of the dancing that followed the successful double launch. It mysteriously then adds the comment: 'We believe there has not occurred in the history of such ceremonies, another instance of an individual launching two ships from one yard in one tide.'[5] The reporter evidently had somehow forgotten that Sir Hugh's. daughter had christened the second ship and was an individual in her own right! Perhaps the explanation lies in the fact that it was not the norm at that time to put the names of ladies in newspapers.

At the end of the eighteenth century it appears to have become increasingly common for ladies to attend ship launches alongside distinguished gentlemen. This is illustrated by a lovely etching of the launching of the *Prince of Wales* at Portsmouth on 28 June 1794 in the presence of King George III and Queen Charlotte and with 'launching colours' flying (Illustration No. 17).

The etching, described by those who created it as 'the exact representation' of the launch, shows elegantly dressed ladies being very much in attendance and adding colour and style to the patriotic occasion. After this event it was only a short step before ladies were themselves invited to launch a ship.

Custom introduced by Prince Regent?

It is often said that it was in 1811 during the period of the Prince Regent that the custom was started of asking a lady to perform the ceremony of naming a new naval ship. Is this true? *The Admiralty Manual of Seamanship* 1951 edition[6] states: 'Until 1811 the ceremony for HM ships was always performed by a Royal Personage or a Royal Dockyard Commissioner but in that year the Prince Regent introduced the custom of allowing ladies to perform it.'

The use of the word 'allowing' in the manual perhaps indicates that the change of practice was somewhat viewed as a concession by the gentlemen!

A formal directive from the Prince Regent to which this custom can be attributed has not been found by the author but during the period of his rule as Regent (1811–20) there were a number of occasions when a new naval ship at its launch was named by a lady.

The first is the launch at Plymouth of the 98-gun ship, again called the *Union*, built after the model of HMS *Victory*, on 16 September 1811, on which a report was written in the *Naval Chronicle:*[7]

the usual ceremonies in the naming of the ship having been performed by Miss Williams of Scorrier House, the dogshores of the Union were knocked away, and with majesty impossible to be described, she spurned the waters of the receding tide, and soon rode triumphantly on that element of which she is so magnificent an ornament. The coup d'oeil at the awful and impressive moment of her departure from the stocks was truly electrifying ...

On 23 January 1811 the Prince Regent had issued an Order in Council to commence work on a breakwater at Plymouth in order to provide better shelter for ships in the harbour. Among the parties involved in this project were John Williams of Scorrier House, who owned quarries, and members of the Fox family of Falmouth. An order to commence construction was given on 22 June 1811. A formal contract to quarry rock and convey it to the wharf ready for the building of the breakwater was signed in 1812 after the launch of the *Union*. The construction of the breakwater at Plymouth was a project of great interest to the Prince Regent and there was, therefore, good reason for him to have invited the daughter of one of the main contractors to have the honour of naming the *Union*. Unfortunately many of the Williams' family archives were subsequently destroyed in a fire at Scorrier House in 1908, and so the Williams family now has no record of exactly how or when the invitation came to be given. Nor does any of the contemporaneous correspondence between the Navy Board and Plymouth Dockyard, which authorised the launch and issued regulations for it, mention Miss Williams or make anything of the fact that a lady was being given this honour. The reports from the Dockyard and the instructions from the Navy Board on the subject of the launches of new ships stick to the usual formal language of a report from the Dockyard that the ship is in all respects ready for launch on a specified date if the Navy Board so approves and in reply the Dockyard being instructed and required by the Navy Board to launch on that date. There is no discussion in this typical, stereotyped exchange as to who will have the honour of naming the ship, nor does the reporter in the *Navy Chronicle* think it worthy of comment that the 'usual ceremonies' had been performed by a lady.

The next possible launch by a lady relates to Princess Charlotte of Wales, the daughter of the Prince Regent and Caroline of Brunswick, who was born on 7 January 1796. The *Naval Chronicle* contains the following report of the launch of the frigate *Maidstone* of 36 guns at Deptford on 18 October 1811:

> The launch took place, not in the river but in a basin within the yard, on one side of which lay the King's yacht, her quarter deck arranged as was understood for the reception of her Royal Highness, the Princess Charlotte of Wales who, however, did not arrive.[8]

Princess Charlotte would have been fifteen at the time of this launch. That she was expected to attend the launch is not in question but we do not know for sure that she was to have the honour of naming the ship. The relationship with her father was not an easy one. Soon after the birth of Charlotte, the Prince Regent became estranged from his wife and, on his orders, she was brought up separately by governesses with only limited access to her mother. It would not, therefore, have been surprising if Charlotte felt resentful and one way of making her feelings known would have been to defy her father's wish that she launch this ship. Again, the formal correspondence between the Dockyard and the Navy Board omits any mention of the possible attendance or role of Princess Charlotte and limits its report to the fact that: 'In obedience to your direction ... we beg leave to acquaint you that yesterday afternoon we launched from slip No. 2 to the basin ... ship *Maidstone* of 36 guns ...'[9] We can only surmise that the Prince Regent was keen to give his daughter a public but enjoyable duty but this did not work out for whatever reason. She was later to defy her father by rejecting the suitor her father had chosen for her. She insisted on marrying Leopold of Saxe Gotha for love and tragically died while giving birth to a child in November 1817, when just twenty-one years old.

What we do know is that at the Royal Dockyard in Chatham on 28 March 1815 the *Howe*, a first-rate warship of 120 guns, was christened at her launch by Lady Torrington. She had excellent naval connections, being the daughter of Sir Robert Barlow, Comptroller of the Navy and Superintendent at Chatham, and the wife of Admiral Lord Torrington.

He was the son of George Byng, First Viscount Torrington (1633–1733), who had been First Lord of the Admiralty between 1689 and 1690.

Again, the *Naval Chronicle* has the report of the launch:

At a quarter past two the Commissioner, Sir Robert Barlow, accompanied by his daughter, Lady Torrington, by Admiral Lord Torrington and other persons of distinction, were introduced into a place appointed at her head [of the ship]. Some bottles of wine being produced the builder Mr Perkins, poured out several glasses, which he handed to Lady Torrington and the Nobility around and 'the Howe and success to her being drunk', Lady Torrington took a bottle of port which she brake against the cut – water,[10] agreeable to the ancient mode of christening. At a quarter before 3 o'clock, all being ready, Mr Perkins gave order for knocking away the triggers and with slight assistance from the Samson Jacks the Howe with great majesty and precision slid into the bosom of her element, amidst the cheers of as great an assemblage as ever was known on a similar occasion.[11]

While no evidence has to date been found that the Prince Regent, in 1811 or subsequently, formally directed that naval ships might from that date forward be christened by ladies, there were clearly good reasons for him to have suggested that the three ladies in question should have the honour. As noted, Miss Williams of Scorrier House was the daughter of one of the constructors of the Plymouth breakwater, a project in which the Prince Regent took a great deal of personal interest; Her Royal Highness Princess Charlotte of Wales was his daughter; and Lady Torrington was the daughter of the Comptroller of the Navy and superintendent of the Royal Dockyard at Chatham where the *Howe* was built. However, it is safe to conclude that it was during the Regency that a pattern can first be discerned of ladies being invited to christen naval ships; and that this is probably how the custom started. What is also interesting is that in none of these reports was anything made of the fact that it was a lady, not a gentleman, who was launching and christening a ship. Again, the explanation may lie in the social customs of the day and the reluctance to mention the names of ladies in the press.

Just why the custom was started is more speculative. It has been suggested that 'it amused the Prince Regent's many girlfriends and caused excitement among them'.[12] However attractive this may be as a theory, there is no suggestion that Miss Williams of Scorrier House or Lady Torrington were girlfriends of the Prince Regent, so a verdict of not proven would have to be returned on this theory. Perhaps the answer is simply that the Prince Regent clearly enjoyed the company of women and perhaps saw an opportunity to extend his patronage to women in this way. Alternatively, since popularity of the royalty mattered after the French Revolution, which had only recently occurred, and the Prince Regent, not being well loved by the people due to the way he treated his wife and daughter and with his private and public life being generally regarded as a scandal, maybe saw it as a means to court public affection.

Sailors have a long-held superstition that it is bad luck for women to be on board their ship, fearing that their presence would anger the sea gods and result in the ship encountering bad weather or some other misfortune. Could this account for the reluctance on the part of gentlemen to invite ladies to christen ships? The author's view is that this superstition was not a factor; rather the change in practice of inviting ladies to launch came about by reason of their increased attendance at ship launches at the end of the eighteenth century and the Prince Regent's wish to extend his patronage to women. Besides, by the time of the Regency the 'standing cup' ceremony had been discontinued and the naming ceremony took place on the quayside, so any lady invited to name a ship did not need to step on board to perform the ceremony and risk angering the sea gods.

The invitation to ladies to launch naval ships was not to exclude Lords of the Admiralty and other distinguished gentlemen of the day from continuing to perform this honour after 1811. A brief survey of launches between 1811 and 1818 show that most launch ceremonies of naval ships during this period continued to be performed by the First Lord of the Admiralty and other gentlemen of distinction; but the custom of inviting ladies, having been started, gradually gathered momentum, but never to the total exclusion of gentlemen. There continued to be launch ceremonies carried out by male members of the Royal family and Royal Dockyard Commissioners, a good example being the launch ceremony for HMS *Dreadnought* performed in Portsmouth on 10 February 1906 by King Edward VII.

Christening bottle to be attached by lanyard

A much-told story is that, soon after the custom of inviting ladies to launch naval ships started, a lady threw the christening bottle at the bow of a ship with such force that it missed the hull altogether and injured a spectator, who then sued the Admiralty in damages.[13] The result of this incident was said to be the requirement by the Admiralty that the christening bottle should henceforward be attached by a lanyard to the ship being launched.[14]

It is a colourful story. However, the author has again been unable to find concrete evidence of the event: neither the claim by the injured spectator nor the Admiralty directive relating to the lanyard. Some possible indirect evidence is to be found in an account in the *Naval Chronicle* of the launch on 15 October 1818 of the 74-gun *Talavera* at Woolwich Dockyard, which includes the following passage on another launch by a lady:

> The Hon. Miss Townshend (daughter of Viscount Sydney)[15] was conducted to the bow of the ship, and a bottle of Madeira, suspended by a small cord from the upper part of the vessel, was put into her hand. She flung the bottle against the jibs, and called, or christened, the ship – *Talavera*.[16]

It is significant that the writer of the report thought it important to mention the fact that the christening bottle was 'suspended by a small cord from the upper part of the vessel'. This suggests, possibly, that the incident relating to the injured spectator had happened or at least that the Admiralty directive requiring the christening bottle to be tied by a lanyard to the ship had been issued only a short time before the launch of *Talavera* in 1818, so that his readers would have readily understood the significance of this detail.

By 1821 the custom of inviting ladies to name ships, whether naval or merchant, seems to have been enthusiastically adopted in Ipswich at least, where no fewer than four ships built in the town that year were recorded as being named by a lady.[17] One of them was 'a lady from London who threw the christening bottle in good style'[18] before the schooner *Henry* went down the ways for Truro owners. When Lady Harland launched an East Indiaman at the Halifax yard a few weeks later she said: 'May God bless the good ship *William Fairlie*.'[19]In the US it was in 1828 that the first lady christened a naval ship, the *Concord*, but her identity is not known, only that she was 'a young lady of Portsmouth'.[20] However, as noted, the social norms at that time in the US as well as in England were to avoid mentioning ladies by name in the press.

'Sponsor' or 'godmother'

A lady who has the honour of naming a naval ship is often known as her 'sponsor', or in the case of a merchant ship as her 'godmother'. The roles of a sponsor and a godmother are similar and it would appear to be a matter of tradition, rather than any difference in substance, that determines that it is 'sponsors' for naval ships and 'godmothers' for merchant ships; but these terms have not always been been consistently used.

Sponsors

At a Christian baptism or christening of a child the godparents are called upon to be 'sponsors', a word that is derived from the Latin *sponsum*, meaning promise. They make solemn promises on the infant's part to keep God's commandments until the child is old enough to take responsibility for himself or herself. Having made this sacred vow, the godparents will naturally want to take a special interest in the wellbeing, education and upbringing of their godchild. When it comes to sponsors of ships there is, of course, no element of making a promise on behalf of the ship but the ship's sponsor, having been honoured to name a ship, will naturally want to take a special interest in her during her life and in the sailors who man her.

Role of sponsor or godmother

Sponsors or godmothers play a unique role in the life of a ship. As they christen their ships, bestowing upon them the chosen name, they become part of that ship's history. As we learnt earlier, at the moment of christening the ship ceases to be just a hull number or an 'it', but becomes a 'her' with a chosen name and individual personality.

The crew of a ship may change many times over during the life of a ship but the sponsor remains the same. Most sponsors form a warm and lasting relationship with their ships, an affiliation that is rewarding to both. In this respect they are genuinely like godmothers of children. They are there to take a special interest and many sponsors try to visit their ships as frequently as possible, in the same way that a godparent wants to see his or her godchild.

For example, the author has heard of one sponsor who makes a special effort to visit the Royal Naval ship of which she is the sponsor at least once a year whenever she calls at a convenient port and cooks a special fruit cake for the ship's company each Christmas.

Role of sponsor formalised in US

In the US the role of the sponsor of US naval ships has been formalised. In 1908 there was formed an exclusive Society of Sponsors of the US Navy, membership of which is restricted to ladies who have been a sponsor of a US naval ship. The society was founded by Miss (Annie) Keith Frazier (Somerville), sponsor of the USS *Tennessee,* and Miss Mary Campbell (Underwood), sponsor of USS *Birmingham*, with the support of the Secretary of the Navy and President Roosevelt. Mrs Keith Frazier Somerville wrote about the society's history:

> It all started in 1907 when I saw in a newspaper account of the launching of the cruiser *Birmingham* where it had been suggested there that the girls who had christened ships in the US Navy should form a society. The idea intrigued me and I sat down immediately and wrote Mary Campbell, Sponsor of the *Birmingham* and asked if anything had been done about such a society and if not why didn't we try to organise one. She replied that nothing had been done and she thought it would be fun to try – but how.[21]

Mrs Keith Frazier Somerville was the daughter of the Senator for Tennessee and through his good executive offices an introduction to the

Secretary of the Navy and in due course to President Roosevelt ensured that the idea had backing at the most senior level in Washington.

The society held its first meeting at Willard Hotel, Washington DC, on 18 February 1908 and were guests that evening of the President for the Army-Navy reception (see Illustration No. 18 for a lovely picture of the founding lady sponsors, all very smartly dressed for this special occasion). For many years the annual meeting of the society was held at the Willard Hotel.

The sponsor of a US Navy ship sometimes attends keel-laying but has a defined role at christening, commissioning and at decommissioning. At the launch of a ship of the US Navy the sponsor says: 'In the name of the United States I christen thee …'. At the commissioning ceremony the sponsor gives the word to the ship's company: 'Man our ship and bring her to life,' to which the traditional reply is: 'Aye, aye Ma'am,' and the crew then board the ship; all present rejoice and break out in thunderous applause. It is a very patriotic and proud moment for all. The motto of the society is 'Don't give up the ship', reinforcing the bond that exists between each sponsor and her ship. The role of a sponsor is described on the society's website:

> Far beyond participation in ceremonial milestones, sponsorship represents a lifelong relationship with the ship and her crew. While this bond begins with the ship's christening and the initial crew it will ideally extend throughout the ship's service life and even beyond. Sponsors are encouraged to make every effort to foster this special relationship and to maintain contact with initial and successive captains and the amazing men and women who comprise her crew. This can be as simple as exchanging emails or holiday questions and participating in sail away and home coming.[22]

For every ship there will be a list of commanding officers, some of whom may be remembered for their distinguished service, others not; but for the entire life of a ship there is only one sponsor and the sponsor will always be a part of the crew and her name will live on with the ship.

In the US it is not unusual for the lady sponsor to be accompanied by daughters or special friends, so called 'matrons of honour', to assist the sponsor at the christening. The President of the Society attends all christenings and commissioning of US Naval ships during her time in office and does a report for the society; it has become the tradition to end her report of each such event with the words 'It was a great Navy day!'

A sponsor usually makes a gift to her ship at the time of her christening, in much the same way as a godparent does at the baptism of a child. This gift is then displayed on board the ship during her life. There is provision in the US for the Secretary of the Navy to lend or give the sponsor of a US naval ship a name plate or any article of negligible or sentimental value from that ship.

The Society of Sponsors of the US Navy has published a record of the launching of all US naval ships from 1797 to date with details of the name of the sponsor, the reason for the name chosen for the ship, frequently a distinguished naval officer, with biographical details and frequently a description of the launch. The society has included among its members such distinguished First Ladies as Barbara Bush, Nancy Reagan, Jacqueline Kennedy and Michelle Obama. Three nuns who participated in the launch of the destroyer *Laboon* in 1993 are also members, in honour of their late brother, Father John Francis Laboon (1921–88), a chaplain of the Chaplains Corps who was awarded the Silver Star for his heroism in the Second World War.

How is a sponsor nominated?

US Navy ship

In the old days it was the custom for the builder of a US Navy ship to invite a sponsor to break a bottle of wine or water and bestow the name upon the ship. This custom has changed so that it is now the practice for the Secretary of the Navy to request the governor of the state in which the ship is being constructed to nominate the sponsor for a ship to be named for a state, or when ships are to be named for individuals it is customary for the Navy Department to nominate as sponsor some member of the family of the officer or distinguished civilian for whom the ship is named. Most ships have only one sponsor but, as we have seen with the Destroyer *Laboon,* sometimes two or more are nominated if they have a close relationship with the person in whose honour the ship is to be named. Another interesting example is the USS *Winston S. Churchill*, which has two sponsors: Lady Soames, daughter of Sir Winston Churchill, and Mrs Janet Cohen, the wife of the former Secretary of Defence, William Cohen.

Royal Navy ships

The sponsor for Royal Navy ships and submarines are today chosen by the First Sea Lord, who invites the lady he has chosen to accept the honour. The sponsors are drawn from the Royal household, from the wives of political or military figures or is the wife of a senior serving Admiral of the Royal Navy. The First Sea Lord informs the Secretary of Defence of his appointment of sponsors for ships and submarines. For example, Admiral Sir Mark Stanhope, as First Sea Lord, invited HM Queen Elizabeth II to be the sponsor of the new 65,000-ton aircraft carrier HMS *Queen Elizabeth* constructed in Rosyth Dockyard previously mentioned, an invitation she accepted.

A navy ship's original sponsor is unique: a US naval ship and a Royal Navy ship can only have one true sponsor, the original sponsor, the lady who broke the bottle and gave the ship her name and her personality. If the sponsor dies while the Royal Navy ship is still in service, the ship may have a 'friend' but not another sponsor. A recent example is the aircraft carrier HMS *Illustrious*, where HRH Princess Margaret was the sponsor. When Margaret died, Queen Elizabeth II gave permission for her daughter, Sarah Chatto, to become the ship's 'friend'; she took over the role and took an active interest in the ship up to and including her decommissioning. It is anticipated that King Charles III may in due course appoint a ship's 'friend' for HMS Queen Elizabeth following the death of her sponsor The late Queen. Similarly, in the US upon the death of a sponsor no new sponsor is named, but matrons of honour who assisted the sponsor at the christening or a member of the sponsor's family may continue unofficially to maintain the special relationship with the ship enjoyed by the sponsor until her death.

The Society for Sponsors of the US Navy was also responsible for the introduction of the Prayer for Our Navy in 1914,[23] which for many years formed a central part of the religious service upon the launch and naming of ships of the US Navy.

Association of sponsors to be formed in UK?

Although there has been some suggestion that a similar society of sponsors of Royal Naval Ships be established in the UK, at present one does not exist and the Society of Sponsors of the US Navy is, therefore, currently unique. As the wife of a former First Sea Lord has told the author: 'There is very little by way of guidance for launchers of ships in the UK. We are there to support the ship through her life in whatever ways we can but there is no association of launchers ...'. In 2011, in an effort to start such a society in the UK, an invitation was issued to some forty ladies, who had all launched the navy's current ships, to a lunch aptly titled for 'Ladies who Launch', from which the title to this chapter is derived. Although the occasion apparently met with great enthusiasm, the idea of a society for sponsors of Royal Navy Ships has not yet been taken up. Since 2011 there has been one further reception for lady sponsors held in February 2018, at Admiralty House Portsmouth, the home of the Second Sea Lord, which twenty-two lady sponsors attended. A British society is a great idea and it is to be hoped that one will be formed in the not too distant future.

Chapter 9

Launches at Royal Dockyards

T here were special procedures, colourful customs and traditions for launches of naval ships constructed at Royal Dockyards.

Location

Royal Dockyards (also known as 'Royal Naval Dockyards') in England where naval ships were constructed, based or refitted, were first established during the reign of King Henry VII. Portsmouth was the first to be created in 1496 with the construction of a dry dock. Woolwich in 1512 and Deptford in 1513 on the Thames, near to King Henry VIII's palace at Greenwich, soon followed. The other places where principal Royal Dockyards have been located in England have been at Harwich, Sheerness, Chatham and Plymouth (where in 1843 the Dockyard became known as Devonport), in Wales at Pembroke Dock and, in Scotland, at Rosyth. There were also Royal Dockyards in the British colonies, but their main activity was maintenance and repair of ships rather than shipbuilding.

Naval Overseer at private yards

The essence of Royal Dockyards was that they must be Government concerns in the ownership of the Crown. However, at various times, in order to complement the limited shipbuilding performed at the Royal Dockyards,[1] naval ships were also built in private yards under the supervision of an officer from a Royal Dockyard known as a Naval Overseer – a good example being Buckler's Hard on the Beaulieu river. But, even in the case of naval ships built in private yards, fitting out was frequently done in a Royal Dockyard, so that in the case of naval ships constructed at Buckler's Hard, after launch the hull was towed to Portsmouth Royal Dockyard for completion.

Buckler's Hard

The private shipyard at Buckler's Hard has been substantially preserved and the attractive street with the original shipyard workers brick houses leading down to the river makes for an interesting visit today. The large house nearest to the river, which belonged to the shipyard owner John Adams, as well as the site of some of the launch ways, can also still be seen. Visitors may, however, have some difficulty in imagining from what is left of this site that 'the stout oak-built ships which were launched there from 1743 to 1818 helped in no small degree to lay the foundations of our empire. During the Napoleonic wars they took part in nearly every fight of importance …'[2]

The procedure for the launch of a naval ship at Buckler's Hard was that, when ready for launching, a party of some 200 riggers, supervised by a master rigger, was requested to be sent over from Portsmouth Royal Dockyard. A 'cradle' or 'bulgways' as it was sometimes called and timber props were also requested, as well as flagstaffs for the 'launching colours' described below. The cradle comprising long pieces of timber and props were used to support the hull during launch. Slideways were built from the building blocks at the stern of the ship down to the water, which were then greased. The weight of the ship was gradually transferred from the blocks on which it was built onto the cradle.[3]

On launch days at Buckler's Hard:

A great concourse of very genteel people assembled on the occasion, about 150 of whom stayed for dinner and the day was spent with great conviviality. It must have been a fine sight to see, with the band playing 'God save the King' and 'Off she goes' as hats were taken off amidst ringing cheers, ships like Nelson's *Agamemnon* take the water …[4]

Timber in the royal forests, such as the New Forest, was reserved for use in Royal Dockyards. A private contractor such as Henry Adams, who built some twenty-five naval ships at Buckler's Hard between 1749 and 1794, including *Euryalus*, *Swiftsure* and *Agamemnon*, all of which were in Nelson's fleet at the Battle of Trafalgar, was obliged to source timber from private estates. Upon a successful launch, the Naval Overseer reported to the Navy Board that the ship was 'launched and delivered safe into the hands of the officer appointed to receive her'.[5] If there was no damage and the hull had been 'built agreeably to contract' the Naval Overseer also signed a document certifying a 'perfect bill' so that the private contractor could claim payment from the Admiralty. In order to ensure punctual completion of the hull, the contract with the private contractor would usually provide that, if launching was delayed without just cause, a fine, or 'mulct' as it was called, was to be deducted from the final payment.

After a successful launch the hull was then towed by a fleet of rowing boats, manned by the riggers, down the Beaulieu river into the Solent and onwards into Portsmouth. With a rather unwieldy hull in tow it must on occasion have been a long and strenuous trip, taking 'two or three days'[6] for the 8-mile journey. Once at Portsmouth the masts, rigging and any iron work were completed.

Managed by the Navy Board – Permission to launch

Management of the Royal Dockyards was the responsibility of the Navy Board.[7] This was represented in each Royal Dockyard by the resident Commissioner. The principal officer at each yard in charge of shipbuilding was the Master Shipwright. The permission of the Navy Board was always needed before a ship was launched.

Typically the Commissioner at the relevant Dockyard would report to the Navy Board that a ship was 'in all respects ready for launching' on a date specified and asking what name should be given to the new ship. The Navy Board's standard reply, usually in the form of a warrant, was that the Dockyard was 'hereby directed and required to cause the ship to be launched' on the date stated, specifying the name to be given to the ship and that it then be entered on the list of the Navy. Sometimes additional directions relating to the launch were given. The instructions issued by Captain Robert Fanshawe, Commissioner at Plymouth dockyard, in September 1811 prior to the launch of *Union*, is a good example. This is the same 98-gun ship mentioned in the previous chapter as an early example of a ship being named by a lady and which was constructed on the model of Nelson's *Victory*. The Napoleonic wars were in progress at the time, so additional security was needed. Captain Fanshawe directed that prior to its launch extra watchmen were to secure the hull day and night, no strangers were to be admitted to the various stores in the dockyard, no foreigners whatsoever were to be allowed into the dockyard on the date of the launch; and special arrangements were made to marshal the multitude of spectators which were expected (50,000 attended the launch) and finally 'no persons except those belonging to the yard necessary to be employed on the occasion are to remain on board the ship at the time of launching her'.[8] After a successful launch the Commissioner reported this event to the Navy Board, which then issued instructions as to the fitting out and commissioning of the new ship or that the ship 'was to be laid up in ordinary to season', meaning that only her lower masts were stepped before being laid up in reserve in the Royal Dockyard.[9]

Launching Colours

Early shipbuilding at Royal Dockyards was mainly carried out in docks, with the hull on completion being floated out on an incoming tide through the opening of the dock gates. Naval ships, when launched, were empty shells without guns, stores, masts or other fittings, which were added after launch in the fitting out process. Although the launched hull had no stepped masts, in the eighteenth century it was nonetheless the practice at launch to fly large flags, known as the 'launching colours', from tall flagstaffs stepped in place of the masts. The flags flown were usually the Red Ensign, Admiralty Flag, Union Jack and, if the King was present at the launch, the Royal Standard[10] (see Illustration No. 17). If the contemporary paintings or etchings are a true representation, such float outs were attended by comparatively few spectators during the beginning and middle of the eighteenth century. By the end of the eighteenth century these events had become much more popular with large crowds in attendance, no doubt influenced by the greater attendance of members of the Royal family and then the onset of the Napoleonic Wars (1803–15) and with many of those attending being actually on board the ship as it was launched (see etching of launch of *Prince of Wales* in

Portsmouth in 1794, Illustration No. 17).With the dry dockyard capacity at Royal Dockyards being increasingly needed in time of war for repairs and maintenance, the practice of constructing ships on slipways grew; the completed hulls then being usually launched down the slipways stern first but still flying 'launching colours'. By the twentieth century the flags flown at naval ship launches at Royal Dockyards were diminutive by comparison to the large 'launching colours' of earlier years.

As we have already seen, in Stuart times the naming ceremony of a naval ship took place on the 'poop deck' *after* launch, with the Sovereign or a male dignitary appointed by the Sovereign toasting the ship and naming it in the so-called 'standing cup' ceremony.[11] As the ceremony changed in the late seventeenth century to the ceremonial breaking of a bottle against the bow *at the moment of entry into the water*, the dignitaries could watch the event from specially constructed booths on the shore rather than standing on deck. A launch down a slipway was in any case a much more exciting event for spectators.

Royal booths

For the launch of the third-rate 74-gun HMS *Grafton* at Deptford in 1771 there is among the papers of the 4th Earl of Sandwich a memorandum dealing with the arrangements.[12] George III was to be present, with 'Royal booths' erected on the side of the launching slip on the Starboard quarter of the ship for his use. The memorandum details with a sketch plan how the frigate *Levant* and what must have been a splendid array of five royal yachts, *Mary*, *William and Mary*, *Fubbs*, *Catherine* and *Augusta* (from whose decks other distinguished guests were to witness the launch), were to be deployed in an inverted V formation in the river in front of the launching slip. 'The whole to be dressed with colours.' Detailed instructions were also given, by reference to flag signals, the boatswain's pipe of the *Levant* and the firing of one of the *Levant*'s guns, as to when the ships in the formation were to be manned, when salutes and 'three cheers' were to be given and when to 'let fly the Colours'. In short, it was an elaborately orchestrated colourful naval ceremony in the presence of the King to celebrate the launching of the latest addition to his navy.

Patriotic spectators

Between 1798 and 1805 the fear of invasion from Napoleon and the importance of the navy for the nation's defence served to 'encourage patriotic emotion at the launch of a warship'.[13] The result, as noted above, was that huge crowds began to attend the launch of new warships. The launch of *Prince of Wales* at Portsmouth on 28 June 1794 and of *Queen Charlotte* at Deptford on 17 July 1810 each attracted crowds of over 100,000. These ship launches at Royal Dockyards then became noisy, well-attended events, with bands playing, the National Anthem being sung, the noise of volleys being fired from gun salutes and the shouts of a patriotic crowd, in marked contrast to the quieter events of the early eighteenth century. From the beginning of the nineteenth century, launches at Royal Dockyards were also advertised in newspapers through so called 'Launch Notices', which became part of the daily news cycle.

Signal to announce launches

The increasing number of spectators attending the ship launches in the early nineteenth century caused safety issues for the Dockyard. At the launch of *Queen Charlotte* in 1810 it was reported in the *Naval Chronicle*[14] that the launch went off 'a full twenty minutes before it was expected which nearly had been the cause of many and serious accidents in consequence of the number of boats which were hovering in and about the ship'. The reporter suggested that in future it might be 'advisable to have a gun to be fired, by way of caution … just before the knocking down of the dog shores … The expense and trouble would be so trifling as not to bear mentioning, in comparison with the loss of a life and perhaps of many.'

   This sensible suggestion was taken up and there are many reports of subsequent launches at Royal Dockyards where 'the discharge of a single heavy gun'[15] signalled to spectators that the launching operation was about to begin.

Pembroke Dock – a town built to build ships

Pembroke Dock was the last but one Royal dockyard to be established, in October 1815, this being effected by an Order in Council of the Prince

Regent. The issue of this Order in Council regularised the informal arrangements that the navy already had at Milford Haven, a well-sheltered natural harbour. When the dock was started there was little or no housing for dock workers and the town, which grew up around the Dockyard and which was separate from Pembroke town, came to be known as 'Pembroke Dock'. It was literally a town built to build ships. During the 106 years of its working life the Dockyard produced 250 ships for the navy and five royal yachts launched from thirteen building slips – the largest number of such slips of any Royal Dockyard – and it also had one graving dock. For over a century it was the principal shipbuilding yard in the country. Unlike other Royal Dockyards that had repair, maintenance, building and fitting out facilities, Pembroke Dock was a specialist shipbuilding facility. It was the only Royal Dockyard in Wales and, despite the downturn in demand for navy ships after the end of the Napoleonic war, Pembroke Dock somehow managed to grow in the first fifty years of the nineteenth century.

Pembroke was never a naval base for the provisioning of naval ships or the training of naval personnel, and was under the direction of a Captain Superintendent rather than a Commissioner, indicating its lower status in the eyes of the Navy Board. For much of its life the ships it built and launched were fitted out elsewhere, usually at Plymouth or Portsmouth. Although Pembroke Dockyard, because of its extensive shipbuilding facilities, is of great interest in the context of ship launches, its lack of other facilities and its remoteness meant that it was always a bit of a 'Cinderella yard'.[16] In brief, Pembroke Dock was a town that lived for and by the Dockyard but never achieved the same status as other Royal Dockyards.

Launch of HMS Caesar at Pembroke Dock

The extent of the town's support for the activities in the Dockyard is well illustrated by the calamitous launch of HMS *Caesar*, which was originally planned for Thursday, 21 July 1853 but which was finally achieved seventeen days later. After being named by Lady Georgiana Balfour, the ship went off down the slipway but stuck after going about half her length with the after part clear of the slip and unsupported as the tide fell. The next day, Friday, further attempts to pull the ship off using steam ships also failed. It was then that the town's people stepped in: 'on Saturday all the casks of the town were borrowed, and it was gratifying to see the alacrity with which these were furnished by the publicans and others – the former in some instances actually emptying both beer and porter into tubs and vats'.[17] These emptied wooden casks were positioned under the stern of the ship to lift it. In the minds of the town's people there could be nothing worse for the reputation of the Dockyard than a failed launch. The livelihood of the Dockyard and in turn of the inhabitants of the town depended entirely on the continuing output of completed hulls, launched successfully.

The cause of the calamitous launch could not be determined. One rumour was that the ship had been cursed by an old lady who it is said was denied access to the Dockyard to attend the launch. It was on Sunday morning, 17 August, seventeen days later, that the ship began to move after camels made of wood, in addition to the barrels, had been constructed under the ship to lift it. It was during the hours of the divine service that a bugle was heard summoning any remaining dockyard workers to return to the Dockyard. 'This resulted in the very natural but unseemly effort that followed. All the people hastily left the places of worship, and, moved by one impulse, ran to the Dockyard to see the ship go off.'[18] In the event, despite the tireless efforts of the dock workers, successful launch did not occur until the next tide later that evening. Colourful as the story of the curse may be, it is generally thought that the failure to launch was due to the timber used in the construction of the launching ways being too soft, fir being used instead of oak in a false economy; and further that the tallow used to grease the ways was of inferior quality. What is sadly not recorded is whether the publicans and other town's people who had so loyally supported the Dockyard in its hour of need were compensated for the loss of their wooden barrels, let alone the contents!

The town campaigned long and hard for fitting out facilities to be established at Pembroke Dockyard. There were comments in the local press about the useless expense and risk of towing newly launched ships to a fitting out port elsewhere that might be avoided by making Pembroke Dockyard a fitting out dock as well as a shipbuilding centre. Although engines and boilers were sometimes installed at Hobbs Point, it was not until 1903 that the cruiser *Essex* became the first ship launched at the Dockyard to be fully fitted out there. The lack of fitting out facilities meant that the Dockyard's work on a shipbuilding order often finished at the stage of launch. Launch days, therefore, had extra significance at Pembroke Dockyard, not only as patriotic events in the manner celebrated at other Royal Dockyards, but as *the* event – the successful launch – which marked the completion of the Dockyard's work on a particular order.

Launch days at Pembroke Dock

On launch days, except in wartime, the gates of the Dockyard were opened to the public and frequently attracted a large crowd of spectators, not just from the town but from Cardiff, Swansea and other places along the Great Western line, which had reached Pembroke Dock in 1864 and which organised special excursion trains to bring in crowds to witness the spectacle. Although admittance to the dockyard for a launch was often by ticket, on other occasions the policemen on the gates were authorised to admit 'all respectable people without distinction'. Security concerns, however, dictated that, once inside the yard, the movement of visitors was often restricted to the launch area.

In press reports of launches at Pembroke Dock the town on launch days was often described as being 'en fete'. Schools in the town were sometimes closed in the afternoon to enable people from the town to attend; and workers employed in building the ship to be launched were granted a half day holiday with pay and worked the remainder of the day with unpaid overtime. Government ships in the Haven would be dressed overall with flags. The booths for the spectators would be decorated with flowers, bunting and flags. 'The gay dresses of the numerous ladies and the bright uniform of the naval and military officers adding lustre to the event.'[19] It would have been a colourful scene. Music at such events was provided by the Dockyard band or regimental bands from the garrison in the town to entertain the spectators in the booths waiting for the launch ceremony to start. In the Heritage Centre at Pembroke Dock, housed in what was the former Dockyard chapel, there is included among the many exhibits a launch programme for HMS *Defence* dated 27 April 1907. This contains a programme of waltzes, marches, dances and sea songs to be played at the launch by the Volunteer Battalion Welsh Regiment. As the new ship went down the slipway, with the usual vociferous cheers from all the spectators in the booths and at every vantage point, it was the custom for 'Rule Britannia' to be played by the band, followed by the National Anthem. These ship launches at Pembroke Dockyard, like those performed at other Royal Dockyards, were indeed patriotic, colourful and stirring events.

Singing

In addition to the music from the bands at Pembroke Dockyard, in the best Welsh tradition, there was singing. Following the introduction of the short religious service to be performed by the Dockyard chaplain at the launch of naval ships, the choir from the Dockyard Chapel at Pembroke sang Psalm 107 during the standard service. On visits to the dockyard by royalty or other prestigious dignitaries, usually to attend a ship launch, large choirs of children sang a greeting to the distinguished visitors or entertained the guests with songs after the launch. The celebration frequently ended with dinner being given at Admiralty House at the invitation of the Captain Superintendent for invited guests.

Refreshment for dockyard workers

For the workers at the Dockyard a ship launch was the moment at which their efforts were rewarded with beer. For example, in 1691 the Commissioner at Chatham Sir Edward Gregory, wrote to the Navy Board: 'I will allow some strong beer to give the men a drink when they dock or launch a ship.'[20] The Commissioner at Deptford similarly wrote to the Navy Board in 1695 that: 'In accordance with your command I have bought 6 firkins of liquor for the launching of the 3rd rate.'[21] By way of comparison, at Buckler's Hard, which it will be recalled was a private yard, on the evening of a launch Henry Adams entertained his important guests at the Master Builder's house but the workmen were entertained on another day.[22]

Launch of submarines at Chatham

At Chatham, which in the twentieth century became a specialist constructor of submarines, there were two different traditions relating to the launch of submarines constructed inside covered slipways. At the end of the religious service the order would be given 'Stand by to launch', followed by the report 'Ready for launch', at which point the lady sponsor named the ship by breaking a bottle of wine against the bows. The General Manager then invited the sponsor to launch the ship, following which she cut the trigger rope with a mallet and chisel, which freed up the last restraint to the launch of the submarine. After the launch three cheers for the sponsor were called and she in turn called for three cheers for the men who built the submarine. The second tradition was that after the launch the lady sponsor was invited to take the salute, from a dais in the road outside the construction slipway, of a march past from active Navy personnel or Royal Marines and the military bands that had participated in the launch ceremony.

Tradition of gratuity of silver plate to Master Shipwright

It was a well-established and enduring custom in Royal Dockyards starting in the seventeenth century that a Master Shipwright, on the successful launch of a new ship for the navy, received a piece of silver plate from the King. This was always expressed as a gratuity, but in reality it became a more or less fixed supplement to wages.

Master Shipwrights in Royal Dockyards in the sixteenth, seventeenth and eighteenth centuries were not well paid for their skill and responsibility. The pay in private shipyards was somewhat better but there was less job security and no pension arrangements.[23] It is not surprising, therefore, to find that many of the Master Shipwrights at Royal Dockyards looked for other means to supplement their income.

It is in this context that the custom of a gift of silver plate being made by the King to the Master Shipwright on launch of a new ship for his navy must be viewed. For Master Shipwrights with a comparatively low income the gratuity of silver plate was without doubt a significant perk and one to be cherished.

Origin of the custom

So when did the custom start? We know from the autobiography of Phineas Pett that in 1610 it was usual for the 'ancient custom' of the 'standing cup' to be performed on the occasion of the launch of a new ship 'by drinking part of the wine, giving the ship her name and heaving the standing cup overboard'.[24] What was different on the launch of the *Prince Royal* at Woolwich on 25 July 1610 was that on this occasion the 'standing cup' was not thrown overboard. Phineas colourfully describes what happened:

> His Highness *[Prince Henry]* then, standing upon the poop, with a selected company only, besides the trumpets, with a great deal of expression of princely joy, and with the ceremony of drinking in the great standing cup, threw all the wine forwards towards the half deck, and solemnly calling her by name of the *Prince Royal*, the trumpets sounding all the while, with many gracious words to me, gave the standing cup into mine own hands ...[25]

Later at dinner, after the departure of Prince Henry to Greenwich, Phineas, in the company of the Comptroller of the Navy, Sir Henry Palmer and others, 'drank Prince Henry's health round, to Hansel[26] the standing cup given at the launching'.

Commentators have speculated as to whether this was the start of the custom of giving silver plate to Master Shipwrights: 'Maybe it had been decided by this time that a better use might be made of a silver cup than throwing it overboard ...'[27]

Samuel Pepys, then Naval Administrator, in an entry in his famous diary for 25 October 1664 reports buying on behalf of King Charles II a piece of plate for the Master Shipwright Christopher Pett in preparation for the launch at Woolwich of *Royal Katherine*, which was to take place the next day. His entry for the day of the launch records:[28] 'I staid with them while the ship was launched, which was done with great success, and the King did very much like the ship saying that she had the best bow that ever he saw.' After the launching: 'I sent for Mr Pett and put the Flaggon into the Duke's hand [presumably the Duke of York, afterwards James II] and he, in the presence of the King, did give it, Mr Pett taking it upon his knee.'

The practice was well established by this time and in a Memorandum and Conclusions of the Navy Board[29] there is a fascinating table itemising the pieces of silver plate given to Master Shipwrights on the launch of naval ships during the period from 1660 to 1679:

> Bills passed for pieces of plate given by His Majesty to the builders undermentioned as a gratuity for their services in building the shipps there also expressed with the Duke of Yorkes arms with an anchor through with this subscription under it.
>
> Att the launching of his Majesty's shipp … day of… 166 built at… by… his Majesty's Master shipwright there burthen … Tunns, Menn … Gunns …

There is then set out a table showing the following particulars in columns: 'Builders name/Rate/Shipp built/where built/when built/tunns/ menn/gunns/nature of the plate/price of the plate.' The 'Builders name' column contained the name of the Master Shipwright.

The table itemises particulars for plate given on the launch of twenty-nine naval ships between 1660 and 1679, specifying the nature of the plate and the price. From this we can deduce that there had been established by this period what was, in effect, a more or less fixed tariff for the type and value of plate to be given for the launch of a certain size of ship. For example a 'State plate and cupp' costing £29 for construction in 1677 of *Resolution*, a Rate 3 ship of 833 tons with 340 men and 70 guns, and a 'flaggon' costing £16 for the construction of a Rate 4 ship, *St David*, built in 1667 of 663 tons, 220 men and 52 guns, and a 'tankard' costing £14 for the construction of smaller ships. What is also of note is that the wording to be inscribed on such plate was made standard.

An analysis of this table shows that during these nineteen to twenty years some Master Shipwrights received several items of plate. We can only speculate as to whether they kept it or sold it to supplement their income. What is clear is that the plate, although it was a gratuity, represented a substantial increment to their salaries. Illustration No. 19 gives some examples of the plate awarded to Master Shipwrights.

Disputes as to entitlement to the gratuity

Inevitably with a gratuity of this nature and value, disputes did sometimes arise as to whether the plate had been properly earned. Robert Lee, Master Shipwright at Chatham 1660–98, was in charge of the second rebuilding of *Sovereign* of the Seas in 1685 and requested the grant of a piece of silver as a reward. While this was customary when the building of a new ship was completed, rebuilding posed a problem of interpretation of the rules of the navy for Samuel Pepys.[30] At Plymouth in 1698 a shipwright endeavoured, unsuccessfully, to have a fourth rate launched before the ship was fully ready with the intent to claim the silver plate gratuity before he left his employment in the shipyard.[31] At Woolwich in 1746, where there was a handover between one Master Shipwright and another just before a launch, the new Master Shipwright, who took over charge of the arrangements on the launching day and saw the ship launched safely, claimed the grant of the plate.[32]

Attempts to abolish the custom

In 1801 the officers at Royal Dockyards were given increased salaries and their allowances and other perks were abolished. However, there seems to have been doubt as to whether this general abolition of allowances included an abolition of the gratuity to Master Shipwrights of the piece of plate upon the launch of a new ship. On 17 July 1801 the Navy Board felt it necessary to issue the following guidance:

> It having been usual when a ship has been launched to present the Master Shipwright with a piece of plate or money to a certain amount according to the rate of the ship as expressed in the Board minute of 31 January 1800 and all allowances whatever now being taken from the officers of His Majesty's yards, the Board desire that when any application of this kind is made in future it may not be paid until it has been considered whether this allowance was also intended to be taken away.[33]

This did not convince the Master Shipwrights. Those from the five Royal Dockyards then in existence on 17 April 1805 evidently thought that, despite the salary increase, the gratuity should be retained. In what must have been an unusual step at that time, and perhaps indicating the strength of their opinion on the subject, they combined together to write a joint letter to the Navy Board asking it to continue 'the long accustomed Allowance of a Piece of Plate on the launching of a ship ... and which is esteemed by us far above its intrinsic value arising from that laudable pride which every man feels who has been the Principal in conducting the executive part [in the construction of] of the great machine, a ship'.[34]

It was a clever line to take; the Navy Board had just increased salaries to all officers at Royal Dockyards and clearly intended these to replace all allowances and perks. An economic argument based on level of salaries was, therefore, unlikely to have succeeded. The Master Shipwrights instead based their case for retaining the gratuity on pride in their workmanship and, from the King's point of view, the need to ensure that naval ships continued to be built to the highest standard. The Master Shipwrights' appeal was initially rejected but on 10 August 1814 the custom of the plate gratuity was once again restored, although reducing its value to £50 for three-deckers and £40 for two-deckers. However, the debate continued as to whether the Dockyards were at liberty, instead of the gift of plate, to pay the Master Shipwright the money that was allowed for the plate. On 2 February 1815 the Navy Board stated that their Lordships desired that the pieces of plate only be given on these occasions and that they should bear an engraved inscription stating it to have been presented to the officer by order of the Lord Commissioners of the Admiralty in consideration of the building and launching of the ship under his direction.[35]

The cash alternative mentioned in the Navy Board's note of 17 July 1801 continued to be discussed. Many successful Master Shipwrights, instead of accumulating a collection of silver plate, which may not have been so easy to sell, would have preferred a gift of cash. This cash alternative was eventually established. For example, we find that in 1858 on the launch at Pembroke Dock of HMS *Windsor Castle*, the Master Shipwright 'received a donation for £40 for the launching of the ship'.[36] The custom of a gratuity in cash continued at least until the last quarter of the nineteenth century and was formally enshrined in the Dockyard

Instructions 1875 applicable to all Royal Dockyards where provision was made for the payment to the Chief Constructor (the title then given to a Master Shipwright) of a gratuity for the safe launching of naval ships or floating them out of dock after building in dock.[37] It is not clear when it was finally phased out, but the 1904 Home Dockyard Regulations make no provision for such a gratuity.

Launching caskets

Another tradition at ship launches in Royal Dockyards, already mentioned in relation to the launch of submarines at Chatham, was the use of a mallet and chisel to symbolically start the launch procedure by severing the line that held the last retaining dog shores, thereby setting the ship free. The mallet and chisel were crafted individually for each launch, usually in wood but sometimes in silver. After use in the launch procedure, the mallet and chisel were then presented to the dignitary performing the ceremony as a souvenir of the occasion contained in a special wooden or silver box, known as a launch box or casket. Some launch caskets had in the lid beautiful pen and ink or watercolour drawings of the ship being launched and were typically inscribed with the date of the launch and the name of the Master Shipwright or Chief Constructor responsible for construction of the ship. They were sometimes lined with velvet or silk.

The author is lucky enough to be the owner of one such launch casket, the beautiful example made for the launch of HMS *Alert*, which took place at Sheerness in 1894 (Illustration No. 20). It is inscribed:

HMS ALERT
Launched at Sheerness, December 1894
By Mrs Fellowes and separately by John Fellowes, RN, CB Captain
Superintendent /HH Ash Esqr Chief Constructor

As a small Royal Dockyard, the senior officer at Sheerness was a Captain Superintendent rather than a resident Commissioner, the title given to the senior officer at more major Royal Dockyards. By virtue of the Dockyard Instructions of 1875, 'Chief Instructor' was the new title given to Master Shipwrights.

The tradition appears to have commenced around the 1850s. In the National Maritime Museum there is exhibited the launching box with its mallet and chisel used by Lady Milford to launch the royal yacht *Victoria and Albert* at Pembroke Dock on 16 January 1855. It became an almost universal tradition for launches at Royal Dockyards thereafter. It was especially popular for the launch of the Dreadnought battleships from Royal Dockyards, the first of which was HMS *Dreadnought* launched on 10 February 1906. Its launch heralded the start of a great battleship construction race between Great Britain and Germany, which finally came to a head at the Battle of Jutland in June 1916, the largest sea battle of the First World War, albeit inconclusive. Altogether seventeen Dreadnoughts were constructed in the Royal Dockyards.

Timber used from HMS Victory

The launching caskets presented to the sponsors of the Dreadnought battleships at Royal Dockyards were often symbolically made out of timber taken from Nelson's flagship HMS *Victory*, so bringing his myth into the heart of the event. The caskets were, as mentioned, almost invariably made individually for each launching ceremony and therefore unique in design but following a similar pattern. The launching of the Dreadnought battleships, like the launches from the Royal Dockyards in the 1790's, were patriotic, well-attended public spectacles. Some 60,000 people attended the launch of HMS *Iron Duke* at Portsmouth in 1912, and this figure was greatly exceeded on the launching on 16 October 1913 of HMS *Queen Elizabeth*, the ceremony being performed by Lady Meux, wife of the Commander in Chief. 'Each of the launches had its distinct coterie of admirals, aristocrats, politicians, naval officers and senior dockyard officials, their wives and daughters and the massed ranks of manual workers.'[38]

'Most of the women wear broad brimmed hats with layered flowers and ribbons as befitted a celebratory occasion.'[39]

Launching ceremony using mallet and chisel described

The launching ceremony commenced with the naming of the ship by an eminent lady. At a given signal she swung a bottle of Empire wine, usually Australian, against the hull and uttered the traditional words: 'I wish good luck to the [name of ship] and to all who sail in her.' This ceremony was met by a burst of spontaneous cheering. On a given signal the dockyard workers then started to knock down the final blocks beneath the ship restraining her. On the launch platform the Chief Constructor removed a chisel from the launch casket and handed it to the lady sponsor, who struck it with the mallet, severing the launch rope, situated at the bows on an oak rosette. The cutting of the rope released the half-ton weights that knocked aside the last of the dog shores.

As the ship moved down the slipway, the Royal Marines band played 'Rule Britannia', the crowds cheered and handkerchiefs and hats were waved. 'For many observers these were quasi-magical moments of grandeur; a time to express and articulate deeply held imperial values.'[40]

The idea of using timber from HMS *Victory* to make the launch casket may have started with the making of one for HMS *Royal Albert*, the launch of which was performed by Queen Victoria at Woolwich on 13 May 1854. This casket subsequently became the property of Queen Elizabeth II and is displayed at the National Maritime Museum. The launching casket is a blue-covered case lined with blue velvet containing mallet, chisel and silver plaque and the inscription reads:

> This mallet & chisel (made from a piece of *Victory*'s hull) liberated the Dog Shores at the launch of *THE ROYAL ALBERT* at Woolwich on the 13th May 1854. The ship was named by Her Majesty the Queen. *The Royal Albert*, designed & partly built by the late Oliver Lang Esqur, was completed and launched by William McPherson Rice Esqr, Master Shipwright.[41]

Home Dockyard Regulations

Following the abolition of the Navy Board in 1832 the Admiralty Board assumed administration of the Royal Dockyards. The Dockyard Instructions 1875 issued on 1 July 1875 and subsequently the Home Dockyard Regulations of various dates provided general rules relating to the administration of the Royal Dockyards and contained a number of specific regulations relating to launches of naval ships. The principle was formalised that Admiralty approval was needed before the launch of a naval ship and that an immediate report should be given to the Admiralty once the launch or floating out had occurred. While a well-organised launch with sufficiency of ceremony did a lot of good for the morale of the workforce in the Royal Dockyard, this had to be balanced against the need to control public expenditure. Many of the regulations on launching were, therefore, designed to control the cost of such launch ceremonies. They required the Superintendent at the relevant Royal Dockyard to be guided by the latest Admiralty instruction as to the erection of booths for visitors, which 'official visitors' were to be accommodated on the launching platform, the appropriation of tickets and the admission of the public. Estimates for the total expenditure were required to be submitted in advance for approval by the Admiralty. No doubt as a result of previous wars against the French, it was also stipulated that only wines which are 'products of British Empire are to be used for the naming ceremony'.[42] This usually meant that Australian wine was used. The sums that could be expended on launch caskets were revised from time to time. For example, in the 1925 Regulations, a launching box, including mallet and chisel, were still included in the estimate of expenses but limited in amount 'except where Royal personages are concerned or some very special function is contemplated',[43] to £30 for vessels of 5,000 tons displacement and upwards and to £20 below 5,000 tons displacement. An Admiralty Fleet Order of 1932, which was incorporated in 1939 into an addendum[44] to the Home Dockyard Regulations, limited the cost of launch boxes to £40, except where 'Royal personages are concerned or some very special function is contemplated'. It also stipulated that in the case of launches of 'second importance', for example sloops, destroyers and submarines or smaller craft, while the Superintendent at the relevant Dockyard was now free to choose the lady to perform the naming ceremony (which had previously been a decision for the Admiralty for all newly constructed naval ships of whatever size), she was no longer to be presented with a launch box but 'with a souvenir which is to be made in the dockyard at a cost not exceeding £10'. The colourful launch box tradition seems to have gradually died out when increasingly in the twentieth century naval ships ceased to be built at Royal Dockyards and were instead constructed at the yards of private contractors.

General note on closure of Royal Dockyards

Harwich ceased to be a Royal Dockyard in 1713, while Woolwich and Deptford ceased in 1869. The last Royal Dockyard to be established was at Rosyth in 1903, as a naval base and dockyard. By 1906, when the Dreadnought battleships were being constructed, this could only be achieved at Portsmouth and Devonport. Pembroke Dock and Chatham were not given enlarged facilities and Pembroke Dock accordingly specialised in building cruisers and Chatham in building cruisers and submarines. Pembroke ceased to undertake formal dockyard work in 1926. Sheerness closed as a naval base in 1960. In 1984 Chatham closed and Portsmouth ceased to be a Royal Dockyard. As from 1987 the two remaining Royal Dockyards at Devonport and Rosyth were placed under private ownership.

Chapter 10

Religious Service at the Launch of Naval Ships

British naval ships

When HM Queen Elizabeth II named the new aircraft carrier HMS *Queen Elizabeth* at Rosyth Dockyard in Fife on 4 July 2014, she followed a long tradition of monarchs who have christened naval ships. Her words of prayer 'May God bless her and all who sail in her' were preceded by a religious ceremony conducted by the Chaplain of the Fleet, the Reverend Scott James Brown CBE QHC. This chapter reviews the history behind this short religious ceremony, how it originated and how it has evolved and changed.

In many ancient cultures a variety of traditions have been developed to bless new ships or to make an invocation to the gods in order to ask for protection for sailors and their ships from the dangers of the sea.

Little or no religious ceremony

In a country such as England, where the Church has played such a prominent role in our history, it might have been expected that a strong religious element would always have been included in the ceremony for the naming and launching of warships; and that the order of religious service would be one that has been followed by tradition down the centuries. This, surprisingly, is not the case. Between the Reformation and 1875 the christening and launch ceremonies for naval ships contained little or no religious element. There was no invocation or prayer for the new ship and those who would sail in her.

Hallowing

Even prior to the Reformation there are only a few reported instances of a religious participation in the naming of naval ships. In 1418 the Bishop of

Bangor was commissioned by the Council of Henry V to proceed at public expense from London to Southampton to 'hallow' or bless his new ship *Grace Dieu*.[1] In 1514, prior to his break with Rome, Henry VIII issued a warrant to the keeper of the royal wardrobe to deliver 20 ells (about 22.8 metres) of linen cloth for the 'hallowing' of his ship *Henry Grace a Dieu*.[2] We have no contemporaneous guidance on how this linen was to be used but Phineas Pett (1570–1647), who was Master Shipwright at the Royal Dockyard at Woolwich, writing in his diary in 1610 about preparations for the launching of *Prince Royal*, describes how the poop and quarter deck of that ship were to be decorated with fine cloth in readiness for the launch; so we can perhaps assume that something similar was intended for *Henry Grace a Dieu*:

> Now began we on all sides to make preparations for the launching
> of the ship, and for that purpose there was provided a rich standard
> of taffety,[3] very fairly gilt with gold, with His Majesty's arms, to
> be placed upon the poop, and a very large ensign of crimson rich
> taffety, with a canton of the Prince's crest upon the quarter deck,
> and all other ornaments were carefully provided for, befitting that
> purpose.[4]

The reference to 'ornaments' may well be a reference to the 'standing cup' to be used to christen the ship and these would have been on the poop deck. Later in his diary it is recorded that: 'The drums and trumpets [were] placed on poop and forecastle and the wind instruments by them, so that nothing was wanting to so great a royalty that could be desired.'[5] From this we have a fairly clear picture of the main elements of colourful launching ceremony that was under preparation: decoration of the poop and quarter deck with the cloth bearing the royal arms, filling the 'standing cup' on the poop deck with wine in readiness for naming of the ship and placing the musical accompaniment on standby.

The 'standing cup' ceremony itself has already been described in detail[6] and in the context of this chapter on religious ceremonies it is sufficient to note that the 'standing cup' ceremony was devoid of any religious element; it contained a secular wish for 'success' of the 'ship royal' and was more akin to a pagan libation, recalling the ancient Greek ritual of a deposition sacrifice, where the cup was thrown into the sea in order to favour the powerful sea gods and appease the evil spirits of the deep.[7] The religious content to the ceremony that had been found in the ceremonies for the launch of *Grace Dieu* and *Henry Grace a Dieu* in earlier Tudor times was absent. There was no blessing of the ship. There were no prayers.

Members of the royal family were customarily the 'sponsors' of English warships in early Tudor times but with the Reformation under King Henry VIII and the recognition that the leadership of the Church was vested in the Sovereign rather than the Pope, the clergy in England had no role in the ceremony for the launch and naming of naval ships. This contrasts with the ship christening ceremonies in Catholic countries, where, down the ages, blessing of a new ship by a priest was the invariable practice.

As we have seen, the colourful 'standing cup' ceremony was replaced at the end of the seventeenth century by the practice of breaking a bottle across the bow, this ceremony from the time of the Prince Regent often but not invariably being conducted by a lady; but the religious element was still absent.

Catholic countries

In the meantime, in Catholic countries the religious ceremony continued. From the diary of Henry Teonge,[8] an English cleric and between 1675–79 a Royal Naval chaplain, we have the following colourful description of the christening of a man-of-war in Malta on 22 February 1676 attended by 'knights', thought to be from the Roman Catholic military religious order of St John of Malta:

> This day we saw a great deal of solemnity at the launching of a new brigantine of twenty-three oars, built on the shore near the water. They hoisted three flags in her yesterday and this day by 12 they had turned her head near the water; when as a great multitude of people gathered together, with several of their knights and men of quality and a crowd of friars and churchmen.

They were at least two hours in their benedictions, the nature of hymns or anthems or other their ceremonies; their trumpets and other music playing often. At last two friars and an attendant went in to her, and kneeling down prayed half an hour, and laid their hands on every mast and other places of the vessel and sprinkled her all over with holy water. Then they came out and hoisted a pendent to signify that she was a man-of-war; and then at once thrust her into the water ...

Teonge, as an English cleric, would naturally have taken good note of all the religious elements of this ceremony.

There were no such blessings for new ships launched in England at that time. Launch of the flagship *Queen Charlotte* in 1810 at Deptford inspired J.T. Barker to preach a colourful sermon with ten religious lessons derived from the 'amazing spectacle' of the launch attended by 'multitudes' and based on the text James Chapter 3 v 4 'Behold also the ships'. But this was not a religious service forming part of the launching ceremony with a blessing for the ship and for the seamen who would serve in her, but rather a sermon given after the event.

Introduction of religious service for naval ships

In England, it was not until 1875 that the then First Lord of the Admiralty, George Hunt,[9] after consulting with the Archbishop of Canterbury, ordered the observance of a religious ceremony at the launch of naval ships built at Royal Dockyards.[10] There survives some interesting correspondence between the First Lord of the Admiralty, Queen Victoria and Archbishop Tait.[11] It was acknowledged by the First Lord of the Admiralty, 'if he was rightly informed', that England was the only country in Europe at that time where there was no religious ceremony used on such occasions. Queen Victoria was at first sceptical about the introduction of such a religious service. She expressed concern – being before the advent of the microphone – that on occasions where great crowds are assembled very few persons can hear the prayers that are offered and that, therefore, the form of service should be kept short[11]. Her advice was followed then and to this day.

In the House of Commons on 16 February 1875, Mr Edward Reed, MP for Pembroke and himself a naval architect and the designer of many ships during that period, and whom we have previously encountered in his capacity as the chairman of the public inquiry into the *Daphne* launch disaster that was to occur in 1883, questioned the First Lord of the Admiralty 'as to whether in those cases in which the launch takes place in tidal rivers and harbours with strong currents, the dockyard officers and private contractors have been, or are to be, released from all responsibility for any accidents and disasters that may arise from the suspension during the ceremony of the important and often critical mechanical operations involved in the launching of heavy ships'. The First Lord of the Admiralty replied that he believed that 'the introduction of this service, which would be a very short one, would be so timed as in no way to interfere with the launching of ships' and consequently 'the liabilities and responsibilities of those persons [the officers and contractors] will not be increased'.[12]

Although Mr Reed did not mention this ship by name, in making the reference in the House of Commons to 'important and often critical mechanical operations in the launching of heavy ships' it seems likely that he was thinking of the problems encountered the previous year, 1874, in the launch of the heavy ironclad frigate *Independenzia*, mention of which has already been made in relation to the problems of ships becoming stuck on the ways.[13] It will be recalled that, although he was not responsible for the launch arrangements, this ship had been designed by Mr Reed.

But, to return to the introduction of a religious service at the launch of naval ships, this background explains the historical and practical reasons why the original form of service entitled 'Service for the launching of ships of her Majesty's Navy' is so short. It was ordered by the Admiralty in 1875 to be used at all naval dockyards upon the launching of any ship to be added to the list of her Majesty's Navy and to be performed on such occasions by the Dockyard chaplain.[14]

Constitutional issue with Scotland

With the independence of the Church of Scotland being recognised in the 1706 Act of Union between England and Scotland, Rev. K.M. Phian, convenor of the Church of Scotland Army and Navy Chaplains, complained that what was proposed by the First Lord of the Admiralty raised a constitutional question. His concern was the use in Scotland of a form of service drawn up by the Archbishop of Canterbury and the impropriety of a public religious service being performed in Scotland at the direction of a Government department conducted by a minister not of the national church. The Admiralty replied that the form of prayer for the launching of ships in Her Majesty's navy ships was not put out by the authority of the Archbishop of Canterbury, but under the authority of the Admiralty. And so, with all the religious, constitutional and operational problems finally overcome, a short form of divine service was adopted for the launching of ships of the Royal Navy. The only disappointment, which somewhat detracted from the significance of the introduction of this religious service, was that when it was issued it was printed on a rather drab Ministry of Defence form, simply numbered 'D10'[15], a copy of which, as amended, is to be found in Appendix II.

Naval ships built by private contractors

This form of religious service was designed for the launch of naval ships built in Royal Dockyards to be conducted by the Dockyard chaplain. But, by the end of the nineteenth century naval ships were, in increasing volume, also being constructed in the shipyards of private contractors usually under the supervision of a Naval Overseer. This required the Admiralty to address the question as to what religious service should be conducted on the launch of those naval ships that were not built in Royal Dockyards. The Admiralty's answer was to require that the Naval Overseer arrange that such ships would also be launched using the religious service 'usual in HM's service'. However, since these private shipyards did not have their own 'Dockyard Chaplain' to conduct such a service, the contractor was free to choose its own clergy to officiate with the proviso that timely notice of the name of the officiating clergy chosen by the contractor was to be given to the Admiralty for approval.[16]

Now, after all the years with no religious element to the christening ceremony of naval ships, this omission had been corrected. From this moment, for the first time since the Reformation, the ceremony for the launching and naming of naval ships would be conducted by a member of the Royal family, or a lady sponsor, performing the ceremony in conjunction with the clergy.

First naval ship to be launched with new religious service

Appropriately, a few months after the introduction of the new form of religious service, Archbishop Tait was personally invited by the First Lord of the Admiralty to conduct the religious service[17] upon the occasion of the launch in the Royal Dockyard in Chatham on 7 April 1875 of the ironclad battleship HMS *Alexandra*, to be 'christened' by the then Princess of Wales, Princess Alexandra. An etching of this occasion is to be found in the *Illustrated London News* issue of 17 April 1875, which shows the Archbishop in his clerical robes standing next to the Princess of Wales (Illustration No. 22).

It is thought that HMS *Alexandra* is the only ship in the British Navy to be launched with the Christian name or title of a Princess of Wales.

HMS *Alexandra* is often stated to be the first naval ship launched at which the form of religious service was used, but it seems that this is not the case. At the launch of HMS *Dreadnought* at Pembroke Dock on 8 March 1875 it was reported in the local press[18] that the form of religious service 'recently prepared by the Archbishop of Canterbury' was conducted by the Dockyard chaplain. Even this may not have been the very first such occasion.

It appears that the launch of HM Dockyard tug *Perseverance* at Devonport may in fact have been the actual first. Admiral Sir Herbert King-Hall, in his *Memoirs and Traditions*, writes:

It was during the period of my father's appointment [as Superintendent] at Devonport Dockyard that the practice started. The practice was due to my father, who being a religious man, suggested to the Admiralty the desirability of a service on such occasions. This was approved, and the first of Her Majesty's ships which benefited by the new service was Her Majesty's dockyard tug *Perseverance* launched in 1875 at Devonport Dockyard by one of my sisters.[19]

That launch was, it seems, a few months before the launch of HMS *Dreadnought* at Pembroke Dock. Whichever was the first ship is not so important, what is significant is that from 1875, three centuries after the Reformation, there *was* once again to be a religious service performed in this country at the launch of naval ships. The author has been unable to verify Admiral Sir Herbert King-Hall's claim that it was his father's influence that was behind George Hunt's decision to introduce this religious service in 1875.

Announcement of religious service

In addition to the noise from the large throng of people present when a ship is about to be launched, there is frequently also the noise of the blocks being knocked away beneath the ship preparatory to the launch, both of which could, as Queen Victoria had wisely noted, make it difficult for the religious service to be heard. In order that the prayers be heard there was started in some dockyards the custom of ringing a bell or the sounding of a bugle to announce the start of the divine service and 'to secure order'.[20] At the launch of HMS *Duke of Edinburgh* at Pembroke Dockyard on 14 June 1904 a bugle was sounded to herald this moment. The *Pembroke Dock and Pembroke Gazette* reported: 'The bugle call on this occasion called for silence. The hammers stopped their clamour, and the people stilled their voices, while for once the voice of the Chaplain could be distinctly heard reciting the beautiful words of the Psalm "They that go down to the sea in ships".'[21] In 1964, at the launch in Chatham of a submarine for the Canadian Navy, visitors were given the following guidance on the launching procedure: 'After the Buglers have sounded the opening fanfare the Dockyard Chaplain will conduct the service, particulars of which are contained in the centre of this Programme.'[22] This modern-day use of a bugle to call for silence for prayers recalls a similar practice of having a trumpet or herald demand silence to announce the start of Athenian fleet sacrificial and purification ceremonies many centuries earlier prior to their fleets going to war by sea.

Dockyard chapel choir at launch service

At launch services led by the Dockyard chaplain in Pembroke Dock, a psalm and the hymn 'Eternal Father strong to save' were sometimes sung by the choir from the Dockyard chapel.[23] The chapel at Pembroke Dock was constructed by the Admiralty for the religious instruction of its employees and was completed in 1833–34. Mrs Stuart Peters, writing in 1905,[24] said that the music rendered in the chapel 'is specially good' and the singing from the chapel choir, when it participated in ship launches at Pembroke Dock, as well as the music played by the local military bands, must have been an uplifting feature.

The only other Georgian chapel at a Royal Dockyard is believed to be at Chatham, completed in 1808. A photograph taken at the launch of the mine-laying submarine HMS *Grampus* at No. 7 Slip on 25 February 1936 shows a choir from the Dockyard chapel with a Royal Marine band in attendance for the launching ceremony.[25]

Responsibility for organising launching ceremony and religious service for naval ships today

After 1875 the form of religious service for the launch of ships constructed at naval shipyards was revised from time to time but was still kept short in accordance with Queen Victoria's wishes. What has changed in recent years is that ships for the Royal Navy are no longer built at Royal Dockyards owned by the Crown but entirely by private contractors.

The responsibility for organising the launching ceremony and order of religious service on such occasions today rests with the private contractor in conjunction with the commanding officer of the new ship; and the person invited to conduct the religious service is sometimes a member of the local clergy and sometimes the Chaplain of the Fleet, in accordance with the preference of the contractor and the commanding officer. For example, in the case of the launch and christening of the aircraft carriers *Illustrious* and *Ark Royal* at Swan Hunter's shipyard on the Tyne in 1978 and 1981 and of *Invincible* at Vickers shipyard at Barrow-in-Furness in 1977, the religious service was on each occasion conducted by local clergy. The form of service, still short, varies on each occasion and is now frequently printed in a rather smarter format than the old Form D10.

The Form D10 ends with the words: 'After this [the religious service] the ceremony of launching shall proceed with the usual formalities.'

The Rosyth Dockyard, formerly a Royal Dockyard, where the new aircraft carrier HMS *Queen Elizabeth* was assembled and floated up, was privatised in 1997 and is now owned by Babcock Marine. The form of service prescribed under the Home Dockyard Regulations for use at the launch of naval ships at Royal Dockyards did not apply to such a christening. After all, in the case of a naval ship built by a private contractor, the Crown, acting through the Ministry of Defence, does not own the hull at the time of launch or, in this case of this ship at the time of her naming in the dry dock. Ownership until delivery after completion of the construction remains vested in the private contractor. In the eyes of the Royal Navy the key form of religious service for naval ships today is the commissioning service, when the Royal Navy takes the ship over from the shipbuilder.

For this reason, the form of religious service upon the occasion of the naming of the new aircraft carrier HMS *Queen Elizabeth* did not follow the D10 order of service for the launching of ships of her Majesty's Navy but was designed specifically for this event by the shipbuilder, the Aircraft Carrier Alliance, in conjunction with the commanding officer, Commodore Jerry Kyd, and their chosen officiant, The Rev. Scott James Brown. He was an ideal choice to conduct a naming ceremony for a naval ship in Scotland, being not only the Chaplain of the Fleet but also a Presbyterian minister. The religious service that he conducted was, however, still short – as Queen Victoria had first suggested in 1875. After opening prayers led by the Chaplain of the Fleet it consisted of the Lord's Prayer, the Naval Prayer, the Naval Hymn and the Blessing. The service was set out in a *'Naming Ceremony Event Programme'* produced and printed on smart blue paper especially for the occasion, in contrast to the drab standard D-10 form.

US Navy ships

The earliest recorded christening of a US warship was on 21 October 1797 when Captain James Sever named the USS *Constitution* at Navy Yard, Boston, Massachusetts. He broke a bottle of choice Madeira wine from the cellar of the Honourable Thomas Russell, a leading Boston merchant, over her bow before, being the third attempt to launch her, she slid down the launching ways into Boston harbour. There is no recorded religious element to this launching ceremony. USS *Constitution*, one of six frigates authorised for construction by the Naval Act of 1794, is the world's oldest ship still afloat and now moored at Charlestown Navy Yard, Boston.

First recorded religious service for US Navy ship

The first recorded instance of any religious service at the launchings of a US Navy ship prior to 1914 is at the launching and naming of USS *Princeton* on 5 September 1843, which preceded the introduction in 1875 of the form of religious service upon the launch of naval ships in Queen Victoria's navy. Just before the vessel was released, Captain Stockton, US Navy, who was in charge, assembled those on board and the following prayer was offered by Rev. Doctor Suddards:

> Eternal God, Creator of the Universe, Governor of Nations. Humbly we prostrate ourselves before Thee and ask Thy blessing. Most humbly we beseech Thee with Thy favour to behold and bless Thy servant the President of the United States and all the officers of the Government. May the vessel about to be launched be guarded by Thy gracious Providence and care. May it not bear the sword in vain, but as the minister of God be a terror to those who do evil and a defense to those who do well. Graciously bless its officers and men. May love of country be engraven on their hearts. Remember in mercy both arms of our National defense, and may virtue, honor and religion pervade all their ranks. Bless all nations and individuals on earth and hasten the time when the benefits of holy religion shall have so prevailed that none shall wage war again for the purpose of aggression and none shall need it as a means of defense. All of which blessings we ask in the name of Him who taught us to say: 'Our Father who art in Heaven'...[26]

Prayer for our Navy

In 1914 the custom of prayer at the launching of US battleships was established through the efforts of the Society of Sponsors of the US. As noted already, this society was formed in 1898 and continues today and is composed of women who have taken part in the time-honoured tradition of christening a ship to be commissioned in the US Navy.[27] The prayer offered by Reverend Suddards became known as the 'Prayer for Our Navy' or the 'Navy Prayer' and is still used at each meeting and board meeting of the society.

A copy of this historic prayer was forwarded to the Secretary of State of the Navy with a petition that an adapted form of the prayer be offered at launchings of US Navy battleships.

Following the suggestion of the Society of Sponsors, the first reported occasion on which the launch of a US battleship was preceded by a prayer is that of USS *Oklahoma* at Camden, New Jersey, on 23 March 1914. The *New York Times* recorded: 'Bishop E.E. Hoss of Mukogee Oklahoma in a brief invocation dedicated the dreadnought to "the errands of peace and Christianity". The invocation was at the suggestion of Mrs Reynold Hall, President of the Ship Sponsors Society.[28] The suggestion made by the Society of Sponsors was supported by the Secretary of the Navy, who adopted the idea that in future a prayer will be part of the ceremony of the launching of US battleships.

Today it remains the custom for an invocation or prayer to be offered by a US Navy chaplain at the launching of any new ship that is to be commissioned into the US Navy. However, as in the case of the religious service for the launch of British naval ships, there is now no prescribed form of service or prayer. The form of Prayer for our Navy first offered by Rev. Doctor Suddards in 1843 has been modified from time to time and is no longer used for launching ceremonies of ships of the US Navy. It is up to the chaplain leading the religious service that precedes the launch to offer whatever prayers he considers appropriate for the occasion. The discretion is left up to the individual chaplain, not the Chief of Chaplains.

Chapter 11

Royal Launching and Christening of Ships

Royal tradition

Naming or christening of ships has long been a royal tradition in most European monarchies and this is especially true in this country. The British Royal family has down the ages had a special relationship with naval ships, which have played such a key role in the defence of the realm. For many centuries naval ships have been called 'His or Her Majesty's ships' or 'His or Her Britannic Majesty's ships', emphasising the close bond between the Sovereign and the navy. Later the full style was abbreviated to 'HMS'. So it is not all that surprising that Kings and Queens in this country have frequently launched and christened naval ships, whether constructed in Royal Dockyards or in the yards of private contractors.

Launches attended by 'Royal Personages'

The Home Dockyard Regulations that from the late nineteenth century regulated launches of naval ships constructed at Royal Dockyards included special provisions for those attended by 'Royal Personages'; but senior naval officers or Commissioners at the Royal Dockyards also carried out these ceremonies. When a member of the royal family attended such a launch the Regulations permitted higher expenditure on the celebratory lunch and the cost of making the unique commemorative launch casket, including the mallet and chisel, presented to the royal sponsor.[1]

Launch of royal yachts – rarely attended by member of royal family

When it comes to British royal yachts it might have been expected that members of the Royal family would invariably have attended the launch and christened the yacht in person. Surprisingly, this has rarely been the case. The pattern seems to have been that the royal yachts were launched, often without any ceremony, and christened at a later date but then often not by a member of the Royal family. There have been some notable exceptions, of course.

In 1604 Phineas Pett, a member of the distinguished shipbuilding family, received instructions from Lord High Admiral Howard 'commanding me with all possible speed to build a little vessel for the young prince Henry' (the eldest son of King James), then ten years old, 'in order to disport himself in about London Bridge and acquaint his Grace with shipping and the manner of that element'. The little vessel was by the keel 25ft and 12ft in breadth 'garnished with painting and carving within board and without'. Mr Pett describes how he 'wrought upon her as well day as all night by torch and candle lights'. Some six to seven weeks after laying the keel the yacht was launched on 6 March 1604 'with a noise of trumpets, drums and such like ceremonies at such time used'.[2] The yacht was then brought up the Thames and anchored at Paul's wharf. A few days later, on 22 March, the young Prince Henry 'according to the manner in such cases used with a great bowl of wine christened the ship and called her by the name of the *Disdain*'.[3] *Disdain* was the first royal yacht to be built solely for pleasure. This is an early, but as we shall learn, rare example of a royal yacht being named by a member of the royal family, but the naming was not at launch but several days after it.

Continuing with the theme of a royal 'little vessel', mention has already been made of King Charles II's enthusiasm for yachts. Between 1660 and 1688 as many as twenty-six yachts were built in Royal Dockyards, fourteen being still in existence in December 1688, at the time of King James' abdication. In addition to personal use they were employed on state and naval services, especially in emergencies; and some were armed with a few cannon. The deployment of five royal yachts upon the occasion of the launch of the third rate HMS *Grafton* at Deptford on 26 September 1771[4] already described was a unique display of such yachts. The yachts were *Mary*, *William and Mary*, *Fubbs*, *Catherine* (originally *Katherine*) and *Augusta*, constructed at various dates between 1677 and 1694. The name

Fubbs came from the nickname of one of King Charles II's mistresses, Louis de Kerouille, Duchess of Portsmouth, 'fubbs' meaning plump or chubby, a fashionable female form at that time! It became the tradition for King Charles II to name his yachts after his favourites! So far as known none of these yachts were formally christened by a member of the royal family. The concept of the royal yachts just being used for pleasure died out on the death of Charles II.

When the yacht *Royal Sovereign* was launched in 1804 it was reported in the *Naval Chronicle* that 'when she was launched she was christened in the usual manner'[5] but the report does not say by whom or describe the ceremony. Again, in 1817 there is a full account of the launch of the royal yacht *Royal George* reported as being 'sent afloat with martial pomp and ceremony in the presence of the then Duke of York, the Lords of the Admiralty and a great assemblage of notabilities'[6] but again the report is strangely silent on whether she was christened and, if so, by whom. The name given to this yacht was in honour of George, Prince of Wales, then the Prince Regent, and was used by him for visits to inspect the construction of the breakwater at Plymouth, a project in which, as noted earlier, he took a keen interest.

Queen Victoria inherited the *Royal George*, a sailing yacht, from her uncle William IV but found it too slow for her liking and in October 1842 she ordered the 225ft double paddle steam yacht *Victoria and Albert* from Pembroke Royal Dockyard. Since Queen Victoria had taken such a personal interest in this yacht it might have been expected that she or a member of the royal family would have wanted to christen her, but this did not occur. This yacht was designed by Sir William Symonds, Surveyor of the Navy, was launched on 16 April 1843 and 'at the express desire of her Majesty'[7] was christened by Lady Cawdor. We do not know why she was chosen for this honour but her husband, Lord Cawdor, had been the bearer of Queen Victoria's ivory rod at her coronation.

A replacement yacht, *Victoria and Albert II*, was launched at Pembroke Royal Dockyard on 16 January 1855. The Dockyard had wished Queen Victoria to be present at the launching but the building berth was needed and it was not possible to find a convenient date in her schedule, and so she asked Lady Milford to do the honours. This yacht was the principal floating palace of Queen Victoria for half a century. After Prince Albert died in 1861 it was said that everywhere she turned her eye on this yacht reminded Victoria of her young married life. She resisted as long as she could the introduction of electric light and would never consent to the removal of the silver candlesticks. She held out too against the building of a further new yacht, but imperial competition between Russia, Germany and Britain was such that Britain, as the leading maritime nation of the day, had to have and to display the biggest and the best.

Yachts of Russian Imperial family

The new Russian imperial yacht *Standart* had been launched at Burmeister & Wain in Copenhagen on 21 March 1895 in a special canal cut in the ice (see Illustration No. 37) but due to the extreme winter Tsar Nicholas II was unable to attend the ceremony; but members of the Danish royal family did attend.[8] In general, however, the Russian Imperial family had a rather better record than their British counterparts when it came to attending the launches of the various yachts built for them. Of the nine principal yachts launched between 1851 and 1895 for the Russian Tsar, either the Tsar or his heir, the Tsarevich, or a younger son of the Tsar, attended the launch of at least three.[9] These were in 1871 *Derzhava*,[10] in 1890 *Polyarnaya Zvezda*[11] – these two yachts being built in St Petersburg – and in 1880 *Livadia*,[12] built in Govan, Scotland. The difference in practice may perhaps be explained by the fact that the Tsar's attendance at the launch of ships of the Russian Imperial Navy was regarded an important symbol and an opportunity to demonstrate imperial power; and failure by the Tsar or a member of his family to make an appearance at such a public ceremony might have been interpreted as a loss of authority.[13]

In Germany the Kaiser's imperial yacht SMY *Hohenzollern* was built by Vulkan Shipbuilding Company in Stettin and had been launched on 27 June 1892, when she was christened by the Kaiser's consort, Empress Auguste Viktoria. Both this yacht and Nicholas II's *Standart* were modern, propeller-driven ships, while Queen Victoria's yacht was a double paddle steamer. So, Queen Victoria finally gave in to pressure from the Government to have a bigger and technically better yacht built and it was ordered in 1897, again from Pembroke Dock.

Less well known is the royal yacht *Osborne*, a paddle yacht that was designed by Edward Reed, the same well-known naval architect of the day whom we have already come across on a number of occasions in this book. This yacht was launched at Pembroke Dock on 19 December 1870, again not by a royal but by Countess Cawdor. The yacht was used almost exclusively by the Prince and Princess of Wales, who later became King Edward VII and Queen Alexandra, and was frequently to be seen at Cowes.

Victoria and Albert III was launched at Pembroke Royal Dockyard on 9 May 1899. Here at last we find a launching and christening of a royal yacht by a member of the royal family, the Duchess of York (later to become Queen Mary when her husband became King George V). She was accompanied to the launch by the Duke of Connaught, Queen Victoria's son, who was standing in for the Duke of York, who was ill. 'The Dockyard Chaplain, Rev. George Goodenough, led the service supported by the Dockyard chapel choir' and then 'the Duchess broke the bottle of wine against the bows, naming the ship *Victoria and Albert*'.[14] It was a memorable event in the history of the Royal Dockyard attended by thousands of visitors. Unfortunately this glittering event was soon overshadowed by the mishap that occurred when the new yacht subsequently keeled over 20 degrees when being floated out of dry dock. It appears that there was excess weight in her upper structure that altered her metacentre, causing instability. Victoria never stepped on board her new yacht.

Christening by a reigning monarch

If we do not count the naming of the yachts *Disdain* in 1604 by Prince Henry and of *Saudadoes* in 1670 by Queen Catherine, the Portuguese wife of King Charles II, neither of whom were monarchs – and which were also both namings after launch – it was not until the launch of the royal yacht *Britannia* on 16 April 1953 at John Brown & Co. shipyard by HM Queen Elizabeth II that we find a *reigning* monarch launching and christening at launch a royal yacht in this country. That is a surprise if it is recalled that there had been eighty-three royal yachts since the restoration of the monarchy in 1660.

Launch of RY Britannia

It was a truly historic event. It had taken all that time for a launching and christening by a reigning monarch of a royal yacht to happen. It was the first ship launched and christened by Queen Elizabeth II since her accession to the throne and, unless a replacement is built – which is discussed below – it is ironic that the first royal yacht to be named by a reigning monarch may prove to be the last to have been built for the British royal family, at least for some time. The RY *Britannia* was also the first royal yacht not to have been built and launched at Pembroke Dock since the 1840s.

A replacement for *Victoria and Albert III* had been first considered in 1938 but these plans had been interrupted by the Second World War and were not resumed until 1951. King George VI had taken a keen interest in the project and told the Admiralty that he wanted the design of the future yacht to incorporate rapid conversion to a hospital ship in the event of war. Sadly, by the time the plans were revived, the King's health was failing and he died four months before the keel was laid.

George VI, in the conditions of post-war austerity, had wanted in the interests of economy for as many items as possible to be transferred from *Victoria and Albert III* and a number of these, including furniture and bed linen, were brought over.

On the day of the launch at John Brown's shipyard on the Clyde it was a wet and windy day but thousands turned out to welcome Queen Elizabeth II and the Duke of Edinburgh. The Queen arrived dressed in black since she was still in court mourning for the death of Queen Mary. This was the first launching she attended after her accession to the throne. She had last been at Brown's shipyard for the launch of *Caronia* in 1947 and previous to that for the launch of the battleship HMS *Vanguard* in 1944.

As has been observed already, launch of a ship is an anxious moment even for the most experienced naval architect and the launch of the royal yacht in the presence of the Queen was no ordinary affair. Sir John Brown remarked: 'The launch calculations were my responsibility ensuring that the royal yacht would act properly. Thus, any launch is a nervous time for the Naval Architect. Things can happen …'.[15]

All went well.

Elizabeth used a bottle of Empire wine instead of the traditional champagne for the christening, symbolising that the royal yacht was to be the link with the Commonwealth as well as a royal naval ship. The yacht was launched flying the Union Jack, Admiralty flag and White Ensign. In view of the ship's dual role, as a royal yacht in time of peace but a naval hospital ship in time of war, on the express instructions of the Queen, she was not launched with the Royal Standard flying but with the White Ensign, signifying her status as a naval ship. The name of the yacht had been a well-kept secret until the moment her name was pronounced.

In her speech immediately after the launch, Elizabeth wished to emphasize the role played by her father in the planning and design of the yacht. 'I am sure that all you present here realise how much the building of this ship meant to the late King, my father.'[16]

She went on to say that both King George VI and she regarded the yacht as a necessity to enable the Head of the British Commonwealth to visit more easily the members of the Commonwealth, many of them outlying islands best reached by sea; but in the event of war the yacht would serve as a hospital ship.

In this respect RY *Britannia* was quite unlike any other royal yacht; she was also a non-combatant ship of the Royal Navy. In January 1985 the royal yacht was on her way to Australia to meet Queen Elizabeth II for a state visit to the Pacific Islands when news broke of civil war in the former British colony of Aden. The Queen sent orders that the whole ship, including the State apartments, were to be made available to rescued evacuees. The royal yacht was able to pick up 'a total of 152 people of 26 nationalities and one French dog'.[17] More people, including the British Ambassador, were rescued by *Britannia* in the next days from both Khormaksar as well as Little Aden. The unique status of the royal yacht as a non-combatant ship allowed her to go closer to the shore than other vessels. During her period of commission she was not, however, ever deployed as a hospital ship but did much to help boost trade for the UK, when used in trade missions overseas.

In 1997 Prime Minister John Major had authorised the drawing up of plans for a replacement yacht but these were shelved when the

Labour Government under Tony Blair announced on 10 October 1997 that *Britannia* would not be refitted or replaced. The RY *Britannia* was much loved by Queen Elizabeth II and the Duke of Edinburgh, and at her decommissioning in 1997 it is said that the Queen wept in public. At various times since her decommissioning there has been discussion about a replacement yacht being built to help to boost trade deals for the UK; but to date this project has not materialised.

Launch of three 'Queens' by three Royal Queens

There have been other memorable launches and christenings by the royal family in the last eighty years or so, of merchant ships as well as Royal Navy ships, of which a few should be mentioned. Even if the stories of these launches have been told many times before, no book on ship launches would be complete without including the story of the launches of Cunard's three famous liners, the 'Queens', by three Royal Queens.

The launch of the *Queen Mary* at John Brown's yard on 26 September 1934 is one. Cunard intended to name the ship *Victoria* in line with the company's tradition of their ships ending in 'ia' but when the company's representatives asked King George V's permission to name the liner after 'the greatest Queen of Britain' he, evidently misunderstanding the question, said his wife would be delighted. And so the story goes, the delegation had no choice but to report that Hull No. 534 would be called *Queen Mary*.

Before the final decision could be made on the name of Hull 534 there was an obstacle to be overcome. There was another ship in existence with the name *Queen Mary* owned by Williamson-Buchanan Steamers Ltd of Glasgow. Following discussion with that company and, by agreement with the Board of Trade, that ship was renamed *Queen Mary II* so as to make way for Cunard to name its ship '*Queen Mary*.'[18]

The launch itself was a significant symbol of the resurgence of British shipbuilding following the economic depression of the early 1930s. Construction of Hull 534 had commenced in December 1930 but a year later the work was suspended, not cancelled, at the request of Cunard due to its lack of funds and the worldwide economic downturn. Cunard, in desperation, applied to the British Government for a loan to complete the construction, which was granted on condition that Cunard would merge with White Star Line. Once this merger had been concluded on 10 May 1934, work on the liner resumed, to the intense relief of the workforce on Clydebank.

At launch on 26 September 1934 the *Queen Mary* was 1,019.4ft long overall and displaced 77,400 long tons. Some deepening of the river had to be carried out to cope with the size of this new ship. The Clyde Navigation Trust dredged around the shipyard and widened the Clyde at the entrance to the Cart, but the launch of so long and heavy a ship, then the largest liner in the world, into a narrow river was certainly a great engineering challenge for the shipyard. The naval architect of the shipyard, James McNeill, created a model to test the feasibility of the launch: 'a ... model was ... launched into a part of the shipyard model tank in conditions closely simulating the Clyde' including 'an equation to represent the motion of the ship at launch and from this [it was] predicted that the ship would travel 1,194 feet after it was launched – in fact it travelled 1,196 feet.'[19] To check the momentum as the hull entered the water, a set of enormous drag chains, whose total weight aggregated 2,350 tons, were used, connected in bundles to various points along the hull. It is remarkable to note that the shipyard succeeded in arresting the velocity of so long and large a ship in just over 100ft more than its own length. The ship when complete was one of the finest ever built and a flagship on the high seas for British shipbuilding. It is believed that this was the first merchant ship to be launched in the presence of a British monarch and the first naming ceremony of a merchant ship to be performed by a Queen consort.

Before the launch, King George V, in his address said: 'Today we come to the task of sending on her way the stateliest ship now in being.'[20] Queen Mary then christened the liner with a bottle of Australian wine in heavy rain witnessed by 200,000 people. Cutting the cord that released the christening bottle with a pair of golden scissors, she said: 'I am happy to name this ship *Queen Mary*. I wish success to her and all who sail in her.'[21] The ship's name had been kept secret until she announced it. When she returned to Balmoral after the christening she wrote in her diary: 'Went to a splendid stand [at shipyard of John Brown & Co. Ltd], G [King George V] read an address. I cut a string to release the bottle of wine & pressed a button which released the enormous ship & she took to the water in a beautiful manner – a most impressive sight – unfortunately it rained all the time.'[22] The launch was broadcast to the nation through the agency of the BBC and it is believed to be the first time that such an event had been broadcast.

In February 1936 Cunard announced its intention to build a running mate to *Queen Mary*, again to be constructed on Clydebank by John Brown's. The rumour was that she might be called King George V, honouring the husband of Queen Mary, who had died in January 1936. The ships would then be 'the king and queen of the Atlantic'. However, they became 'the queens of the Atlantic' in February 1938 when Cunard revealed that *Queen Elizabeth* was their choice of name for Hull 552. They were honouring the popular Duchess of York, who had become Queen Consort when her husband ascended the throne in December 1936 as George VI. It was originally intended that King George VI and Queen Elizabeth would both attend the launch with Princess Elizabeth and Princess Margaret. In the event, due to the Munich crisis and Neville Chamberlain's discussions with Adolf Hitler on the day before the launch, the King cancelled his journey to Clydebank and directed that the Queen Consort accompanied by Princess Elizabeth and Princess Margaret carry out the programme.[23] Half a million people crowded into the John Brown shipyard for the launching ceremony on 27 September 1938. The event was once again broadcast by the BBC. Microphones had been hidden in the slipway so all could hear the roar as the huge hull went down the ways and into the Clyde. Her length, at 1,031ft overall, was slightly longer than *Queen Mary* and quite a lot heavier: another engineering triumph for John Brown's shipyard.

The Queen Consort, in her launching address, delivered a message from the King. She told them of his deep regret at being unable to be present at the launch, adding: 'He bids the people of this country to be of good cheer, in spite of the dark clouds hanging over them and, indeed, over the whole world.'[24]

As the Queen Consort came to the end of her speech the ship began to move down the launch way. She instantly cut the string, which sent the bottle of Australian wine crashing into the bow of the rapidly receding liner, using the same gold scissors that Queen Mary had used to perform the launching ceremony of her namesake; it had been a close call.

Princess Elizabeth and Princess Margaret had evidently taken a great interest in the whole operation and after the successful launch the shipyard donated a small working model of the launching 'trigger' mechanism to them as a memento of the event.[25]

At the outbreak of the war there was great concern that the sheer bulk of *Queen Elizabeth* lying at Clydebank would have been an unmissable target for German bombers. It was, therefore, decided that she should be put into a condition that would enable her to sail to New York and safety as soon as possible. She was painted grey and taken to the Firth of Clyde on 26 February 1940. From where, without any trials, she sailed without any mishap to New York.

The *Queen Mary* in the meantime had also been painted grey, converted into a troop carrier and armed. Due to her great speed and zig-zag manoeuvres, she was able to successfully outwit the U–boats and transported a million men to war.

After the end of the Second World War John Brown shipyard was again Cunard's chosen shipyard for the construction of another liner, Hull 736, launched on 20 September 1967. Queen Elizabeth II symbolically used the same pair of gold scissors to cut the launch cord her grandmother and mother had used to launch *Queen Mary* and *Queen Elizabeth* in 1934 and 1938.

As was Cunard's practice at the time, the name was not to be publicly revealed until the launch. Dignitaries were invited to 'the launch of Cunard Liner Hull 736' as no name had yet been painted on the bow.

Queen Elizabeth II launched the ship with the words: 'I name this ship Elizabeth the Second. May God bless her and all who sail in her.' The *New York Times* and *The Times*, in their report of the occasion, printed the name as 'Elizabeth II' but when the ship left the shipyard the name on her bow was *Queen Elizabeth 2*. She was later, more colloquially, known as 'QE2'. She became the third 'queen' to be christened by a Royal Queen.

It was a remarkable feat of engineering by John Brown's shipyard to have launched these three great 'queens' safely in the confined waters of the Clyde, using a combination of dredging of the entrance to the River Cart opposite to the shipyard and the skilful deployment of a series of heavy check chains.

Opportunity to make public speech

The christening of ships by a member of the royal family has frequently been the first opportunity for some of them, not including Queen Elizabeth II, to make a speech in public. It has been said that when Queen Mary named *Queen Mary* in 1934: 'The few she spoke as she launched her name sake were the only words she ever said publicly as Queen.'[26] When HRH Princess Margaret christened *Edinburgh Castle* at the shipyard of Harland & Wolff in Belfast on 16 October 1947, it was her first unaccompanied public engagement.[27]

Ships named or launched and named by HRH Princess Elizabeth/HM Queen Elizabeth II

As Princess Elizabeth, Queen Elizabeth II named or launched and named four ships. During her reign as Queen it is thought that she named or launched and named a total of twenty-seven ships (see Appendix I), giving a total of thirty-one. As might be expected since the official headship of the Royal Navy was vested in Queen Elizabeth II and, as noted earlier, Royal Navy ships bear the prefix 'HMS', the largest category is Royal Navy ships, being seven in total.

As we have learned in an earlier chapter, the last naval ship named by Queen Elizabeth II was the new aircraft carrier HMS *Queen Elizabeth*, named in dry dock in Rosyth on 4 July 2014. The Queen christened the ship with a bottle of Islay malt whisky against the hull, rather than the more traditional champagne. It marked the first time in more than fifteen years that the Queen had christened a Royal Navy ship. In her speech she included the following words:

'Wherever this ship may serve, whatever tasks may be asked of her, let all those who serve on her know that on this day she was blessed with the prayers of us all for her success and for her safe return to calm waters.'[28]

Naming of lifeboats

There are also strong connections between the Royal family and the RNLI. Apart from HRH the Duke of Kent's role as RNLI President, HM Queen Elizabeth II, during her reign, named at least five lifeboats. In 1993 Queen

Elizabeth II named the lifeboat *Her Majesty the Queen* at Ramsgate, marking the fortieth anniversary of her reign. It was the third lifeboat to be named after Queen Elizabeth II and the first time a reigning monarch had named a lifeboat in their name. In 2011 Prince William and his then fiancée, Catherine Middleton, chose the naming of Trearddur Bay's new lifeboat as their first official joint engagement. Prince William's work as an RAF search and rescue pilot has given him a close affinity to the work of the RNLI.

Naming outside Great Britain

The Queen's only naming of a ship outside Great Britain was in June 1973 when she named the training ship *Playfair* in Toronto. It is believed to be the only Canadian ship to be named by a reigning monarch.

Naming of cruise ships

The Queen also named a number of cruise ships, including *Oriana*, *Queen Mary 2*, *Queen Elizabeth* and, on 10 March 2015, P and O Cruises' latest liner, *Britannia*. Since the latter was, as already noted, the name of the royal yacht much loved by the Queen there must, it is conjectured, have been some extensive correspondence between P and O Cruises and Buckingham Palace to secure permission to use the same name for this new cruise ship. It must have been a difficult and nostalgic moment too for the Queen at the naming ceremony in Southampton. In October 2014 P and O Cruises acquired the Union Jack that was previously flown on the royal yacht. It is understood that it will be displayed in the new cruise ship when royal visitors are on board or on special occasions. The flag was flown on the occasion of the naming by the Queen on 10 March 2015 and can only have added further to the feeling of nostalgia for the royal yacht.

Chapter 12

Venice's Unique Ring Ceremony

Unique

In this special launch ceremony in the *Arsenale* in Venice large
commemorative copper rings, after being blessed by a Catholic
priest, were hung by a ribbon from the stern of an Italian naval ship
as it was launched, so as to be the first thing to touch the water. This
launch ceremony is unique: unique because almost all other launch or
naming ceremonies of ships are performed at the bow or on the 'poop'
deck; unique because the ring ceremony symbolically recalls the historic
'marriage with the sea' ceremony that is unique to Venice; and unique
because it only applied to Italian royal naval ships constructed in Venice's
Arsenale for a very short period, between 1891 and 1914.

Marriage with the sea ceremony

In order to understand the significance and symbolism of these rings we
need to recall the ancient tradition in Venice of the so-called *Sposalizio
del Mare* – 'Marriage with the Sea' – ceremony. The Venetians have for
many centuries recognised that they owe their very existence to the sea
surrounding their lagoon. In the fourth century the population of the
villages and towns of *Istia* and *Venetia* fled from the invading Goths and
Barbarians. With their seafaring experience the Venetians were able to
find refuge in the islands of the lagoon. This lagoon over time became
the source of Venetian trade and power. So Venetians have always had a
special bond with the lagoon.

At the end of the tenth century a ceremony was initiated by Doge
Pietro Orseolo II involving the Doge, members of the Council, the
clergy and citizens of Venice going to the port of Saint Nicolo do Lido
on Ascension Day for a blessing of the Adriatic Sea. The Doge would

travel to the ceremony in a carved and gilded galley called the *Bucintoro*.[1] The Doge, dressed in fine gold robes, sat in a special throne at the stern. A figurehead of a lady holding a sword and scales known as 'Venice of Justice' adorned the bow. The figurehead from the 1526 barge is to be found today in the *Museo Storico Navale* in Venice; and similar figures adorned subsequent *Bucintori*. These galleys, propelled by oars, were not the personal property of the Doge but very much ships of state, ceremonial state barges of *La Serenissima*, a frequently used name for the Republic of Venice.

This ancient ceremony was given almost sacred significance by Pope Alexander III in 1176. The Pope wished to thank Venice for its services in the struggle against the Holy Roman Emperor Frederick I. The Pope drew a ring from his finger and gave it to the Doge, Sebastiano Ziani, and bade him cast such a one into the sea each year on Ascension Day, and so wed the sea. The ceremony took place in front of the church of San Nicolo al Lido, which houses some of the relics of Saint Nicholas, the patron saint of sailors. From this date, on Ascension Day every year, the Doge dropped a consecrated ring into the sea with the Latin words *Desponsamus te, mare, in signum veri perpetuique domini* – we wed thee, sea, in the sign of the true and everlasting Lord. Venice and the sea were declared to be indissolubly one.

The 'marriage with the sea' ceremony has been a tradition of Venice down the centuries and is still celebrated today aboard a smaller barge called the *Bissona Serenissima* but no longer involving the throwing of a precious ring into the water.

Introduction of ring ceremony

In 1866 the war of independence with Prussia led to the annexation of the Republic of Venice to the Kingdom of Italy under Victor Emmanuel as King. Naval ships built in the *Arsenale* at Venice would now be 'Royal Ships'. The Royal Italian Navy, in homage to Venice, wanted the Venetian tradition of 'marriage with the sea' to become part of the official ceremony for the launching of naval ships built in the *Arsenale*. A new ritual was, therefore, introduced by the Director of the *Arsenale*, Commendatore Canevaro, with the approval of the Minister of Marine:[2] symbolic rings made of copper were to be blessed by a priest and hung by ribbon from the stern of the ship being launched, so as to be the first thing to touch the water, thereby recalling the unity with the sea that is at the heart of Venice's ancient 'marriage with the sea' ceremony. The more important the ship, the larger the ring and the more precious the stones used to decorate it. The wording inscribed on the ring was not standard but individually composed for each launch. It was considered that, if a ship had symbolically been married with the sea, this was a good omen for its future. In this way the special status of Venice would be preserved despite its inclusion in an enlarged and unified Kingdom of Italy. The ring ceremony was unique to naval ships built in the *Arsenale* in Venice and did not extend to naval ships built at shipyards elsewhere in Italy.

Prior to the introduction of the new ritual, naval ships built at the *Arsenale* were blessed by a Catholic priest before being launched and christened with a bottle of champagne in the traditional way.

First launch with ceremonial ring

The first ship launch at which the new ring ritual was performed was the *Corazzata Sicilia* launched on 6 July 1891, where the *Madrina del varo* – godmother – was Princess Margherita of Savoy, Queen of Italy. She was consort to Umberto I, who had become King of Italy in 1878. After her marriage Princess Margherita did much to promote the new royal house of the united Italy. Her role as godmother of this new ship at which this new ring ritual at Venice was to be performed was, therefore, particularly significant, emphasising that she was not only Princess of Savoy but Queen of a unified Italy, of which Venice was now a part. The ring was donated by the Princess herself and blessed by the Patriarch of Venice, Cardinal Agostini. The ring was decorated with the heraldic emblem of the House of Savoy and inscribed with the name 'Margherita di Savoia, Regina d'Italia' – Margherita of Savoy, Queen of Italy – on the top and the words *Madrina del varo* – godmother of the launch – on the bottom (Illustration No. 23).

Conservation of ceremonial ring in captain's cabin

At launches at the *Arsenale* after the *Corazzata Sicilia* the ring was usually inscribed with the name of the launched ship, the date of the launch and the name of the *Madrina del varo*, but there was no standard wording for this inscription. The rings were often decorated with precious stones, being more or less precious according to the importance of the ship being launched. The larger rings were about 6in across measured from the outer diameter. After the launch the rings were recovered and conserved aboard the ship in a custom-built decorated coffer, usually displayed in the captain's cabin. Three of the godmothers of naval ships built at the *Arsenale* during this period were members of the Italian Royal family, SM Margherita di Savoia, Queen of Italy, SAR Elena Principessa di Napoli and SAR Isabella Duchessa di Genova. The ceremonial rings for the ships they launched were all donated by these royal godmothers and all of them are now displayed in the *Museo Storico Navale* in Venice as well as an example of a decorated coffer.

Confusion between rituals

This new ring ceremony ritual, once introduced, was generally followed for naval ships built at the *Arsenale*, in substitution for the old ceremony of blessing of the ship by a Catholic priest followed by christening with a bottle of champagne. However, at the launch of *Esploratore Quarto*, an explorer vessel, on 19 August 1911 there was confusion between the two rituals and those responsible wanted to have the ring ceremony followed by baptism of the ship with a bottle of champagne, which was contrary to the new ritual introduced by the director of the *Arsenale*. The godmother threw the bottle three times and it failed to break, only breaking at the fourth attempt. The failure of the bottle to break and the confusion with the new ritual evidently did not create a good impression.

Launch of cruiser Ammiraglio di Saint Bon

One of the largest rings on display at the *Museo Storico Navale* is that for the launch of *R. Corazzata Ammiraglio di Saint Bon* on 29 April 1897, which was donated by the godmother of the launch, Elena Principessa di Napoli. The Princess was the daughter of King Nicholas I of Montenegro and in 1896 married Victor Emmanuel, who in 1900 became Victor Emmanuel III of Italy. This battleship was a pre-dreadnought of 111.8 metres length armed with four 10in guns and having a top speed of 18 knots. She served in the Italian–Turkish war of 1911–12 but was obsolescent by the start of the First World War.

Since the ceremonial ring ceremony in Venice's *Arsenale* is so unusual there has been included below a full account of the launch of *R. Corozzata Ammiraglio di Saint Bon* from which the colour and pageantry of these unique launch ceremonies in Venice, performed with a ring at the stern of the ship, can be more readily appreciated. Illustration No. 24 also portrays this colourful ceremony.

An Account of the launch of cruiser Ammiraglio di Saint Bon on 29 April 1897[3]

Admission to the *Arsenale* for the launch of royal naval cruiser *Ammiraglio di Saint Bon* on 29 April 1897 was by ticket only with extra security in place with numerous *carabinieri* in attendance and certain streets and canals around the *Arsenale* being closed off.

The arrival of guests for the ceremony was in accordance with a pre-arranged time schedule.

At 11am the rain started to fall and there was a lot of commotion and discussion in the stands because the opening of umbrellas impeded the view until the umbrellas were closed again.

At 11.15am Government ministers, including Benedetto Brin, Minister of the Navy, arrived to take their official seats in the royal stand alongside diplomats and admirals and were greeted with a salute from a battalion of marines. The royal stand was decorated with white, red, blue and gold velvet fabrics.

At 11.34am the Patriarch of Venice, Cardinal Sarto, arrived, dressed in purple and wearing his mitre. He was accompanied by Canons and certain other clerics, one of whom was carrying a cross. The Patriarch's official seats were in a stand decorated in red and yellow.

At 11.50am a fusillade of cannon shots announced the arrival at Piazza San Marco of Vittorio Emmanuel, Principe di Napoli, in the uniform of a general and wearing a plumaged helmet. Elena Principessa di Napoli, who was to be the godmother at the launch of the ship, accompanied him wearing a white dress with a red transparent collar and a hat that was white with ribbons and flowers which were red and pink. They both

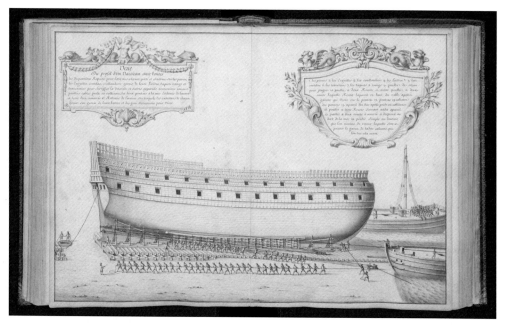

1. Lancement par l'avant sous Louis XIV – bow-first launch in reign of Louis XIV, at Arsenal Toulon, Album de Colbert 1670. © Defence Historique Service, CHA, Vincennes, document number SH140.

2. Site of former launching slip at Buckler's Hard, a private shipyard on the River Beaulieu where ships for Nelson's navy were constructed in the eighteenth century, the slip being set at a fine angle to the river to increase launching space. Courtesy of the author.

3. Bow-first launch of polytherme cargo ship *Ivondro* at Chantiers France-Gironde, Dunkirk, 27 September 1968. Courtesy Collection Musée portuaire de Dunkerque Fonds Ateliers et chantiers de France (ACF).

4. Dramatic picture of side launch of US Shipping Board's First World War Laker, SS *Lake Fernando*, at Buffalo Dry Dock Company, Lake Erie, in 1919. The hull, shown here on its side, seconds later righted itself with the back wash. Courtesy Detroit Historical Society Image ID 2014.002.728.

5. Dramatic picture of sideways launch of cruise liner *Homeric* on 28 September 1985 at the shipyard of Meyer Werft in Papenburg, Germany, showing the huge side wash. Courtesy Meyer Werft GmbH & Co. KG.

6. Aerial picture of sideways launch of liner *Homeric* at the shipyard of Meyer Werft in Papenburg, Germany, on 28 September 1985 illustrating the narrow space in which the launch was effected. Courtesy Meyer Werft GmbH & Co. KG.

7. Launch over compressed vulcanised rubber launching airbags at Jejiang on 5 June 2012 of a 73,000-dwt ship. The airbags were manufactured by Shandong Nanhai Airbag Engineering Co. Ltd, Shandong, China. Courtesy of the same company.

8. Launch of RMS *Titanic*, Harland & Wolff, Belfast, on 31 May 1911. Photo by R.J. Welch (1859–1936). © National Museums NI Collection Harland & Wolff, Ulster Folk & Transport Museum, HOYFM.HW. HI558.

9. Launch of aircraft carrier HMS *Formidable* at Harland & Wolff's shipyard, Belfast on 17 August 1939. Shipyard workers are shown surveying the damage after the fore poppet under the bow collapsed on launch. The hull, after launching itself, can be clearly seen in the right-hand side background after being brought under control by tugs. Courtesy Hulton Archive/Getty Images.

10. Launch of aircraft carrier HMS *Formidable* at Harland & Wolff's shipyard, Belfast, on 17 August 1939. This photo, looking towards the viewing stand, further illustrates the collapse of the fore poppet. Spectators and dockyard workers stand in shock at this unexpected turn of events. Photo R.J. Welch (1859–1936). © National Museums NI Collection Harland & Wolff, Ulster Folk & Transport Museum, HOYFM. HW.7191.

11. The *Daphne* tragedy 1883. Accident on the River Clyde at the launch of small steamer SS *Daphne* at the shipyard of Messrs Alexander Stephen & Sons, Linthouse, on 3 July 1883 when it heeled over after clearing the launch ways and capsized. Some 124 men were drowned. The steamer is seen here on its side at low water. © CSG CIC Glasgow Museums and Libraries Collection: The Mitchell Library, Special Collections.

12. SS *Principessa Jolanda*, seen heeling heavily to port after launch, coast of Riva Trigano, near Genoa, Italy, 22 September 1907. Courtesy Alamy.

13. SS *Great Eastern* launch in 1857, Brunel and three assistants are the men wearing top hats on the launching platform. Courtesy of Brunel University London Archives and Special Collections.

14. SS *Great Eastern* at Millwall on 5 December 1857, sideways to the River Thames showing the enormous size of the ship and the extent of the launching challenge for Brunel. Photo by Robert Howlett (English, 1831–58). Courtesy George Eastman Museum, Rochester, NY 14607 ref.1981.1647.0057.

15. Dramatic picture of the launch of RMS *Mauretania* on 20 September 1906 into the River Tyne at the shipyard of Swan Hunter Wigham Richardson. The picture illustrates the challenge faced by the shipyard of launching in confined waters, the then largest ship in the world. Courtesy Newcastle City Library, Local Studies and Family History Centre.

16. Collision on the River Tyne of newly launched cargo ship *Crosby* with the world's first turbine-powered vessel SY *Turbinia* on 11 January 1907. *Crosby* on launch carried away her check chains (never properly attached). *Turbinia* was nearly cut in two by the impact. Courtesy Tyne and Wear Archives & Museums/Bridgeman images.

17. Launch of HMS *Prince of Wales* 1794. 'Exact Representation of the Launching of *Prince of Wales* Man-of-war before their Majesties at Portsmouth' with 'launching colours', produced on 1 October 1794 by Joshua Cristall (artist) and Barlow (engraver). Courtesy National Maritime Museum, Greenwich, London, PU 6038.

18. Society of Sponsors of the US Navy. Meeting of the Founding Sponsors at Willard Hotel, Washington DC, 18 February 1908. Naval History & Heritage Command: Photo Section NH 98298.

Left: 19. Silver plate awarded to Master Shipwrights upon launch of a ship: silver tankard commemorating the launch of third rate HMS *Captain* at Woolwich in 1743 (Maker Thomas Farren) and a pair of silver candlesticks commemorating the launch of the fifth rate HMS *Faversham* at Plymouth in 1712 (Maker John Bache). © National Maritime Museum, Greenwich, London, PLT 20208 D4623.

Below: 20. Launch casket made of satinwood with mallet and chisel for HMS *Alert,* Sheerness, 28 December 1894. Courtesy the author.

BAPTEME OU BENEDICTION DE LA GALERE.

21. Bapteme ou benediction de la galere (christening or blessing of a galley). A Catholic priest is seen standing with a cross in the bow of the boat about to be launched. The expectant spectators afloat in the boats opposite the launch way suggest that the launch is to take place as soon as the religious ceremony is completed. Etching by Jacques Rigaud (1681–1754) and thought to date from 1721. Courtesy Bibliotheque municipale de Rouen. (Cote: Est. A. Hedou 915-003.)

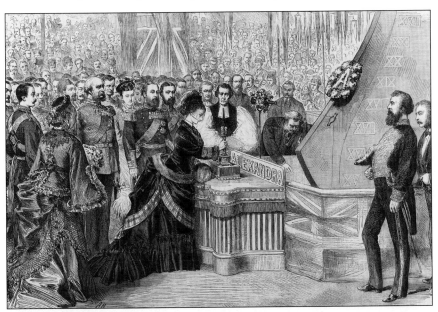

22. Launch of ironclad HMS *Alexandra* at Chatham Dockyard, 7 April 1875, by the Princess of Wales, Princess Alexandra. To the right of the Princess is Archbishop Tait who together with the First Lord of the Admiralty obtained the approval of Queen Victoria to introduce the form of the religious service for the launching of ships in Her Majesty's Navy. The launch was one of the first at which the new form of service was used.
© Illustrated London News Ltd/ Mary Evans April 1875 Supplement, Image 12013789.

23. Commemorative ring from launch of *R. Corazzata Scilia* at *Arsenale*, Venice, 6 July 1891, now exhibited at *Museo Storico Navale*, Venice. Photo taken by the Author with kind permission of *Museo Storico Navale*, Venice.

24. Launch of *R Corazzata Ammiraglio di Saint Bon* in the *Arsenale* of Venice, 29 April 1897. Note the ribbon hanging down from the stern of the ship to which a copper ring will be attached and which symbolically will be the first thing to touch the water at launch. The godmother, Elena Principessa di Napoli, can be seen stepping onto the pontoon to the right. Courtesy *Ufficio Storico Marina Militare* (Italian Navy Historical Office).

25. Commemorative ring from launch of corvette *R. Cristoforo Colombo* at *Arsenale*, Venice, 24 September 1892, now exhibited at *Museo Storico Navale*, Venice. Photo taken by the author with kind permission of *Museo Storico Navale*, Venice.

26. Launch of *R Corazzata Ammiraglio di Saint Bon,* 29 April 1897, inside the *Arsenale*, Venice, with spectators in the covered stands in the background. Courtesy *Ufficio Storico Marina Militare* (Italian Navy Historical Office).

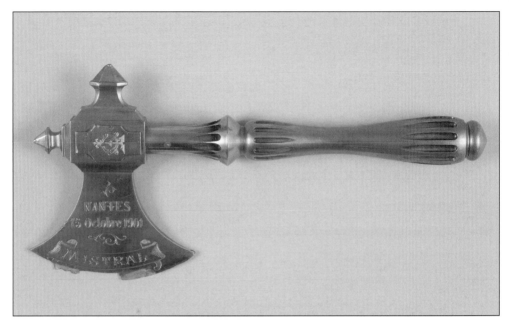

Above: 27. Ceremonial launching axe measuring 14cm x 28.5cm used on the occasion of the launch of the barque *Mistral* on 15 October 1901, built by Ateliers et Chantiers de la Loire, Nantes, to symbolically cut the last rope that attached the ship to the shore. © Musée national de la Marine/Hache No 2008.23.3.

Opposite above: 28. Launch of Imperial Japanese cruiser *Kongo* into the Walney Channel, Barrow-in-Furness, on 18 May 1912, showing the custom of *kusudama* or medicine ball with a red and white balloon suspended from the bow, from which doves and confetti were released as the ship slid down the ways. Courtesy Dock Museum Barrow-in-Furness. Image VPA 3176.

Opposite below: 29. The launch on 10 May 1900 out of the covered yard at Baltic Works, St Petersburg, of the dreadnought battleship *Pobeda* (meaning Victory) of the Peresvet-class. Note the Tsar's ceremonial viewing pavilion. Courtesy Central State Archives of Cinematic, Phonographic and Photographic Documents, St Petersburg, Russian Federation, 2239 1 7348.

Above: 30. The launch of cargo ship SS *Jalabala* on 12 July 1927 at Lithgows Ltd, Port Glasgow. Footage supplied by British Pathe shows the Honourable V.J. Patel, Speaker and President of the Indian Legislative Council, about to smash a coconut against the side of the ship next to the bow, as it slides into the water.

Opposite above: 31. Launch during an air raid of 8,400-dwt cargo ship *North Britain* at the shipyard of John Readhead & Sons Ltd, Newcastle upon Tyne, on 16 September 1940. Courtesy Tyne and Wear Archives and Museums, DS RDD/4/PH/1/519/1/11.

Opposite below: 32. Launch in wartime of Yard No. 523 *Empire Scott* at John Readhead & Sons, on the River Tyne on 10 July 1941. Courtesy Tyne and Wear Archives DS RDD/4/PH/1/523/2(3).

Left: 33. Bottle arrangement for the launch of RMS *Pretoria Castle* at Harland & Wolff on 19 August 1947 showing the 'magic box' that on receipt of radio signals from the ship's godmother in South Africa triggered in Belfast the release of the christening bottle and the launching mechanism. Photo R.J. Welch (1859–1936). © National Museums NI Collection Harland & Wolff, Ulster Folk & Transport Museum, HOYFM. HW. 10541.

Below: 34. RMS *Pretoria Castle* launched by radio signal from South Africa, Harland & Wolff, Belfast, 19 August 1947. Photo R.J. Welch (1859–1936). © National Museums NI Collection Harland & Wolff, Ulster Folk & Transport Museum, HOYFM 10552.

35. Launch of the aft half of Yard No. 233 *Rondefjell* at John Crown & Sons on 9 April 1951 with the name already painted on stern. Photo courtesy Tyne and Wear Archives and Museums, DS. CR/4/PH/1/233/1/3.

36. Mrs Erna Ugelstad ,the wife of one of the directors of the owners, smashing a christening bottle against the bow section of yard No 233 oil tanker Rondefjell at its launch on 15 October 1951 separate from the aft section already launched. Photo courtesy Tyne and Wear Archives and Museums, DS. CR/4/PH /1/233/2/4.

37. Russian Imperial yacht *Standart* launched in a canal cut into the ice at Burmeister & Wain shipyard, Copenhagen, on 21 March 1895. Owner of photo is unknown.

38. Night launch by torchlight of iron screw steamer *Azof* on 17 July 1855 on the River Clyde at the shipyard of Messrs Bourne and Co. Etching. © Illustrated London News/Mary Evans, 11 August 1855, Image 12013704.

39. Venice *Arsenale* – the entrance at *Porta Magna* guarded by the lion of St Mark. Courtesy of Alamy.

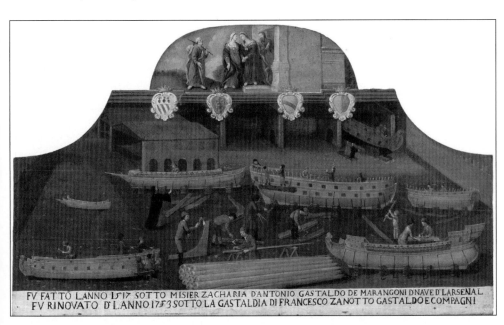

FV FATTO LANNO 1517 SOTTO MISIER ZACHARIA DANTONIO GASTALDO DE MARANGONI DNAVE D'LARSENAL
FV RINOVATO D'LANNO 1753 SOTTO LA GASTALDIA DI FRANCESCO ZANOT TO GASTALDO E COMPAGNI

40. A painted sign, 1517, under Zacharia D'Antonio, steward of the carpenters of Arsenale, showing various stages of construction of a galley. Note completed galley under cover, held in reserve, ready to be launched. 2018 Copyright Photo Archive - Fondazione Musei Civici di Venezia.

Left: 41. The launch of SS *Quistconck* at Hog Island, Pennsylvania, on 5 August 1918. Courtesy of the Atwater Kent Collection, Drexel University, Philadelphia.

Below: 42. The launch of SS *Quistconck* at Hog Island, Pennsylvania, in August 1918. Behind the celebratory lunch tables are the long line of derricks for the multiple construction of ships. Courtesy of the Atwater Kent Collection, Drexel University, Philadelphia.

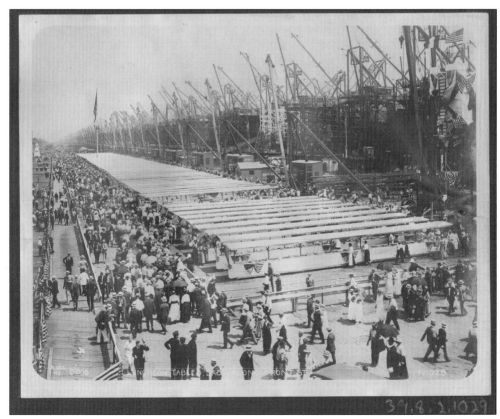

43. Launching ceremony of 'Liberty ship' SS *Patrick Henry*, the first US mass-produced cargo ship during the Second World War, at Bethlehem-Fairfield Shipyard, Baltimore, Maryland, on 27 September 1941. Glasshouse Images/Alamy Stock photo MN77FP.

Left: 44. General de Gaulle, President of France, speaking at the launch of the liner *Le France*, Saint Nazaire, on 11 May 1960 (Photographie Barrault Collection Saint Nazaire Agglomeration Tourisme-Ecomusee. Fonds Chantiers de L'Atlantique).

Below: 45. Launch card for Chinese training ship *Chao Ho*, launched Elswick Yard 23 October 1911. Courtesy Tyne and Wear Archive, DX 1454/1/15/2.

LAUNCH OF THE
· CHINESE ·
TRAINING-CRUISER
"CHAO HO"
From the Elswick Shipyard
Newcastle·on·Tyne.
by Miss AMY LEW

OCTOBER 23ʳᵈ 1911

arrived by gondola and were escorted by 'bissoni'.[4] As they passed down the lagoon they were greeted by a multitude of spectators in gondolas and other boats, and by the ceremonial firing of shots. A lot of Venetians and foreigners wanted to be present at this launch ceremony. Some had arrived in the early hours of the morning, many with packets of provisions for the long wait before the ceremony began. The *Madrina* arrived in a gondola with a four-oar crew followed by two gondolas each of two oars. The arrival of the Prince and Princess at the *Arsenale* was announced by a trumpet call and the Military band, supplemented by a section of the Marine band, played the Royal March.[5] The Prince and Princess were greeted by a group of ministers, admirals and generals. The Prince shook the hands of various people, took the Princess on his arm and they made their way to the official stand of the Patriarch, where an altar had been set up. The Prince and the Patriarch exchanged a few words, shook hands and bowed to one another. The Prince and Princess then proceeded to their official seats, stopping on the way to look at a model of the ship to be launched that was exhibited near their seats.

The Patriarch, accompanied by canons and other clerics and their assistants, in a procession behind the cross, then left the altar and made his way between the official seats onto a temporary pontoon at the stern of the new cruiser on the launch way. As he walked towards the pontoon the Patriarch blessed the workers from the *Arsenale* and members of the public. He was followed by a long procession of people. On arrival at the pontoon the Patriarch repeatedly blessed the new ship [whose name 'R. Corozzata Ammiraglio di Saint Bon' can be clearly seen on the stern of the ship in the photograph of the event].

The Prince and Princess then left their official stand in order to join the Patriarch and clergy on the pontoon below the stern of the cruiser. Cav. Vitale, a knight, then presented the ceremonial ring, contained in a coffer, to the Princess, as the *Madrina del varo* – godmother of the launch. The ring was 15cm in diameter. On the outside of the ring is engraved the lion of Saint Mark and the words 'VARO DELLA R.CORAZZATA AMMIRAGLIO SAN BON 1897' – launch of royal cruiser Admiral San Bon 1897 – and on the inside the name of the godmother and the date of the launch – 'MADRINA ELENA PRINCIPESSA DI NAPOLI 29 APRILE'.

The Princess wanted to know who had made the coffer containing the ceremonial ring and the worker in question from the *Arsenale* was presented to her. The *Madrina* then tied the ceremonial ring to the ribbon. The time was 12.10pm. The ring so tied to the stern was symbolically to be the first thing to enter into the water when the ship was launched down the launch way. The Prince and Cardinal Sarto again shook hands.

A bouquet of white flowers was then presented to the godmother. The Prince and Princess then returned to their official seats alongside the Government ministers and exchanged a few words with the ladies and gentlemen seated around them.

The launch itself then began, this being announced by a trumpet call. The supports or props under the hull were first taken away. In accordance with a new concept invented by Cav. Vitale, the props at the stern were removed first and those at the bow last, so as to ease the descent of the ship down the launch way. When the first prop was removed a naval official was seen to tumble and for a brief moment there was concern that he might be hurt but he was quickly back on his feet. The first prop was taken down at 12.22pm and by 12.34 all props had been taken down. The temporary pontoon was then taken away.

Everyone fell silent and at this moment a bit of anxiety was felt. The workers from the shipyard formed two columns, one on each side of the launch way, and each column picked up a rope in case it was needed to help the ship move down the launch way. Firemen were also standing by. The technical chief of the yard made a last inspection and reported that all was in order.

At 12.41pm the order '*Taglia!*' – Cut it! – was given and a key worker with an axe cut the last ropes holding the ship. The ship was free and started to move down the launch way. This first movement of the ship was greeted by a salute from cannon on board the cruisers *Ammiraglio Monzanbano* and *Ammiraglio Minneapolis*, anchored in the lagoon. The ship on the launch way then came to a stop. At this point different methods were available to help the ship move down the way – hydraulic presses or, if this was not successful, the shipyard workers would pull on the ropes. A little assistance from the hydraulic presses was applied and with thirty-six *Arsenalotti* pulling on the two ropes, which had been wound around two capstans at the stern of the ship, the ship started to move again, majestically.

This movement of the ship down the ways caused commotion among the spectators. [Illustration No. 26]. They removed their hats and, waving their hats and handkerchiefs, shouted '*Viva*' – long life. Some threw multicoloured cards inscribed '*Viva I Principi Di Napoli*!' – long live the Princes of Napoli, others threw cards inscribed '*Viva Vitale*!' – wishing long life to Cav. Vitale – and there were similar messages of long life to other named personnel at the shipyard who had been involved in the construction and launch of the cruiser. As the ship went down the ways the band played the royal march. The movement of the ship into the water created large waves and spectators in the stands S and T were soaked by the waves created by the hull as it entered the water.

After a significant launch such as this, celebrations of the launch usually continued in Venice well into the evening. Such celebrations were colourful events. Since the launch of this ship coincided with the Second International Exhibition of Art being held at the Giardini, the celebrations on this occasion were even more elaborate than was usual for a ship launch on its own. There were lots of concerts and choirs on the Canal Grande, illuminations on the Piazza San Marco and La Riva degli Schiavoni – the bank on the Canal di San Marco opposite to Isola di S Giorgio – illuminations of boats and pontoons in the canals, the flying of balloons with coloured glass, flags displayed from most windows along the canals, singing by choirs, music at the Fenice, feasts in the Castello area of Venice around the *Arsenale* where many of the *Arsenalloti* lived and which continued into the early hours, and at 11pm fireworks. What a celebration throughout Venice!

End of the custom

The use of commemorative rings for the launch of ships at Venice's *Arsenale* started in 1891 and only applied to naval ships, not merchant ships; and in about 1914, with the onset of the First World War, this colourful custom appears to have come to an end. The symbolism of the rings for Venetians, however, is never lost; they are an important reminder of their past, their present and their future: namely, their dependence on and unity with the sea.

Chapter 13

Different Traditions in Different Countries

R ather than including what would inevitably be a rather superficial catalogue of the different launch ceremonies in every major maritime nation, a few examples have been chosen and explored in more detail. As might be expected, these illustrate how the style and content of a ship launch ceremony broadly reflects the different religious beliefs and the different historical and sociopolitical customs and rituals practised in those countries. It is a colourful and diverse pattern.

13.1 Denmark

Little religious element

Unlike in Roman Catholic countries where priests have always played a prominent part in ship launches and christenings, in protestant Denmark after the Reformation in 1536, the clergy have rarely participated and there has been little or no religious element in the naming ceremony of ships, whether naval or merchant. This may come as a bit of a surprise since visitors to Danish churches will frequently find examples of beautifully carved votive ships hanging from the ceiling, evidencing the strong involvement of the church in the lives of seafarers. Some churches also have a distinctive gallery at the back of the church where ships' captains can stand above the rest of the congregation as if they were still in command on the bridge of their ships!

Name to be kept secret until called out

The established practice down the centuries in Denmark, especially in the smaller towns, has been for the ship's name to be 'called out' by a prominent citizen of the village or town before launching; the golden rule being that the name must be kept secret before it is called out. This means that even streamers with the ship's name should not be unfurled and, if the name of the ship has already been painted on the bow or the stern, this should be kept covered until the moment when the name is officially pronounced. The superstitious belief behind this practice appears to be that, if evil powers know the name, they control the ship's destiny. The Danish practice has been followed in the ports of northern Germany.

Attendance of royal family

In the seventeenth century members of the Danish royal family quite frequently attended ship launches, where they made a present to the Master Shipbuilder and gave schnapps to the shipyard workers. A rare example of attendance by the Danish royal family in the nineteenth century is to be found in the launch in 1895 of the Russian Imperial yacht *Standart* at the Burmeister and Wain shipyard in Copenhagen, described in a later chapter, at which the yacht was also, exceptionally, blessed before launch.[1] The blessing was most likely given by an Orthodox priest, an exception to the Danish practice of not having any clergy present, but which can be readily explained in terms of this being a Russian tradition that was being honoured for a ship built in Denmark for the Russian Imperial family.

Typical launching ceremony in small ports

After ship launchings in Denmark, especially in small ports, toasts of beer, schnapps or punch were drunk and there were feasts for the workers sitting at long tables in the open air or in harbour restaurants, followed by singing and dancing. In typical Danish fashion, speeches were made by anyone who felt the urge to say something.

Christening with ceremonial bottle

After 1900 it became the norm for ships in Denmark to be christened by a sponsor with a bottle, following the practice in England. The oldest picture of the use of a bottle at a launching in Scandinavia appears to be the painting by P.C. Holm in 1869 (Atonaer Museum) of the launching of a barkentine, the *Ernst Dreyer*, at the town of Altona, which was then part of Denmark, but close to Hamburg. The lady sponsor is seen under an umbrella by the prow; she is ready to throw the bottle, which is attached by a lanyard, against the side of the ship, while the workers are knocking out the blocks. The ship is positioned stern first to the water and decorated with flags and wreaths, the latter also being typical for launchings in northern Germany.[2]

Danish flags flown

Danish flags are always proudly flown at ship launches in Denmark, where a lady sponsor is known as a *gudmo(de)r*; but since the 1950s the term *navnemoder* is now more commonly used to avoid confusion with the christening of children in churches.

There was a period in Danish history when warships were neither named nor christened. This practice continued until 1931 when Queen Alexandrine, with a bottle of champagne, christened the royal yacht *Dannebrog*, which, like the British royal yacht *Britannia* (prior to its decommissioning), also served as a naval hospital ship. She used the words: 'I christen you *Dannebrog*. May luck and good fortune go with you and your crew.'

The absence of any religious element in the naming ceremony of Danish naval ships has continued with the naming on 5 July 2014 by Karen Lund, partner of the Danish Defence Minister, of the Danish naval ship *Ark Dania*. She used the words: 'I name this ship *Ark Dania*. May she bring fair winds and good fortune to all who sail in her.'

She smashed a bottle of champagne against the bow and the ship's name, which had until then been covered in a shroud, was unveiled.

Maersk tradition

Again, for the christening of merchant ships in Denmark, although the wording may be seen as a prayer, there is an absence of any express reference to religion. A number of wordings have been used that are similar to that used for naval ships but adding a reference to prosperity of the owner, a typical example being: 'I name you … May luck and good fortune go with you and all that sail in you on the seven seas. May you bring prosperity to your Company and do honour to Denmark.'On 14 June 2013 Ann Maersk Mckinney named *Maersk Mckinney Moller*, then the largest ship in the world, constructed at DSME shipyard in Okpoi, South Korea, after her late father with the following (abbreviated) words, which do contain a religious prayer at the end and are believed to follow a tradition of naming ceremonies for Maersk ships since 1906 when the company took delivery of its first newly built ship *Peter Maersk*:

> I name you *Maersk Mckinney Moller*. As you sail the seas of the world may your journeys be smooth … May you bring happiness to your crew … May you be a safe haven … and may you bring pride and prosperity to all. I wish you Godspeed.

Prior to the ceremony Maersk would not comment on the big black letters painted on her bow and stern. A cloth covering the name on her bow was unveiled simultaneously with the naming in accordance with the usual long-standing Danish tradition of secrecy about the name before it is called out.

Launch in Jutland

The author's only personal experience of a ship launch in Denmark was at Nordsøvaerftet A/S at Ringkøbing in Jutland in December 1981, where the launch of two river sea vessels, *Union Star* and *Union Mars*, were accomplished. It was snowing and there was concern that the water at the end of the launch way would freeze, making the launches hazardous. The shipyard accordingly had a tug on standby, churning the water with its propeller to stop it freezing. This enabled the launches to proceed successfully. In accordance with Danish tradition the ships' names painted on the bow were covered with a cloth, which was released simultaneously with the names being pronounced by the godmothers. There was no clergyman present to bless the ships. After the successful launch of both ships the guests were glad to warm up at a memorable candlelit dinner with plenty of schnapps, speeches and toasts in true Danish tradition.

13.2 France

Blessing by a priest a long-standing tradition

In France, historically a Catholic country, in contrast to Denmark, blessing of a new ship by a priest before it enters the water at launch has been an almost invariable tradition for many centuries. In the engraving shown at Illustration No. 21 titled 'Bapteme ou Benediction de la Galere' by Jean Baptiste Rigaud, thought to date from after 1721, the Catholic blessing or benediction of a galley being conducted prior to its launch is portrayed. On the foredeck there appears to be a christening ceremony by Catholic priests, one of whom is bearing a cross to which a banner is attached. A cross has also been erected on the beak head of the ship, which is decorated with flags. It is thought that this may be one of the oldest existing representations of a religious ceremony at a ship launch.

Certainly for the ship's crew it has been regarded in France as indispensable for a ship to be blessed at launch since no seafarer would dare to go to sea in an unblessed ship. The French refer in this context to the expression *'un navir qui n'a pas goute au vin goutera au sang'* meaning a ship that has not tasted wine at its christening will taste blood or suffer misfortune. It is a sentiment or superstition shared by seafarers in different countries but normally without using such expressive language! The ritual form of words for the blessing of a new ship in France is: *'Daignez par votre sainte main, Seigneur, benir ce navire et tous ceux qui'l portera'* – 'Deign by your holy hand, Lord, to bless this ship and all those it will carry.'[3] This form of words was used by the Bishop of Nantes, Monseigneur Villepelet, to bless the new liner *Le France* launched on 11 May 1960 in St Nazaire[4] and are very similar to the words of prayer used by HM Queen Elizabeth II when she has named ships in England.[5]

Rites from baptism of children followed

French launchings and christenings of ships in the eighteenth and nineteenth centuries were invariably accompanied by unique rites closely resembling the baptismal ceremony for children. There was a godfather and a godmother. The godfather for a new ship typically presented the godmother with a bouquet of flowers, as both said the ship's name. No bottle was broken but a priest formally pronounced the vessel named and blessed it with holy water. At a reception afterwards the distinguished guests were invited to share a *vin d'honneur* at a ceremonial meal at which speeches were made and toasts drunk.

Secular elements at launches in Northern France

In accounts of the christening of fishing boats and lifeboats in the ports of northern France between the seventeenth and nineteenth centuries the ceremony is typically attended by the local priest (*prete*), a godfather (*parrain*), a godmother (*marraine*), the boat owner and his close relatives. As already noted, the presence of a godfather as well as a godmother is similar to a child's baptism; but in the context of ship launch rituals the presence of two sponsors, a male sponsor and a female sponsor, is a special feature. The religious character of the ceremony was also mingled with some secular and symbolic elements. After blessing of the ship the godfather, the godmother and sometimes the priest standing on the deck and then at each corner of the ship threw a handful of salt and blessed corn over the ship, as symbols of preservation and prosperity. They also sprinkled the ship with holy water reciting ritual phrases in order to ask for the safety of man and the prosperity of his work. This tradition is particularly associated with the small fishing ports of Normandy and those of the Paix de Caux region. The ceremony ended, by custom, with the reciting by everyone present of Te Deum.[6] After this recital the godfather and godmother smashed a bottle of wine against the bow. Holy bread and sugared almonds (*dragees*) were distributed to all the guests, which, again, are also a traditional part of the ceremony for the baptism of children. Finally, all present take part in a celebratory meal with toasts being drunk and a gift being made to the godmother; and sometimes ending with dancing. On occasion it is only the next day that the boat has its first outing in the water!

The tradition of having both a *parrain* and a *marraine* at the launch of a newly built ship has continued but on a far less frequent basis in twentieth-century France. The clear trend in modern times has been for a *marraine* alone to be appointed to whom a bouquet of flowers and occasionally sugared almonds are presented after the successful launch, so continuing the child baptismal tradition.

Final cord cut with ceremonial axe

There is also the tradition of cutting with a ceremonial axe the final cord, often a red, white and blue tricolour ribbon, sometimes called *le ruban liberateur*, which, when cut, symbolically releases the ship from the land. This is reference to a practice – whether legend or historical fact is not known – said to have been employed for the launch of sailing ships in ancient times, and already mentioned in the Chapter on superstitions of sailors[7], when a convict equipped only with an axe was instructed to knock down the last block that retained the ship to the land. If he had the time to run the convict was saved and granted his freedom; if not, he perished under the hull as it slid down the ways. It is easy to see why this alleged practice would have excited the imagination of writers and, in doing so, may have prolonged the legend and given rise to the tradition of the symbolic use of an axe at launches in more modern times.

An axe, when used ceremonially at a ship launch, was typically a unique object of silver or bronze made especially for each occasion. The ceremonial axe had inscribed on its blade the name of the godmother, the date of launch, the flag and name of the owner and the name of the ship. An example is the bronze axe that was used to launch the four-masted steel barque *Mistral* on 15 October 1901 at Nantes (see Illustration No. 27, which is to be found in the Musée National de la Marine in Paris).[8]

In this exhibit the date and the name of the ship are inscribed on the blade of the axe but not the name of the person performing the christening. In Royal Dockyards in England between the middle of the nineteenth century until the onset of the Second World War a similar ritual is to be found but the instrument used for cutting the last cord at the launch of a naval ship was the chisel and the mallet rather than the axe and presented to the ship's sponsor in a launch box.[9] However, the symbolism behind both rituals is the same: the ultimate severing of the new ship from land. The ceremonial axe tradition has quite frequently continued to be used today in France, with a small silver axe being used at launch ceremonies to cut a ceremonial tricolour ribbon that either symbolically releases the last rope attaching the hull to land or by radio signal releases the christening bottle of champagne to crash against the bow. However, the axe ceremony has also on occasion been replaced in France by the godmother being requested to use a pair of silver scissors to cut a tricolour ribbon so as to cause a bottle of wine or champagne to smash against the ship's bow.

Dunkirk traditions

Some unique traditions have applied to launches at the Dunkirk shipyard of Ateliers et Chantiers (ACF), an important shipyard in France between 1898 and 1987. At the start of the launch ceremony they sounded an old naval signal calling for decks to be cleared for action (*le Branle-Bas des Marins de la Garde*) signifying that the launch was imminent. It was also traditional for the French national anthem, *La Marseillaise*, to be played when the newly launched hull first had contact with the water, frequently followed by the singing of a locally inspired and stirring hymn, *l'hymne a Jean Bart*, extolling the bravery and exceptional exploits of a local hero, Jean Bart. Bart was a seventeenth-century privateer in Dunkirk who, despite his humble birth, went on to join the French Navy, rising to the rank of admiral, and was a bold leader. The cantata or hymn to Jean Bart was written to mark the inauguration of a bronze statue in his honour erected in Dunkirk in 1845 but has become a popular local song performed frequently at carnivals as well as ship launches in the town. When the train ferry *Nord-Pas-de-Calais* was launched in April 1987 it was the last occasion before the closure of the yard and poignantly this took place in silence without ceremony or any bottle of champagne and, with a fog coming up, the silence was only broken by the eerie blasts of the sirens on the tugs in the harbour.[10]

Today, despite France becoming more secular, the blessing of a ship at its launch by a Catholic priest accompanied by *La Marraine* remains, as it has for at least the last three centuries, the most significant element of any ship launching and naming ceremony. The smashing of a bottle of wine or champagne against the bow, usually by a lady acting alone as the ship's godmother and the pronouncing of the ship's name is the next element.[11] The day's proceedings always end with a ceremonial dinner for the invited guests at which numerous speeches are made and toasts are drunk. That is a feature that has not changed!

13.3 Greece

Customs derived from ancient Greece

It is to the ancient Greeks that we owe many of the current traditions relating to the naming of ships and the ceremonies celebrated at their launch.

Feminine name

We are accustomed today to a ship becoming, from the moment of its launch, a fictive female person and having a feminine name. This custom is derived from ancient Greece. From at least the fourth century BC the Athenians kept records of their naval ships, equipment and crew, which is a valuable historical source of information on the size, manning and other details of the Athenian navy. The Athenian Naval Lists of 377–322 BC also tell us that during this period it was the practice of the Athenians to give feminine names to their ships. From these lists from that period we have around 300 examples of feminine names given to galleys in the fleet, mostly to trieremes. The names chosen were usually from mythology or the names of lesser deities – but avoiding main deities – or were related to the ships' appearance, for example beauty or speed or simply *Nike*, meaning victory.[12]

Name device on the bow

A ship's name has for many centuries traditionally been painted on either side of her bow. Again, it is to the ancient Greeks that we probably owe this practice through their invention of a 'name device'. In order to enable the ships to be identified easily, the ships of the ancient Greeks bore a distinctive name device, called a *parasemon*, carved or painted on either side of the bow to identify the name. The device might be some form of figurehead, painted decoration, flag or other removable standard or decoration illustrating the ship's name. As has been wisely observed, in an age when there were no telescopes these name devices were more useful than indications of the name in writing.[13] They enabled ships to be readily identified, especially in sea battles where it was vital to know immediately if the warship approaching you, with her bronze ram in the prow ready to smash into you, was friend or foe, as well as to inform spectators standing on the shore observing the battle. As Herodotus records: 'Spectators were aware of *Artemeia*'s prowess since they knew for certain her ship's name device.'[14] What we do not know is whether the ship's name, in addition to the name device, was indicated in writing on the bow,[15] nor as to whether the ships received their names at launch nor who decided on the names, nor whether there was any naming ceremony. It seems likely that the carving of the name devices would have been done before launching. In ancient Greece another way to distinguish ships of one state from those of another was the different statues of images of gods they carried: 'every Athenian ship carried a statue of Pallas Athene and every Carthaginian ship a statue of Ammon, and so forth'.[16]

The modern practice of painting the name on either side of the bow before launch was, therefore, most probably derived from this original name device tradition of ancient Greece. That said, it was surprisingly not until 1873 that British merchantmen were required by law to have their names painted on the bow. An earlier statute of 1786, in the reign of King George III, 'For the Increase and Encouragement of Shipping',[17] made it obligatory within one month of registry to paint in white or yellow the name by which the ship was registered and her port, curiously not on the bow but on the stern. Identification of a ship from a name on the stern had practical disadvantages and nearly 100 years later, in 1873, this was finally amended to require painting of the name on the bow.[18]

We have already noted that it was the normal practice for a seafarer in ancient Greece to offer sacrifices and to pour libations to the gods before setting sail. They set up an altar by the sea shore and with arms aloft called on the gods of the sea to protect them and offered prayers and sang a paean or hymn. On their safe return votive offerings were often given to the gods in thanks for their safe deliverance from the dangers of the sea.[19] It also became the practice for ships to have a guardian deity, those most favoured by seafarers being the Discouri (Castor and Pollux), the patrons of sailors often invoked for favourable winds and the gods of Samothrace, whose mysteries were said to give protection from drowning at sea and safe voyages.[20] The Discouri are colourfully described in a Homeric

Hymn, thought to date from the sixth century BC, as 'the saviours of earth-born men and swift faring ships when wintry blasts rush over the pitiless sea'.[21] The ships of ancient Greece frequently carried a stylis, a pole with a crosspiece set up alongside the stern post that bore a device symbolising the guardian deity of the ship or with the name of the deity actually written out. This was an additional means of identification of a ship. Some ships also carried a portable altar to set up and use for offering sacrifice upon safe arrival and on other occasions when divine aid was sought. This was usually set up on the poop deck in the stern. The Romans also had a tutelary god[22] of the vessel placed on the stern and continued the practice of invoking the gods for favourable weather on their voyages, but did not follow the Greek practice of putting their ship names into feminine form.

Dressing a ship overall at launch

The tradition of a ship at its launch being decked overall with flags, garlands and flowers also has its origin in ancient Greece. The ancient Greeks, in decorating their ships at launch, wished to please the gods and it is to this superstition that we can attribute the colourful practice of dressing a ship overall at its launch.

Launch ceremonies in ancient Greece

As we have observed, sacrifices, libations and other rituals before setting sail were everyday events for the seafarer of ancient Greece but there are, it seems, few references in the writings of that period to formal ship launch ceremonies for newly constructed ships. In *Credulities Past and Present* written by William Jones in 1880 he gives the following description of what he thinks would have occurred at a launching ceremony of a new ship in ancient Greece:[23]

> On completion of a ship it was decked with garlands and flowers and the mariners adorned with crowns. It was launched ... with loud acclamations and other expressions of joy and, being purified with a lighted torch and brimstone ... it was consecrated to the god whose image it carried.

William Jones does not give any textual sources for his description but all the various features of the ship launch ceremony which he describes are to be found in different ancient Greek texts relating to seafarers setting sail or in rites of purification. The earliest detailed description of a formal ship launch ceremony appears to be that written by Apuleius in the second century AD. He was a philosopher and writer fluent in Greek and Latin and was born in Madauros, a Roman colony in North Africa. Apulius was also apparently a follower of the goddess Isis, initially an obscure goddess but who grew in importance, becoming one of the significant deities in Egypt in the Hellenistic period. Apulius wrote a romantic work in Latin called *The Metamorphoses*, more frequently known as *The Golden Ass*, the only Roman novel to have survived in its entirety. The book's main theme is curiosity about the practice of magic, in the study of which the leading character is accidentally transformed into an ass. Its significance here is that it also usefully contains a detailed, but fictional, account of the festival of the launching of a ship, involving an elaborate ceremony of purification and propitious offerings and libations before the launch and ending with a ceremony at the temple of Isis:

> the chief priest named and consecrated to the goddess a ship ... Holding a flaming torch he first pronounced most solemn prayers from his chaste lips, and then with an egg and sulphur he performed over it an elaborate ceremony of purification ... and they poured on the waves libations ...[24]

Of course, this can be easily dismissed as being from a book of fiction, as having been clearly influenced by the liturgy of the goddess Isis and having been written during a period of the Roman empire when prayers for the civil authority were normal practice, but which would have been out of place in a purely Greek context. It is a curious mixture of Egyptian, Greek and Roman cultures and it is not clear to which period in Greek history the launch ceremony that he describes should be attributed. Many of the features were more sophisticated and formal when compared to the much simpler ceremony described by William Jones. Nonetheless, there is also much to suggest that many of the other basic features such as the purification and libations and gift offerings that Apuleius describes are probably a reasonably accurate account of the somewhat similar but much simpler ceremony for a ship launch that would have taken place at an earlier period in ancient Greece.

Purification

In ancient Greek society purification was part of many initiation rituals, especially those associated with the sacred. Fire has purifying power and a lighted torch as a symbol of purification was used by the ancient Greeks in various initiation ceremonies, so it is easy to see how the launch of a new ship and its consecration to the god whose image it carried could be seen to be an appropriate initiation ceremony at which to use lighted torches. Brimstone or sulphur was also used as a purifying agent by the ancient Greeks and when fumigated its vapours helped to ward off disease and, in the belief of the ancient Greeks, evil spirits, which again was entirely appropriate for the protection of a new ship and to give reassurance to its sailors.[25] Finally, as we have seen, the pouring of libations to the gods before setting out on a voyage was an invariable rite for seafarers in ancient Greece.[26] All of this suggests that William Jones' summary of a ship launch ceremony in ancient Greece is substantially accurate, albeit not supported by an exact textual source.

There are also many images on Greek pottery of warriors on ships or about to board ships wearing garlands of olive trees and Aeneas wore a wreath of 'well-trimmed olive' when celebrating a religious service prior to embarking on a voyage.[27] This supports William Jones' reference to mariners at a ship launch wearing crowns. In Athenaus' book *The Learned Banqueters*[28] he describes a very large ship built in Egypt in the third century BC for Ptolemy IV being 'hauled into the water by a large crowd of men accompanied by shouting and trumpets' which again is echoed in William Jones' summary. The only surprising omission from his summary is that he does not mention water, which was the most widespread means of purification in ancient Greece. Centuries later, under the totally different tradition of the Greek Orthodox church, holy water became, and remains today, a central part of the ceremony for the blessing of a new ship in Greece.

Symbolism of a wreath

Before leaving ancient Greece, mention should be made of a late geometric bowl or *krater* from Thebes,[29] thought to be of *c.*735 BC. It depicts a man at the stern of a ship about to step aboard, with the oarsmen in two tiers ready to pull at the oars, who with his right hand grasps the left hand of a woman who in her other hand is holding a wreath. The scene has been the subject of different interpretations relating to mythological scenes but an alternative view is that the scene is one of everyday life, the moment of departure of the captain of a ship stepping on board after saying goodbye to his wife.[30] The wreath, a token of success or of celebration in ancient Greece, is being bestowed by his wife upon the captain and his ship. Is it too fanciful to imagine that the captain has just been appointed to the post or the ship is newly launched and about to set out on her maiden voyage and the wife of the captain is wishing him and his ship success by the symbolic gift of a wreath? There are other pieces of Attic pottery that similarly depict the stern of a ship crowned by a wreath, either as a reward for success already achieved or as a prayer for future success.

Ancient Greece may also be said to have an indirect influence on the modern practice of breaking a bottle of wine against the bow at its launch. As we have learned, the ancient Greeks before setting sail poured libations from the stern into the sea in an act of sacrifice to appease the gods and sometimes this rite was accompanied by a deposition offering of the cup itself being thrown into the sea.[31] Some elements of this practice were reflected in the 'standing cup' ceremony in Royal Dockyards already described:[32] after drinking from the gilt cup on the poop deck as soon as the ship was afloat, the remainder of the wine was thrown forward towards the half deck and the cup was then heaved overboard, a practice that is akin to a deposition sacrifice. As we have seen, this ceremony was then replaced by the practice of breaking a bottle of wine against the bows but retaining the element of sacrifice from the voluntary outpouring of the wine.

Greek Orthodox Church

With the establishment of the Greek Orthodox Church, the Church assumed a central role in the ceremonies for launching and christening of ships in Greece and this has continued until the present day. Typically, in order to conduct the religious service, the Greek Orthodox priest first sets up a simple altar on the dock in front of the bow of the ship or on board the ship with a cross, candlesticks, bowls and sprigs of basil for the blessing and sprinkling of holy water. In the Orthodox Church holy water is seen as a means of blessing and also to repel evil in much the same way as lighted torches and the fumigation of a new ship with brimstone was used by the ancient Greeks to purify and drive away evil spirits.

Prayers are offered and sonorous verses chanted by the lead Orthodox priest conducting the service, frequently accompanied by one or more assistant priests. The priest begs God to grant the newly built ship stability and security and protect her and those who sail in her and keep them from harm, as he saved Noah in his Ark and his disciples in the Sea of Tiberias. The ship is then blessed and, using branches of basil, holy water is sprinkled over the bow of the ship, sometimes symbolically decorated with green garlands as it would have been in ancient times, and over other key places such as the bridge. On occasion the captain of the new ship kisses the cross and is then similarly blessed by the lead Orthodox priest with the sprinkling of holy water on the crown of his head. Basil, as a symbol of new life, is traditionally used in the Greek Orthodox Church for this purpose.

St Nicholas in the Greek Orthodox Church is the patron saint of seafarers and regarded as the master of wind and tempest. Often at launching or naming ceremonies of Greek ships the Greek Orthodox priest blesses and hands to the captain an icon of St Nicholas to be permanently displayed on the bridge of the ship. Traditionally Greek ships never leave port without an icon to St Nicholas and the captain lights a candle in front of the icon praying for safe passage, so the symbolism of the gift of this icon is an important tradition for a new ship at its naming and for the safety of those who will sail in her. On occasion the Orthodox priest hands the captain a formal certificate of sanctification and anoints all present with oil. It will be seen that the ceremonies today under the auspices of the Greek Orthodox Church, although, of course, quite different in terms of religious belief, still have certain similarities to the traditions of the ancient Greeks. There is a need in both ancient and modern times for the sailor to seek external protection for himself and his ship from the dangers of the deep and to give him the confidence to overcome his fears.

The prayers and blessing completed, in modern times the christening of a merchant ship in Greece by a godmother then proceeds in the traditional way by the breaking of a bottle of wine against the bow prior to launch.

13.4 Imperial Japan

Symbolism

Symbolism and tradition have long been features of Japanese ship launches; but, in accordance with Japanese custom, while some of the symbols used have a deep religious or spiritual significance, their launch ceremonies do not appear to have included a religious service as such. A key feature has been the suspension from the bow of a ship as it was launched of a colourful symbol – a globe (*kusudama*) of flowers or a paper globe, decorated in the national colours of red and white, containing doves or pigeons to be liberated at the moment the hull first touched the water. This was often combined with the release of streamers, confetti and firecrackers. As the new ship left the ways in this colourful ceremony, the band traditionally struck up the Japanese national anthem.

The Imperial Japanese Navy is the only world class navy in history that has a definite beginning and an equally definite end.[33] It was formally established in 1869 and ended on 7 April 1945 when the Imperial fleet flagship, *Yamato*, the heaviest battleship ever built, was sunk off Okinawa in the Second World War following a combined air and torpedo assault by the Allies. Seventy-five years is a fairly short time for the life of the navy of a nation but during that period over 300 warships were built and launched for the Imperial Navy, and their launch ceremonies contain some unique and colourful features.

Choice of name

Supreme command of the Imperial Navy was vested in the Emperor himself. After the Imperial Japanese Navy was formed, the tradition was established for the Ministry of Navy to submit suggested names of ships to him for his approval. The procedure was then changed so that the Minister of the Navy submitted two names to the Lord Chamberlain, who then presented these to the Emperor. The Emperor could either pick one of the selected names or choose one of his own. After 1 August 1905 a more standardised procedure was introduced, with battleships being named after provinces of Japan (such as the last flagship, the *Yamato*), first-class cruisers after mountains and second-class cruisers after rivers. In 1921 the Minister of the Navy was given authority to name all ships except battleships, battle cruisers and cruisers, but then was obliged to report the name chosen immediately to the Emperor.

Camellias and suspension of globe below the bow

Camellias in Japan symbolise the divine and are often used in religious and sacred ceremonies.

The principal naval arsenal of the Imperial Navy was at Yokosuka, which was established in the 1870s with the assistance of the French naval architect M. Leonce Verny. It was here in 1877 that a correspondent from *The Times* newspaper witnessed the launch on 13 March of a wooden-hulled sloop of war, the *Amagi*. He described how:

> the master-carpenter took his stand at her forefoot and waving the national flag – a red ball on a white ground, the rising sun – the shores were knocked down as he directed … A very full band, all Japanese, dressed in scarlet jackets and black trousers appeared on the scene and struck what a Frenchman told me was the national air … and steadily the vessel moved down [the ways], gaily decorated with nautical flags and trimmed stem to stern with artificial camellias.[34] From her bowsprit depended an enormous globe of evergreens and flowers, one of the most artistic things I have ever seen … only one thing was missing, I listened in vain for a cheer and saw no christening.[35]

Attendance of the Emperor or member of the Imperial family

This report does not state whether the Emperor or a member of his family attended the launch of *Amagi*, but during the Meiji era (1868–1912) it became traditional for the Emperor or a member of his family to attend the launching of ships of the Imperial Navy and for the Minister of the Navy to christen these ships.

Launch of ships of Imperial Navy at English shipyards

This tradition coincided at the end of the Sino-Japanese war with a significant expansion and modernisation programme for the Imperial Navy. Most of the new ships were built in Japan, but after 1875 when British yards starting building ironclad warships, the Emperor placed large orders with these in preference to those in France. The Elswick yard of Sir W.G. Armstrong Whitworth on the Tyne built the most, a total of thirteen between 1885 and 1905, some of them at the time of their launch being the fastest and heaviest battleships in the world. There was pride in Britain that its yards could produce such great ships but also a sense of chagrin that there were not more of such ships in the Royal Navy.

The first ironclad warship built in England for the Imperial Navy was the *Fu-so*, launched at Samuda's yard at Poplar in April 1877, just a few weeks after the launch of *Amagi*. The difference between their launch ceremonies is of interest. The launch of *Fu-so* was indeed attended by members of the Imperial family, Prince Hachisuka and Prince Nagaoka, as well as the Japanese Minister, Kagenori Ueno. However, on this occasion the tradition was not followed strictly since the ship was christened not by the Minister but by his wife, Mrs Ueno. This was in line with the British practice, which by that time was well established, of inviting ladies to launch and christen ships. In contrast to the *Amagi*, the *Fu-so* was christened properly when a good bottle of champagne was smashed over the ship's bows by Mrs Ueno; there were flags and there were cheers and many toasts, but no dressing of the ship with the symbolic camelia and no artistic globe of evergreens and flowers suspended at the bow.

At subsequent launches of Imperial battleships built in England members of the Imperial family often attended but, if they could not attend, the Japanese Minister, the Japanese Ambassador to London or a senior Japanese diplomat was there; and a christening was almost invariably performed by the wife of the Minister, Ambassador or senior diplomat in attendance, not a member of the Imperial family, even if present. A notable exception was the launch on 4 July 1905 at Vickers yard in Barrow-in-Furness of the pre-dreadnought battleship *Katori* attended by Prince and Princess Arisugawa. On this occasion it was the Princess who started the launch with the release of a bottle of champagne covered in the red and white colours of Japan. This may perhaps be explained by the fact that not only was her husband, the Prince, a member of the Imperial family but by this date, after a distinguished career in the Imperial Navy, he held the rank of admiral. It was, therefore, entirely appropriate that his wife should have the honour of christening this ship, which at the date of its launch was the most powerful warship ever built in England.

Symbolism of release of doves

Another interesting feature of the launch of *Katori* was the Japanese custom of releasing doves or pigeons at the moment the hull enters the water for the first time. The origin of this colourful custom is not known but it is mentioned in *Le Temps* in 1886, which refers to the custom of the Japanese to release hundreds of turtle doves at the moment of launching that 'troubled by the noise and joy of being freed remained for several minutes hovering and fluttering above the heads of spectators'.[36] The letting fly of doves was considered an omen of safe return – because that type of bird when forced from its habitation delights to return – and, therefore, for the Japanese it symbolised a safe homecoming for the ship and her crew. If the doves did not fly away but alighted on the ship being launched, it was believed by the superstitious to be an omen that the ship was doomed to have an unlucky career.

Barrow News carried the following detailed description of the *Katori* launch ceremony:

> The ceremony was one of more than usual interest, as incidental to the launch was not only the breaking of the bottle of wine [by Princess Arisugawa] but the liberation of a pigeon cote, containing twelve birds, which were comfortably ensconced within a red and white draped balloon and which on the ship beginning to glide

down the ways, was so arranged that by the pulling of a cord attached to the bow of the ship, allowed the birds to fly away and also set forth a shower of confetti. This is a feature of Japanese launches and whatever it may lack in practical value, certainly possesses an artistic value which cannot be gainsaid. The doves we might add, after hovering above the vessel sped off, let us hope to spread the good tidings of peace, and so add another symbolic meaning to the fairy like arrangement ...[37]

And, as the *Katori* slid down the ways there were shouts from the Japanese present of *'Banjai'*, meaning long life.

Illustration No. 28 shows the battlecruiser *Kongo* being launched into Walney Channel at Vickers Yard in Barrow-in-Furness on 18 May 1912 with the same custom of *kusudama* or medicine ball, from which doves and confetti were released as the ship slid down the ways.

This ceremonial release of doves or pigeons was carried out at five or more other launches of Japanese warships at English yards between 1900 and 1912. It appears that the first such occasion was at the launch of another pre-dreadnought battleship, the *Shikishima*,[38] on 1 November 1898 at Thames Iron Works, Blackwall, when the christening honours were performed by Madame Kato, the wife of the Japanese Minister. On this occasion there was another interesting feature. At the start of the ceremony Madame Kato was presented with 'a beautifully modelled sterling silver knife, the handle being delicately reliefed with Royal chrysanthemums',[39] which are the emblem of the Emperor and are embroidered on the Emperor's standard. The knife was used by Madame Kato not only to release the dog shores to start the launch of the ship down the ways but also 'a pretty cage of red and white silk in which was confined a flock of pigeons', which was 'suspended above the ship with brilliant streamers ...' This was opened simultaneously, allowing the birds to fly free.[40]

Release of Kusudama (medicine balls)

The Japanese custom of the Japanese releasing medicine balls (*kusudama*) suspended from the ship's bow as well as streamers, confetti and balloons at the moment of launching is a symbol of good luck and to spread good tidings of peace. *Kusudama* are believed to have originated from the Heian period of Japanese history (794–1185), when fragrant wood and herbs were placed in a small cloth bag to which long silk threads of different colours were attached. The *Kusudama* were hung in a house to ward off evil spirits and disease. It is, therefore, easy to understand the symbolism of *kusudama* in the context of the launch of a new ship with the need to protect her from evil spirits. Firecrackers are also sometimes set off to complete the colourful, emotive and symbolic moment.

Use of ceremonial axe

The tradition of using an axe at a Japanese ship launching ceremony was first adopted on 24 March 1891 at the launch of the protected cruiser *Hashidate* at the Yokosuka naval arsenal in the presence of Emperor Meiji. The axe was symbolically used to cut the rope that tethered the ship to the place where she was built. The ceremonial axe traditionally has grooves carved into both sides of the blade representing various deities and so conferring divine protection on the ship and those on board. The use of a silver axe at the launch of Japanese ships, not only in the era of the Imperial Navy but subsequently for all Japanese ship launches, has become a standard tradition with the name of the ship, date and location of the launching and name of the sponsor engraved or carved on the axe handle. In modern times Japanese shipbuilders traditionally order the crafting of a special axe for each new ship and after launching present this to the ship's owner as a commemorative gift of the occasion.

Although at the launch of naval ships from Royal Dockyards in England in the nineteenth and early twentieth centuries we find a similar tradition in the use of a mallet and chisel for symbolically severing the tether to the shore, the use of a grooved silver axe at ship launches is unique to Japan.

Rice cake, balloons and confetti

In smaller shipyards in Japan or on the launch of fishing vessels, the custom is to throw rice cakes (*mochi*) from the ship's bow immediately prior to launch as a substitute for medicine balls. By throwing *mochi* the

Japanese symbolically sanctify the ship and pray for its safety and success. This is not a religious service as such but again the religious symbolism is clearly there.

The release of balloons and the showering of confetti, always confetti and lots of it – from the bow – continues to be a traditional feature of the launch of Japanese ships even today.

13.5 Imperial Russia

Names chosen by the Tsar

During the Romanov dynasty it was a firmly established tradition that the names of Russian warships were personally chosen or approved by the Tsar. The very first Imperial Russian warship was the *Orel* (the Eagle) launched on 19 May 1668 on the bank of the Oka river. Tsar Alexei Mikhalovich decreed that: 'The ship that is built in the village of Dedinovo is to be named *"Orel"*. Two eagles must be placed at the rostrum and the stern of the ship and the standards must be embroidered with eagles too.' The double eagle became the traditional decoration of all Russian warships.

It was Peter the Great who personally established the Imperial Russian Navy as a fighting force on 20 October 1696 and he carried on the tradition of personally choosing or approving the names of his warships. To him is ascribed the statement: 'A Ruler that has but an army has one hand but he who has a navy has both.'[41] He had the vision that if Russia was to expand then it must rule the seas; the Baltic was practically a Swedish lake, the Black Sea belonged to the Turks and to the north the coastline was on the shores of the inhospitable Arctic ocean. Determined that Russia should become a naval power, the Tsar travelled to England in 1697 to learn the art of shipbuilding at first hand, staying in Deptford so as to be close to the Royal Dockyard there.

In 1703 he founded the city of St Petersburg on the River Neva and established the Admiralty shipyard in 1704 to construct his navy. During his reign the naval ships were named after places where great battles had been won or after admirals who had distinguished themselves in battle, a tradition that has continued with names of famous ships often being repeated. A good example is the 54-gun ship of the line *Poltava*, the first vessel to be launched from the Admiralty shipyard in St Petersburg on 15 June 1712. The launch was attended by Peter the Great and all his family. She was named after the decisive victory that Peter himself had won over the Swedes in 1709 at Poltava in the Ukraine. Some seven ships of the Imperial Russian Navy have subsequently been given this famous name.

The tradition of the Tsar naming or approving the names of navy ships submitted to him by the Chief of Naval Staff continued until the end of the Romanov dynasty with the assassination of Tsar Nicholas II in 1917. The cruiser *Aurora* built at the New Admiralty in St Petersburg and now moored as a museum on the banks of the Neva is best known for its role in the 1917 revolution. On 25 October 1917 the proclamation of Lenin to the 'Citizens of Russia' informing them of the overthrow of the Provisional Government was broadcast from this ship's radio. Less well known perhaps is how this cruiser came to be named *Aurora*. The names suggested to Tsar Nicholas II were *Varyag*, *Bogatyr*, *Polkan*, *Neptune* and *Aurora*. The Tsar chose the latter in order to honour the memory of the sailing frigate *Aurora*. This had been launched on 27 July 1835 in St Petersburg and had taken a heroic part in defending the town of Petropavlovsk in Kamchatka in the Crimean War, which was besieged between 1853 and 1856. So this was another example of the tradition of taking the name of a famous ship of the past and repeating it by giving it to a new ship.[42] Although the Tsar, when he chose the same name for the new cruiser, was clearly thinking of the valiant actions of the sailing frigate in the Crimean War that had previously had this name, he might also have recalled that *Aurora* is also the Goddess of Dawn in Roman mythology. Little did the Tsar realise at the time of her launch on 11 May 1900 that this new cruiser was to play such a key part in the dawn of a new political era in Russian history. How ironic that he chose this name!

Launches of warships were patriotic events attended by the Tsar and his family

Launches of warships for the Imperial Navy were patriotic public spectacles attended by the Tsar and his family with guards of honour to inspect, flags flying, bands playing and salutes fired as well as thousands of smartly dressed public and senior members of the military and of the Imperial Russian Navy. In Imperial Russia, as with other imperial powers from that period, the launch of a new battleship was frequently an occasion of great pageant and expression of patriotic emotion. One such occasion was the launch on 5 July 1839 of the 120/128-gun *Rossiia*[43] at the New Admiralty shipyard at St Petersburg during the reign of Tsar Nicholas I. As she emerged from the covered yard, with large 'launching colours' flying, she was greeted by a huge crowd. The pier was filled with dignitaries. In front of the yard in the Neva was a flotilla of rowing boats adorned with flags and with the crew standing with their oars held aloft in a salute. Behind them ships of the line were deployed, dressed overall and with their yard arms manned with sailors to honour the latest addition to the Imperial fleet.[44] The launch of an imperial naval ship was a carefully staged celebration that demonstrated the power of Imperial Russia and the authority of its Tsar. The personal attendance by the Tsar and his family at such a celebration was seen as an important symbol of that power. This contrasts with the launch of royal yachts in England during the same period, when Queen Victoria did not attend any.[45]

Illustration No. 29, which is a photo of the launch of the battleship *Pobeda* on 10 May 1900 out of the covered yard at Baltic Works St Petersburg, also shows the Imperial ceremonial pavilion erected just outside the dockyard and decorated with garlands to enable Tsar Nicholas II's family to witness the launch. The covered yard, from which the battleship emerges so dramatically, is typical of the construction method in Russia, enabling work to continue in the cold winter months. The ceremonial pavilion is also a typical ornament for these launches of ships of the Imperial Russian navy at that time.

Naval pageantry and demonstration of imperial power

Although no such pavilion is shown in the image of the launch of *Rossiia*, typically, the Tsar, his family and other distinguished guests witnessed the launch from a special pavilion erected on the quayside of the shipyard. On the launch of Russian Imperial yacht *Polyarnaya Zvezda* (Polar Star) on 19 May 1890 at Baltiskiy Zavod shipyard in St

Petersburg, an even more elaborate pavilion was erected, in the form of an old Russian tower in traditional Slavic style, decorated with the white, blue and red tricolour of the Russian state and two ornamental higher towers topped with the Imperial double eagle emblem. Here Tsar Alexander III, the Tsarina[46] and senior officials from the Imperial Navy viewed the launch. On arrival at the yard the Tsar and Tsarina were met by the commander of the yacht. The ship's guard saluted to the music of the choir of the naval college. After inspection of the yacht the Tsar and Tsarina proceeded to the pavilion, where there was a model and drawings of the yacht on display. From a contemporaneous engraving we can see in the background a line of seagoing ships that had come from Kronstadt[47] to take part in the event, stretching from the Nikolaevsky Bridge[48] to the seashore. Sailors manned the yard arms and on the successful launch joined the loud chorus of 'hurrah' in what had clearly become a traditional mode of salute for these launch ceremonies of the Imperial Navy. In the lithograph there also appears to be a cannon firing a salute from one of the ships to greet the new vessel as it entered the water. A sailor in the stern of the new yacht, as it is launched from the covered yard, is lowering the Russian naval ensign in a formal salute to the Tsar, who is clearly seen standing in the front row of the pavilion. The report records that: 'At two minutes to one, the yacht, with the Tsar's two-headed eagle on the prow, moved and rolled down into the water. The launch was greeted with the roar of the salute, the sound of a hymn and many thousands of lengthy 'hurrahs' from the crew, the workers and spectators.'[49] After the launch the Tsar and the Tsarina were collected by the Tsar's personal cutter *Peterhof*, also shown in the lithograph flying his personal standard on the foredeck and the Russian naval ensign aft. At the palace of Grand Duke Aleksey Alexandrovich, the Admiral General, lunch had been prepared, to which the senior officers of the naval department and commanders of the fleet were invited.[50] It is hard to imagine greater naval pageantry and a greater demonstration of imperial power!

Ceremonies not confined to St Petersburg

These ceremonies were not confined to St Petersburg. There is a contemporaneous report in *Niva Magazine* 1902[51] on the launch of the cruiser *Ochakov* in Sevastopol on 21 September 1902 conducted with similar pomp in the presence of Tsar Nicholas II and the Tsarina. This shows that an open pavilion was constructed on the jetty for the Tsar and distinguished guests, the ladies being smartly dressed in white with white hats and the naval officers in the white uniform of the Russian Imperial Navy.

After inspecting the guard of honour the Tsar and Tsarina proceeded on board the cruiser and received a deputation from the town and the fortress of Ochakov, a small city in the south of Ukraine after which the cruiser was named. Proceeding back to the imperial pavilion on the jetty, which was covered with blue fabric and white swags, the Tsar then ordered that the launch should begin. The report continues:

> The command was given 'Cut the restraints!'
> After about three minutes the newly born offspring of the Black Sea fleet quickly and smoothly began to descend into the sea. In another minute *Ochakov* was riding at anchor, proudly turning her hull.
> As soon as she moved, the ship's crew and the guard of honour saluted, music played a welcoming song and a hymn and His Majesty's standard was raised. At that moment the whole ship was decked with flags and a deafening salute roared forth.[52]

Since the name of the cruiser had already been selected by the Tsar it does not appear from this and other reports of ship launches from that period that the Tsar or Tsarina called out the name of the new ship as it was launched or ever christened her with a bottle of wine. This suggests that the role of the Tsar at ship launch ceremonies, with the name of the ship having been already chosen by him, was rather to give imperial support to the newest addition to the fleet by attending the launch in person, often accompanied by his family, to inspect the guard of honour and the ship's company and order the launch to begin. The ceremony was designed to be a public display of imperial power. Further, the Tsars loved military and naval spectacles and uniforms and what better opportunity for both than the launch of a new cruiser for the Imperial navy.

Were the Imperial naval ships named by the Tsar at launch ceremonies?

The author has been unable to find any example of the launch in Russia of an Imperial Russian naval ship at which the ship was actually named by the Tsar or Tsarina at the ceremony itself. The exception is the launch of a Russian Imperial ship constructed outside Russia. The Russian Imperial yacht *Livadia*,[53] a so-called 'round ship' – an innovative design of Russian Admiral Popov – was launched in 1880 at John Elder & Sons, Govan, in the presence of Grand Duke Alexei Alexandrovich. It is reported that after the religious ceremony (see below) the Duchess of Hamilton gracefully christened the ship;[54] but this was a launch of a Russian Imperial yacht in Scotland not in Russia, so local customs for the christening of ships may have prevailed. *Livadia* was one of the most unusual imperial yachts ever built. The hull was like a turbot in shape, 259ft long and 153ft in beam with three funnels set athwartwards. The inside was a lavish palace raised on the top of the steel turbot that had an unusual outside decking.[55] The Tsar and Tsarina suffered from sea sickness and the instruction was to produce a ship that did not roll; but, even if seasickness was addressed by the design, the problem with the ship was that she slammed so badly in heavy weather that she had to be put into drydock at Sevastopol to repair the damage. As a result she had only a short career as an imperial yacht.

Traditional gift of bread and salt

One of the oldest Russian traditions on the arrival of important and respected guests is the presentation to the guest of bread and salt as a sign of hospitality. At the launch of the battleship *Prince Suvorov* at the Baltic and Machine Works in St Petersburg on 25 September 1902, Tsar Nicholas II, on arrival in the shipyard, was presented with bread and salt by a deputation from the shipyard workmen. In response to this gesture of support the Tsar took the opportunity to make a short speech, which interestingly reflects the difficult political mood of the time:

> Thank you for the bread and salt and the expression of your feelings.

Work honestly, conduct yourselves calmly and let's not trouble ourselves with evil people who are as much enemies to you as they are to me.

It is certain that from now on you will maintain the good name of the Baltic Shipyard.

In response to these memorable words it is reported that there was a warm and lengthy 'hurrah' from the shipyard workers, indicating their approval and support for the Tsar.[56]

Blessing by Orthodox Priest

In the Romanov dynasty the Russian Orthodox church had a key role in imperial life. In the early days of the Imperial Russian Navy officers came from the aristocracy who were members of the Orthodox Church and it was the practice for an Orthodox priest to be part of the crew of the larger ships. The naval statutes of Peter the Great required the chaplains on board his ships to conduct services on Sundays and feast days. Against this background it is easy to understand why, from the earliest days of the Imperial Russian Navy, it was the practice for ships to be blessed at their launch by priests. The launch of the *Orel* in 1668:

was attended by the Superior of the Kolomna Temple of St. John the Baptist and a local priest; a religious service and public prayers were conducted and the ship's flags and emblems were consecrated before the launch down a slipway.[57]

Sprinkling of holy water over all parts of the ship at launch was a key feature of the religious ceremony, with chants being sung, burning of incense and the carrying of lighted candles. The practice of blessing of Imperial Russian ships at launch also extended to ships built outside Russia. On the launch in Scotland of the Russian Imperial yacht *Livadia*, mentioned earlier, now it was reported that:

the ceremony of blessing of the vessel according to the rites of the Greek church was then commenced. The service which was choral was performed by Revd M. Smirnoff and two assistants who wore the sacred robes of the church and there was in attendance a small choir from the Greek Church in London. The interesting ceremony was brought to a close by the Revd gentleman sprinkling the ship with holy water.[58]

There are photographs in the archives of Burmeister & Wain in Copenhagen of two Russian Orthodox priests attending the launch of a Russian ship built at that yard, thought to be the cruiser *Boyarin* in 1900, with six attendants holding bowls to contain holy water for the purpose of sprinkling all parts of the ship in a blessing. In 1906, at the launch at Vickers shipyard in Barrow-in-Furness of the battleship *Rurik,* it was reported in the local press that a Greek Orthodox priest sprinkled the ship with holy water before she left the stocks. The *North Western Daily Mail* on 19 November 1906 added: 'In Russia we understand that the priest also sprinkles the decks of the boat before launch.' From these accounts we can assume such a form of religious service and blessing by a Russian Orthodox priest, or, when none was available, by a Greek Orthodox priest was universal practice at the launch of a new ship during the period of the Romanov dynasty (1613–1917) and was followed whether the ship was constructed in Russia or elsewhere.

Blessing of Russian naval ships today

So did the practice continue after the end of the Romanov era? Inquiries made in modern Russia demonstrate the extent to which some of the traditions of the launch ceremony for Imperial Russian ships from the days of the Tsars continue to be practised today, while others have naturally been changed.

In today's Russian navy there are two ceremonies: the first when the ship is launched and the second when it is handed over to her owner, the Russian navy.

The tradition of the Romanov period when the name of a Russian Imperial Navy ship was always chosen by the Tsar has, as might be expected, been changed. The procedure today for selection of the name of a Russian naval ship is that a name is first selected by a Special

Department of the Ministry of Defence and is then confirmed by an official decree of the Russian Fleet Commander, thus stepping into the role previously enjoyed by the Tsar.

From a recent launch in Russia we have learnt that as soon as the bottom of the hull touched the water for the first time, the ship's sponsor, a lady, threw a bottle of champagne tied with light blue ribbon against the side of the ship. It appears that there are no traditional words said on such occasions, nor did the sponsor call out the name of the ship, which follows the Romanov practice that since the Tsar had already chosen the name there was no need for it to be repeated at launch. However, the involvement of a lady sponsor and the breaking of a bottle against the side of the ship are new customs reflecting modern traditions adopted in other countries.

At the second ceremony when the ship was completed and ready to be handed over by the shipyard to her owner, the Russian navy, a Russian Orthodox priest was in attendance. First the priest said prayers and blessed the national flag, which was sprinkled with holy water and then raised, symbolising that the ship was now part of the Russian navy, recalling a similar consecration ceremony for the launch of the *Orel* in 1668. Then the priest continued his prayers and blessed the deck of the ship and afterwards the cabins inside the ship, sprinkling holy water in each place. From this we can reasonably conclude that elements of the naming procedure and the religious ceremony for the consecration of naval ships by the Orthodox Church started in the Imperial era, but now in modernised form, remain part of the ceremony for the launching and commissioning of ships in the Russian navy of today.

13.6 India

Launch ceremonies reflect different cultures and religions

India's maritime history predates the birth of Western civilisation and there were advanced shipbuilding skills on the continent, particularly among the Parsees, well before the arrival of the British. The services of one such Parsee, Lovji Nusserwanjee Wadia, were secured by the British East

India Company in 1736. The Wadia family came from Surat, which was a major shipbuilding centre before the rise of Bombay, and brought with them both shipbuilding skills and ancient Zoroastrian[59] traditions. The development and achievements of Bombay Dockyard in the eighteenth and nineteenth centuries were largely due to the professionalism and integrity of the Wadia family. Lovji and his brother Sorabji built Bombay Drydock, the first such in Asia, in 1750 and eight subsequent generations of the Wadia family were Master Builders in Bombay Dockyard; so that, taken together, members of this family impressively held this position at Bombay Dockyard in an uninterrupted line of succession for 148 years between 1736 and 1884.

This brief account of the launch ceremonies in India is limited to the period between the establishment of Bombay Dockyard and the present day.

The different ship launch ceremonies to be found in India during this period mirror the deep cultural and religious differences that existed between the British during their period of rule and those of other indigenous cultures, particularly the Parsees and the Hindus. As might be expected, ships built in the eighteenth and nineteenth centuries in Bombay were launched in ceremonies that, with some colourful local distinguishing features, more or less followed the pattern set by the British at home. For the Parsees there was the unique tradition, after keel laying and before launch, of driving a ceremonial silver nail into the keel combined with invocations for the ship to be protected. For the Hindus, both before and after the independence of India in 1947, the launch ceremony centred on an invocation to the gods in the form of a *puja*. This was a ritual honouring and connecting with a deity, which included the symbolic offering and breaking of a coconut and seeking a blessing in return. These rituals are described in more detail below, but, illustrate rather well the principle that the nature of a ship launch ritual is very often governed by local religion and then further fashioned over time by tradition and local practice.

The silver nail ceremony

This colourful Zoroastrian ceremony was almost certainly introduced to Bombay Dockyard by the Wadia family. It was not a launching ceremony as such since it took place after the keel had been laid and before launch.[60] However, the invocations for the protection of the ship made at this ceremony are so similar to those performed at launch ceremonies that it is felt appropriate for it to be mentioned briefly here; and for the Zoroastrians it was important that before a new ship was launched the silver nail ceremony should first be performed. A ceremonial silver nail, 6 or 7in long, was specifically crafted for each ceremony and inscribed with details of the ship such as its name, date of build and the names of the Governor of Bombay and the Master Builder. Purification is a central tenet of the Zoroastrian religion and at religious to ceremonies fire must also be present and kept burning with sandal wood and frankincense. At the silver nail ceremony the nail needed to be kept pure before it was inserted into the keel. For this reason it was brought to the ceremony by a Zoroastrian priest, who kept it pure by constantly holding it over a pot of frankincense before it was driven into the keel. The ceremony commenced with an invocation for blessings of the future ship and with verses from the Koran also being recited. The silver nail was then blessed and placed by the priest into the hole in the keel. A ceremonial hammer was then used in turn by the Governor, the Superintendent of the Dockyard and the Master Builder to drive the nail into the keel. The stem was then secured into its place and more invocations pronounced. A sprinkling of rose water over the party was made and sweetmeats distributed. Six shawls – robes of honour – were presented to the builders by the Governor, or in later years by a lady designated for this task, bringing the ceremony to an end.

In his book *The Bombay Dockyard and the Wadia Master Builders*,[61] Rutterjee Ardeshin Wadia sets out a list of the ships built under the supervision of the various Master Builders of his family. The fact that a particular ship had been the subject of a silver nail ceremony was evidently regarded as being significant since in the list of the ships built for the navy between 1805 and 1848 he specifically mentions eleven of these. If the ceremony was only performed for some ships and not others the reason for this distinction is not known.

Launches at Bombay drydock

On 19 June 1810 Jamsetjee Bomanjee Wadia, son of Lovji, launched in the new dockyard in Bombay a third-rate teak gunship for the British,

HMS *Minden*, which has the distinction of being the only ship of the line in the Royal Navy to have been built outside the British Isles. The silver nail ceremony took place on 1 January 1808; and at her launch the *Bombay Courier* reported that 'she was floated into the stream at high water after the usual ceremony of breaking the bottle had been performed by the Honourable Governor, Jonathan Duncan'.[62] The report added that: 'For the skill of its architects, for the superiority of its timber and for the excellence of its docks, Bombay may now claim a distinguished place among naval arsenals.'[63] There is a portrait of Jamsetjee[64] showing him wearing an embroidered Pashmina shawl, a robe of honour indicating high service or great achievement, which, as we have noted, it was the custom of East India Company to give to Master Builders at the silver nail ceremony. In the background to the portrait is HMS *Minden* under construction. On occasion the East India Company also donated to the Master Builder, as a sign of their appreciation of 'his fidelity and services as Head Builder', an engraved silver draughtsmen's ruler, which is also portrayed in the portrait tucked into Jamsetjee's robe. Jamsetjee was the first Parsee to be entrusted by the Admiralty with the building of a man-of-war in India. The Lords of the Admiralty were so impressed with his workmanship that they sent him a letter of appreciation and a piece of silver plate, which, as we have noted, was the traditional gift to Master Shipwrights on the launch of a new naval ship in Royal Dockyards. This took the form of a silver cup, which was inscribed:

> This cup is presented to Jamsetjee Bomanjee by The Right Honourable the Lords Commissioners of the Admiralty in testimony of the sense they entertain of his diligence and skill in building for his Britannic Majesty's Navy, the *Minden* of 74 guns.[65]

And so he had the distinction of being honoured in respect of HMS *Minden* by both the East India Company and the Admiralty in London. He built a total of fourteen ships for the Royal Navy.

One such ship was HMS *Trincomallee* launched at Bombay dockyard by Jamsetjee on 12 October 1817. There is an engraving of the launch showing the hull being floated out of the building dock, bow first, displaying large flags or so-called 'launching colours' on tall flagstaffs which, as we have noted, were typical of launches in Royal Dockyards in England at that time.[66] The silver nail ceremony, considered important by the Wadia family for the well-being of the ship, had taken place earlier on 29 May 1816. Little did Jamsetjee know then how well the ceremony would protect this ship since HMS *Trincomallee* has remarkably survived to this day, being now the central exhibit at the Naval Museum of the Royal Navy in Hartlepool and the oldest British warship still afloat.

Puja and the symbolism of breaking of a coconut

In Hindu culture a coconut, being a fruit containing water (*Nariyal*), is a symbol for good luck and prosperity. Every auspicious work starts with the breaking of a coconut and the offering of *Nariyal* is a traditional ritual in India. The festival *Nariyal Purmina* is celebrated on India's west coast in September at the end of the monsoon season on the date of the full moon. This is the time of the year when the fishing and water trade begin again and, in thanks, people gather on the shore and throw coconuts into the Arabian Sea and make offerings to *Varuna*, the sea god. Painted coconuts are carried on the fishing boats and broken to ensure blessing of the gods. Charles Low mentions this ceremony as already existing in the 1880s and which the English called 'Coconut Day',[67] but it may well have its origin much earlier.

In the Hindu religion *puja* involves honouring and connecting with a deity, and during *puja* Hindus make an offering to that deity and seek a blessing in return. One of the most common offerings is fruit, usually a coconut. It is part of a ritual for everything new and is used at weddings and on the occasion of the start of new enterprises. All religious functions and rituals to mark a new work traditionally start with the offering of a coconut since it is regarded as the symbolic *Ganesh*, the deity that helps in the successful completion of a work undertaken.

It has been said that the splitting of a coconut, which resembles the form of a human head, its dark spots resembling the human eyes, can be interpreted as a substitute for former blood sacrifices. This interpretation when combined with the invocation to the deity has a certain resemblance to the sacrifices offered by ancient Greeks before the start of a seafaring venture; and the three dark spots are also thought to represent the three-eyed Hindu god *Lord Shiva*.

Puja, being grounded on the intimate interaction with deity, does not typically need the ministration of a priest but can be performed by any person who invokes the deity by the making of a gift or reciting a Vedic mantra and then seeks a blessing in return.

It can therefore be readily understood how in India ships constructed outside Bombay Dockyard and outside the period of the British rule have traditionally been launched with a *puja* ceremony – sometimes performed by Hindu priests and sometimes not, in a practice that is becoming more usual today, by reading from ancient Hindu scriptures made by any person, not necessarily a priest, who then invokes the deity and seeks blessings for the ship and her sailors. This includes the ritualistic breaking of a coconut on the bow of the new ship and garlanding the ship with flowers and throwing grains of unbroken rice, the latter being also commonly used in rituals such as a wedding to signify auspiciousness and prosperity.

Breaking of coconut ceremony at launch of ship in Port Glasgow

An interesting example of a coconut being used in this ceremonial way prior to India being granted independence in 1947 is to be found at the launch of the cargo steamship *Jalabala* built at the Lithgows' yard at Port Glasgow in 1927. The ship had been ordered by Scindia Steam Navigation Co. Ltd of Bombay, a company founded in 1919 by Walchand Hirachand, an Indian industrialist who supported the Indian independence movement. Scindia's first ship, SS *Loyalty*, started the India–Europe trade, but the company was then forced by its British competitors to restrict this to Indian coastal waters. The company was referred to widely by Mahatma Gandhi in his columns on the Swadeshi freedom movement. It was, therefore, not surprising that the Honourable V.J. Patel, Speaker and President of the Indian Legislative Council, was invited to launch the ship. A report on the launch in *The Scotsman* for 16 July 1927 states, rather laconically, that 'the launching ceremony was carried out in accordance with Eastern custom'. Fortunately, however, there is also archived a silent film of the launch made by British Pathé, in which Mr Patel, accompanied by two women, dressed in traditional Indian robes, is seen performing the launch ceremony (see Illustration No. 30). The stern of the ship was anointed with oil (it may be that attar was used), garlanded with flowers and a coconut deposited, being typical offerings made to a deity at the commencement of a *puja*. It seems likely that verses from Vedic literature were also recited. The picture shows Mr Patel about to smash a coconut against the side of the ship next to the bow.

He also throws unbroken rice grains against the hull as it moves down the slipway. For the same reason that the film is silent we do not know (but must assume) that Mr Patel named the ship when he smashed the coconut against its side. After the launch we learn from the article in *The Scotsman* that Mr Patel made a speech saying that the launch was a landmark event in the history of Indian shipping since the company was at that time the only surviving purely indigenous shipping company.

The American Bureau of Shipping, in its August 1974 edition of *The Surveyor*, reports that in 1969: 'The first large tanker, the 87,612-dwt *Jawarhalal Nehru*, to be built in Jugoslavia, was sprayed with coconut milk at a point on its bottom where a symbol, signifying the invocation of a Hindu prayer, had been painted.'[68] It seems likely from this report that a *puja* was performed prior to the launch and that the symbol on the ship's bottom was probably painted using the Hindu traditional turmeric or *kumkum* that is frequently used for such ceremonies.

Launch ceremonies for the modern Indian Navy

In the twenty-first century we find examples of ships of the modern Indian Navy being launched with a coconut being broken on the bow by the wife of a senior naval officer after offering prayers in a short *puja* or being christened by such a lady following a *puja* and blessing from a Hindu priest. For example on 17 September 2016, the guided missile destroyer *Mormugao* was named by Mrs Reena Lanbi, wife of Admiral S. Lanbi, after the Mazagon Dockyard priest Shri Puranik had performed *puja* and blessed the ship.

On 26 July 2009 at the Shipbuilding Centre in Visakhapatnam, Gurshuran Kaur, wife of the Indian Prime Minister, Manmohan Singh, in a symbolic ritual, cracked a coconut on the hull of India's first locally built nuclear submarine, INS *Arihant*,[69] on the occasion of its launch by flooding the dry dock in which it was housed. The ritual was described as being in accordance with 'Naval tradition'.

On 20 April 2015, 'in keeping with Indian nautical traditions', the guided missile destroyer *Visakhapatnam* was launched at Mazagon Dock Ltd, Mumbai. After an invocation in a *puja* was recited by Minu Dhowan, wife of the Chief of Naval Staff, she broke a coconut on the ship's bow, named the ship and wished the ship and 'crew to be' good luck.

For the launch of some, it appears mainly smaller, Indian naval ships, after recital of invocations from Atharva Veda, the wife of a senior naval officer ceremoniously applies *kumkum* on the ship's stem before naming the ship and wishing her good luck. *Kumkum* is the red powder made from turmeric that has had religious significance for Hindus for many centuries and is regarded as an auspicious symbol. It is said in certain contexts to be a substitute for a former blood sacrifice.

There is a similarity between all of these ceremonies used at the launch of these new Indian naval ships, all built in India in the last few years under its goal of 'Make in India'. It suggests that the form of the ceremony is now established as a *puja* performed by a priest or an invocation performed by the wife of a senior naval officer, followed in some cases by the breaking of a coconut against the hull or in others by the application to the stem of the ship of *kumkum* and ending with the naming and the wishing of good luck for the ship and her crew. What is also noteworthy is that the ceremony is now, more often than not, performed by a lady. Ship launch rituals continue to evolve in India and to reflect current social norms.

13.7 Ottoman Empire

Chief Astrologer determines auspicious day for the launch

The Ottoman Empire (1299–1922) was a land of ceremonies and protocols. *Monajjim-bashi* were selected from scholars who had graduated from the *madrasahs* (schools). From the sixteenth century they calculated the most auspicious hour for almost all palace-related ceremonies, such as imperial accessions, wars, imperial births, wedding ceremonies as well as ship launches. Launching ceremonies generally took place on an auspicious day as determined by the Chief Astrologer. However, the choice of the day was regarded by some Sultans as ceremonial rather than necessary and it seems that the Sultan made the final decision on the time of launch.

Sultan's attendance obligatory by law

The ceremony commenced with the arrival of the Sultan and other dignitaries. The Sultan's attendance was obligatory under a law dating back to the reign of Suleiman the Lawgiver, who was Sultan between 1520 and 1566. The ship was decorated. The throne for the Sultan was decorated with precious clothes. Written invitations to the launch were sent by the Grand Vizier (Prime Minister of the Ottoman Sultan) to religious leaders and other dignitaries such as the Grand Admiral. Separate pavilions were set up for each dignitary in the arsenal.

Prayers

Just before the launch, prayers were read by the *Seyhulislam*, who was head of the learned class whose duty it was to validate or invalidate a certain action depending on whether it accorded with Islamic law.

Qur'anic verse was recited, appropriately referring to the prophet Noah and the flood. The priest then asked for the blessing of Allah and prayed that the ship may have a prosperous and successful career and would ride safely over the waves in all weather.

The ship was then launched.

Animal sacrifice

Right after the launch animals, usually sheep, were sacrificed and all the participants were given presents by the Sultan according to their rank; for example, the Grand Admiral of the arsenal and other dignitaries of the arsenal were given sable furs, caftans and other robes of honour.[70] Sometimes the Sultan took his stand on a decorated galley. After the launch the participants and the invited guests were given a celebratory meal.

Ship launches were public affairs and relatives and friends of arsenal workers and ordinary people could attend and watch at a certain distance.

Names chosen by the Sultan

Ships were by tradition generally named during the launching ceremony. Names chosen were often heroic or epic, those of wild animals, or religious ones suggestive of asking heavenly aid. It seems that the Sultan had the final say in the name chosen.[71]

Launch ceremonies for ships constructed outside the Ottoman Empire

When, as a result of the vulnerability of wooden warships to explosive shells, ironclad warships were developed in the early part of the second half of the nineteenth century, the Ottoman Empire joined in this revolution. Some ironclad warships were built for the Sultan in his own arsenal in Constantinople, but there were also large orders for these ships placed by the Sultan with shipyards in England and Scotland. What is of interest here is to note the difference between the launch ceremonies at that time for those ships built for the Sultan in Constantinople – and the extent to which the old customs continued there – and those built for the Sultan in England and Scotland, where new customs had started.

Launch of *Hamidiye*

On 5 January 1885 there was launched after some ten years of construction an ironclad ship at the Sultan's arsenal situated on the Golden Horn in Constantinople. In a surprising break with the tradition that ships were not named after a Sultan, this ship was named *Hamidiye* after the Sultan himself. Her iron plating was partly sent out from England and partly manufactured in the Imperial arsenal. Prior to the launch it was reported that:

> The Imam or priest attached to the Arsenal recited the prayers for the Sultan and for the success of the new vessel in her future career. Six sheep were then sacrificed, and at a given signal the

supports were cut away from the monster's sides. The vessel glided into the water slowly and gracefully, to the immense satisfaction of the Minister of Marine and his staff and the thousands who watched the interesting spectacle from the decks of the shipping and the house tops on either side of the Golden Horn.[72]

From this report it appears that the old tradition of animal sacrifice at a ship launch was still being practised in 1885.

Different views on timing of the launch

There is also a report of a launch in Constantinople the next year where a discrepancy arose between the opinions of astrologers, who were always consulted on such occasions, and the wishes of the Sultan over the timing of the launch with the result that, when the Sultan and his guests arrived to witness the launch, they found that it had already happened.[73]

Ships launched in England and Scotland

These prayers, animal sacrifice and opinions of the astrologers were in accordance with well-established Ottoman and religious traditions. They are in sharp contrast to the ceremonies practised at the launch of the many ironclad warships built for the Sultan in the 1860s and 1870s in England and Scotland. From contemporaneous press reports of these launches the ceremonial pattern here was for the ships to be dressed with flags including the Crescent and Star on a red background, being the flag of the Ottoman Empire. The Turkish Ambassador to London, as a more or less invariable practice, attended the launch as the representative of the Sultan and then, more often than not, his wife or his daughter had the honour of christening the ships with a baptismal bottle of wine. Although some expressed the opinion that 'the Koran was transgressed in spirit by the cracking of that baptismal bottle',[74] the nature of the ceremony had more to do with the fact these ships were built in England, where by that date the tradition of ladies christening ships with a bottle of wine was firmly established, rather than any change in the Ottoman practice. That said, such a christening ceremony performed by a lady with a baptismal bottle would not have been contemplated in Constantinople at that time where women did not participate in such ceremonies nor would the use of wine have been thought appropriate.

Gradual secularisation

Over time, after the abolition of the Ottoman Sultanate in 1922 and the recognition of the Grand National Assembly of Turkey, there has been a gradual secularisation with religion playing a less prominent role in launch ceremonies and with a greater participation of women. Verses from the Koran are, however, still frequently recited prior to the launch of ships built for owners in the Republic of Turkey.

Traditionally, until recently, no wine was spilt over the bow of a new ship, but breaking of a bottle of wine against the bow is sometimes practised today in Turkey. Although in Christian countries the blessing of ship with wine has a religious significance, in Turkey it is more a sign of secularisation. Frequently the Turkish flag, which is derived from the flag of the Ottoman Empire, is draped over the bows at the launch, with the ship being decorated overall with flags, red and white balloons and red and white decorative cloth representing the Turkish national colours; and the Turkish national anthem (Independence March) is sung as the new ship enters the water. The draping of cloth with the national colours or flags over the hull has its origin in the custom prevailing in earlier Ottoman times when gift cloths were traditionally draped on the hull of a ship being launched.

13.8 Portugal

Boat blessing and fleet blessing

Boat blessing and fleet blessing ceremonies have a firm historical basis in Portugal, going back to the Age of Exploration in the fifteenth century when such occasions took place before Portuguese explorers set sail from Lisbon to discover and conquer India. The tradition of a new ship being blessed by a Catholic priest and christened with the name of a saint before launch was also firmly established by this time. The Portuguese have a traditional and deep rooted veneration for the clergy.

Henry the Navigator sought and obtained a papal bull for the Portuguese maritime expeditions to West Africa and India with papal forgiveness of sins being granted to those who died in this discovery and conquest. The papal approval in effect made these expeditions into crusades to suppress the growing power of Islam and subject any conquered lands to the Christian faith. Thus, Vasco da Gama went to India to promote the cross as well as to search for spices. This background explains why the Portuguese explorers named their ships after saints, why they had the sign of the cross decorated on their sails and why they planted a cross (*Padrao*) wherever they landed.

Before Vasco da Gama set sail in 1497, on a day 'consecrated to the Virgin Mary [which] had been chosen by court astrologers as auspicious for departure', he was presented with 'a silk banner ... emblazoned with the cross of the Order of Christ'.[75] He took an oath to go and discover the land and the seas of the Orient and to defend the cross unto death. There was a solemn religious ceremony on the shore attended by a large crowd. During the emotional farewell ceremony a Catholic priest led prayers and blessed the voyage. 'Everyone knelt to make a general confession and to receive absolution according to the papal bull which Henry the Navigator had obtained.'[76] The explorers or 'navigators' as they were called were rowed out to their boats amidst the traditional cries of 'Safe Voyage!', and set sail.

The two main ships in the fleet were *Sao Gabriel* commanded by Vasco da Gama himself and *Sao Rafael* commanded by his brother Paulo da Gama. They were sturdy carracks specially built by Bartholomeo Dias and christened with the names of the Archangels 'according a vow made by King Joao before his death'.[77] Both ships had beautiful wooden figure heads of the Archangels on their prows to safeguard them from danger. There was a general belief in the power of the Saints and of the Virgin Mary to exercise a miraculous influence over the destinies of seamen.

Named after saints

Out of the squadron of twelve Portuguese ships taking part in the Spanish Armada in 1588, nine were named after saints. The practice of Portuguese ships first being blessed by a priest, christened with the names of saints and then launched continued into the seventeenth century. The majority of Portuguese ships during the seventeenth century were built at the Ribeira das Naus, the royal dockyards in Lisbon. After the arrival of the Portuguese in Goa, where Admiral Afonso do Albuquerque had first arrived in 1510 in search of spices, shipbuilding was also carried out there, with the main advantage of Goan-built ships being the hardiness of the local teak. The same religious customs at launch were carried out in Goa as were practised in Portugal. For example, in 1636 there is an account of a new galleon being launched in Goa:

> At our being here was launched a new galleon of 14 foot by the keel, as they say being first blessed, christened and named 'el buen Jesus' by the Archbishop that came over in the carrack.[78]

What is of interest in this account is that 'christening' and 'naming' were treated as being somehow different. The concept appears to have been that after the ship was blessed it was then dedicated to, as well as being named after, the saint.

Launches in presence of Royal family

In 1721 we find an example of two 50-gun warships being launched in the presence of the royal family seated in a richly furnished royal box constructed for the occasion. The ships were named *Nossa Senhora da Oliveira* and *Nossa Senhora da Nazario*, both being churches dedicated to Santa Maria. The launch was followed by a customary celebration with Portuguese sweets and whatever drinks took the choice of the guests.[79] The 74-gun man-of-war *Nossa Senhora da Conceicao* was reported to have been similarly launched on 12 July 1733 in the presence of the King, the Prince and Princess of Brasil, *Infantes* (royal children) Dom Peter and Dom Francis and the whole court.[80] Such launches were clearly important events during the period of the monarchy in Portugal to be supported by the whole royal family and its entourage.

Special protection of the saint

The concept behind a ship being named after a saint was, as mentioned, to invoke the special protection of the saint whose name the ship bore. In times of peril it was to the saint whose name was given to the ship and to the image of that saint, which was frequently carried on board, that the prayers of the crew were addressed. This reflected the strong influence of the Jesuit cult of saints and their images.

Change of practice

This practice continued in Portugal until 1770, when under the leadership of Martinho del Melo, Secretary of State of the Navy, the Portuguese navy underwent reform and modernisation. As part of these reforms the old procedure of baptising Portuguese ships with the names of saints was replaced by their baptism with the names of mythical, historical or royal persons. Not surprisingly, the aura of the famous explorers has been preserved, with ships being named after such famous names as Vasco da Gama, Bartolomeu Dias and Alfonso de Albuquerque.

Ceremony today

In today's ceremonies for the launch of a naval ship after conventional speeches and christening by a godmother and launch, the band plays the national anthem – *A Portuguesa* adopted in 1911 – which, appropriate for a ship launch, has as its opening line *'Herois do mar-nobro povo'* – Heroes of the sea, noble people. The Naval guard present arms and the authorities welcome the ship into the fleet 'in the name of the Homeland and the Republic'.[81]

Portuguese merchant ships are similarly blessed by a priest and named by a godmother before launch. On 22 September 1960 a 19,393 grt passenger cargo liner, built by Swan, Hunter & Wigham Richardson Ltd at its Neptune yard on the Tyne for Companhia Nacional de Navegacao (CNN) of Lisbon, was named and launched by Senhora D'Ana Mafalda Guimaraes Jose de Mello, daughter-in-law of the president of the owner. She was named TSS *Principe Perfeito* after Portugal's 'Perfect Prince', King Juao II, who reigned from 1481 to 1495. Prior to being named and launched there was a short religious service conducted by a Catholic priest, accompanied by seven assistants bearing a cross, lit candles and incense. The service ended with the priest sprinkling holy water on the bow using an aspergillum, as a symbol of blessing and baptism. The ship was then named and launched by her godmother. With a length of 625ft, she was the largest ship ever to have been launched at the Neptune yard.

Fishing boats and protection from the 'eyes' of Horus

Special traditions have applied to the launch of new fishing vessels, especially around the famous fishing village of Nazaré, where the best but most dangerous fishing in all of Portugal is carried out. There is a traditional ritual when new fishing boats are constructed and launched. The fishing boats, historically Phoenician in design, are frequently brightly painted with 'eyes' on the bow, supposedly with the magic or apotropaic power to ward off evil and to avert storms. These 'eyes' are probably derived from the Eye of *Horus*, an ancient Egyptian symbol of protection. The 'eyes' may also be seen as a form of animism whereby a soul is attributed to an inanimate object and the sentiment that a ship is a living thing and must see her way. As such it reflects persistence of old beliefs prior to Christianisation. As a living being, a boat must have a face and eyes and the eyes need to be opened immediately prior to launching. The same influence of the all seeing Eye of *Horus* is also to be found in ancient Greece with the practice of painting a large eye on each bow of a warship, which is portrayed in the images of ships painted on vases in the seventh and sixth centuries BC.[82]

However, even with the protection of the 'eyes' the names given to fishing boats frequently have a religious invocation such as the names of saints, which reflects the old tradition of the fifteenth century already described or words seeking divine protection or names of historical character. So, in the case of some fishing boats there is to be found a complex double protection, magical and Christian.

Adiafa and Gueste

After construction of the fishing vessels is complete there is a ceremony called *Adiafa* – the placing of a bunch of flowers on the tip of the prow and *Gueste*, a festival with food, wine and dancing, which is not peculiar to ship launches. When the ship is put into the water for the first time it is usually blessed by a priest. Amulets and good luck charms are also frequently hung in the boat; again a combination of spiritual and magical.

In the Museo Dr Joacquim Manso in Nazare there is a modern watercolour painted in 1976 by Coelho de Silva called *'Bencao dos Barcos'* – Blessing of the Boats – which depicts the typical ceremony of a fishing boat being blessed by a priest who sprinkles it with holy water. Thus, the blessing of ships by a Catholic priest, traditional in Portugal since the Age of Exploration, continues today.

Chapter 14

Unusual Launches and Naming Ceremonies

S hip launches and christenings do not always follow a uniform
pattern.

Sideways launch using elephants

There is an intriguing account from south India in 1775 of the sideways
launching of two frigates, one of 32 guns and the other of 24 guns,
unusually using elephants to push the hull down the launch ways. They
were built in the river at Mangalore, the principal dockyard and arsenal
of Hyder Ally, the de facto ruler of Mysore and who was engaged at that
time in resisting the military advances of the East India Company:

> Instead of the head or stern fronting the river, their broadsides do;
> they are built with their sides parallel to the banks. On my asking
> how they launched them, I was told that when ready, they laid long
> straight timbers squared, which reached from the ship's bottom to
> the water. Then they take away the supports from the side next to
> the river and the ship resting on those timbers, which are greased,
> by the force of elephants, first at one end and then at the other,
> alternately, is pushed into the river.[1]

This is a very early example of sideways launching, a launching method
that was more commonly employed in the nineteenth century by
shipbuilders in the Great Lakes. As we have learned, hydraulic power
was the method used to launch *Great Eastern* sideways in 1858 and the
clear advice that Brunel received from Mr G.W. Bull at Buffalo Shipyard[2]
was that, when launching sideways, care should be taken that both ends
of the hull start down the incline at the same time. Elephant push power
may well have been an effective forerunner of hydraulic power but what

is intriguing is that the elephants pushed at either end 'alternately', which, if this is a correct description of what took place, means that both ends of the hull may not have moved down the launch way at the same time! We shall never know how the elephants prevented the hull moving transversely down the ways, with a potentially disastrous result!

Launch and christening of two Imperial state yachts with the same name by two sisters

What is unusual is to find two state yachts for Imperial Russia being launched and christened by two sisters at the same shipyard in Hull with the same name *Tzarevna* within a short period of one another. Tzarevna means wife of the Tsarevich, being the eldest son and heir of the Tsar of Russia.

The story is that Grand Duke Alexander Alexandrovich became Tsarevich when his elder brother Nicholas died suddenly in 1865. The Grand Duke then married Princess Dagmar of Denmark in 1866 who, after becoming a member of the Orthodox church, changed her name to Maria Feodorovna. The first yacht to be named *Tzarevna*, in honour of his wife, was ordered by Grand Duke Alexander from Earle's Shipbuilding and Engineering Company in Hull and was designed by Edward Reed. He is the same naval architect whom we have encountered in connection with the introduction of a religious service for naval ships in 1875[3] and who led the enquiry into the *Daphne* disaster in 1883[4] but at this time he was Chairman of Earle's. The first yacht of 160 gross tons was launched in the presence of the Grand Duke himself in July 1873 and was christened by Miss Resa Reed, daughter of Mr Edward Reed. She dashed a bottle on the stem and the Tsar's flag was hoisted on the main mast. As a souvenir of the occasion the Grand Duke was presented with a sailor's knife with an ivory handle made in Sheffield on which the arms of Imperial Russia were engraved.[5]

After the launch of the first yacht it was decided that she was not of sufficient size for state purposes and an order for a second yacht was placed, again with Earle's, in the same style of excellence as the first but of 800 gross tons. The launch and naming of the second *Tzarevna* took place on 2 September 1874. On this occasion it was without the presence of the Grand Duke but the christening was conducted by Miss

Cissy Reed, sister to Miss Resa Reed. It was said that this second yacht 'when the finishing touches have been given her will undoubtedly be one of the most commodious, costly and beautiful yachts afloat'.[6] So that is how it came about that two sisters christened two Imperial yachts built in the same shipyard with the same name within fourteen months of one another! The first *Tzarevna* was subsequently renamed *Slavyanka*.

Launch during an air raid

The story of a launch on the Tyne on 16 September 1940, while the air raid sirens howled, illustrates some of the difficulties under which shipbuilding was undertaken in the UK during the Second World War.

Hull No. 519 was an 8,400 dwt cargo ship of typical tramp ship design and size of the time. The ship had been ordered by local shipowner, North Shipping Co. Ltd of Newcastle from shipbuilders John Readhead & Sons Ltd, South Shields, and proved to be the last ship to be built in wartime to a private shipowner's specification. Following delivery of this ship, and thereafter for the duration of the war, all further merchant shipbuilding at Readheads came under the control of the Admiralty, who placed orders for ships of standard design and 9,000–10,000 dwt.[7] The Admiralty appointed managers for each ship, oversaw their construction and approved their name. These standard designs were generally given names commencing with the prefix *'Empire'*.

The story of the launch of *North Britain* was told by Harold Towers, the Managing Director of the yard at the time, to his son Rodney, who has kindly given his permission to include it here. It is also obliquely reported in the local press, with the name of the ship and the yard being omitted by reason of wartime reporting restrictions.

Everything was ready for the launch when the air raid sirens 'burst in with their discordant howl. For a brief second those assembled looked at each other but there was no alarm, no panic, only a feeling of annoyance that the ceremony should be interrupted …'.[8] It was at this point that Harold Towers had to personally ask the young godmother whether she would like to take cover or proceed with the ship's launch and, as the local reporter recorded: 'Without hesitation, without sign of fear or panic, she moved up to the platform and sent the ship on its way down the stocks.'[9]

The moment is captured in Illustration No. 31. On the launching platform are, left to right, wearing the bowler hat, Douglas Grier, shipyard manager; Harold Towers, the Managing Director of the yard; the young lady whose name is not known who was the 'plucky godmother'; and a representative of the owner, North Shipping Co. Ltd, whose identity is not known, with his hands in the air annoyed at the untimely interruption to the launch and apparently praying that no bombs will fall.

'Tyneside workmen admire pluck and, in their admiration, they cheered and cheered again as the ship slid gracefully in to the water.'[10]

As good fortune would have it, the Luftwaffe did not interfere.

The report continues that the courage of the young lady so inspired the workmen that none left their job but carried on with the task of bringing the hull safely alongside. The shipowner, the yard management and the unruffled godmother then retired to the unusual venue of the shipyard office air raid shelter, where they raised toasts to the ship and all who would sail in her.

As the photograph shows, the launching platform was not extensively decorated. This was not the elaborate ceremony normal for peacetime launches. Indeed it was the case that many of the merchant ships launched in the UK during the Second World War on account of the Admiralty were launched without ceremony.

Rodney Towers has commented to the author that in the UK (but not in America) the construction bottleneck during the Second World War was always the building berth. This meant that once a ship was launched there was immediate pressure to get the ship off the berth and to lay the keel for the next ship. This contrasts with the construction of the 'Liberty ships' in the US yards between 1941 and 1945, where there was plenty of room for prefabrication of parts and multiple launches and there were no anxieties about bombs, air raid precautions or blackouts to interrupt production.[11]

Launch by wireless from other side of the world

As a shipbuilder, how do you arrange a ship launch when you discover that the royal sponsor of the ship will, on the intended day of the launch, be 12,000 miles away in Brisbane? Or, in the case of another shipyard, when you discover that the chosen godmother is too frail to travel to the shipyard to perform the ceremony? These were the challenges faced by Vickers-Armstrongs Ltd in December 1934 for the launch in Barrow-in-Furness of the Orient liner RMS *Orion* and by Harland and Wolff in August 1947 for the launch in Belfast of RMS *Pretoria Castle* for Union Castle Mail Steamship Company Ltd. An ingenious solution was found on each occasion using a wireless link.

Launch of Orion

Vickers News described the launch on 7 December 1934 as 'an epoch-making and memorable event' in the history of Barrow shipbuilding when *Orion* was launched by wireless link from Australia by His Royal Highness, the Duke of Gloucester, who at the time was attending a concert in the Brisbane City Hall given by the Returned Sailors and Soldiers and Ex-Service Men's Welcome Committee. Since the ship was intended for the Australian trade it was totally appropriate that the launch should be signalled from Brisbane.[12]

Elaborate arrangements were made by the Post Office authorities in Australia and England. The whole ceremony had a strict timetable working to split seconds. In Barrow, just before the event started preparations for the launch were advanced further than usual with the shores and blocks cleared away under the hull and the ship only being held by the triggers. When His Royal Highness pressed a key in Brisbane Town Hall an electric impulse was carried by land line to the Telegraph Office in Brisbane, then by telegraph line to Melbourne and by beam to London. From there it was picked up by Rugby Radio and directed by land line to Barrow, where it was amplified to sufficient strength to trip both the release of the triggers holding the ship and the bottle-release mechanism.

In Barrow on the launching platform was General Sir Herbert Lawrence, the Chairman of Vickers-Armstrong Ltd, and in Brisbane Town Hall was Sir Allan Anderson, Chairman of the Orient Steam Navigation Company, and HRH the Duke of Gloucester, the latter sitting at a small table on which was set a telegraphist key mounted on polished oak.

The whole ceremony from start to finish was broadcast both in the UK and in Australia and New Zealand, which was in itself unusual;

but not totally without precedent since, as already related, the launch of RMS *Queen Mary* had also been broadcast a few months earlier in September 1934.

In Barrow the launching party heard Sir Alan Anderson start his speech to His Royal Highness in Brisbane, telling him that everything was ready at the shipyard to launch the ship. Almost immediately the voice of His Royal Highness was heard replying to Sir Alan Anderson.

His Royal Highness then pressed the key on the table in front of him transmitting the special launching tone 12,000 miles across the world. This action gave a high-pitched tone to those listening in Barrow and immediately the triggers were released, the bottle of Australian wine smashed against the side and the ship took to the water.

Once the ship was afloat Sir Herbert Lawrence told the Duke that the ship was safely waterborne, amid loud cheers and the playing of the National Anthem; Brisbane, hearing the broadcast, had a sense of what was happening far out of sight on the other side of the world.

It had been an unusual launch, the arrangements for launching by wireless from Australia being unique in the history of shipbuilding at that time. In today's world of satellite communications and video all this would all be child's play but in 1934 it was well described by His Royal Highness as an 'act of magic'! It was certainly technically innovative and unusual.

In wishing her good fortune, the Duke could hardly have foreseen *Orion*'s subsequent career after it was requisitioned in 1939 as a troopship, surviving a serious collision when her steering gear jammed and on several occasions being subjected to heavy enemy attacks.

Pretoria Castle

Fifteen years later but in entirely different circumstances, history was to repeat itself with the launch in Belfast of RMS *Pretoria Castle* from the Queen's Island shipyard of Harland and Wolff. Union Castle Mail Steamship Company Ltd wanted this ship, intended for the Southampton–Cape Town express passenger service, to be launched and named by Mrs Smuts, wife of the Prime Minister of the South African Union, Field Marshal Smuts. Unfortunately Mrs Smuts was too frail to make the journey to Belfast and arrangements were made to launch the ship by radio signals from her home, 12 miles from Pretoria in the Transvaal. Some commentators claimed that this was the first (and possibly only) ship to be launched electronically by radio but they seem to have forgotten the earlier successful launch of *Orion* by this method.

The *Glasgow Herald*[13] described the scene:

> the interest of the platform party centred on a little box – described by a shipyard official as 'the magical box' – to which was attached the wine bottle for the naming ceremony, three microphones, and three coloured bulbs. This box contained a magnet which, when the radio signals were received, released the wine bottle and the launching mechanism or 'trigger' at the centre of the hull.

A photo of the magical box is to be found at Illustration No. 33.

Mrs Smuts was then heard over the radio line naming the ship. The *Glasgow Herald* reporter continues with his description:

> There were two or three whistling noises over the radio system. Apparently these were the operation of the radio signals. Suddenly the wine bottle was released to crash against the ship's hull. Very quickly the giant liner moved away and in a matter of seconds was afloat.

Illustration No. 34 shows the liner as it entered the Lough.

Launch of Russian Imperial yacht in channel cut through the ice

The manner and circumstances of the launch of the Russian Imperial yacht *Standart* on 21 March 1895 at Burmeister & Wain's shipyard in Copenhagen were unusual in many respects; and her subsequent career proved to be unusual too. The ship was launched as an imperial yacht but when she was ordered by Tsar Alexander III in 1893 she was to be a light cruiser for the Imperial Russian Navy. The decision to place the order with Burmeister & Wain was undoubtedly influenced by the Tsar's wife, Tsarina Maria Feodorovna, who was the daughter of King Christian

IX of Denmark, and the close connections between Imperial Russia and Denmark at that time.

On 1 October 1893 the Tsar, Tsarina and their son Nicholas Alexandrovich (the future Tsar Nicholas II) were present at the keel laying but shortly after construction commenced the specification was amended from cruiser to imperial yacht. When Tsar Alexander III died before the ship was ready for launching, his son decided that, as a mark of respect to his father, the ship should be launched on 21 March 1895, the anniversary of his father's birthday.

The winter of 1894–95 was very severe and the entrance to Copenhagen harbour was covered in a thick layer of ice. When Tsar Nicholas II insisted that the launch should proceed '… Burmeister & Wain had to comply with the Emperor's wish [and] … could do nothing else than have a channel cut through the ice and several hundred men were working day and night to prepare a channel long and wide enough to enable the ship to float out safely …'.[14]

As we have noted, the normal tradition was for the Tsar to be present at the launch of ships of the Russian Imperial Navy,[15] but on this occasion the bad weather prevented Nicholas II from attending. On a cold and windy day in Copenhagen, despite all the difficulties, the launch went ahead successfully on the anniversary of Tsar Alexander III's birthday in the special channel cut through the ice (Illustration No. 37). No members of the Russian Imperial family were present but the launch was attended by members of the Danish Royal family, Russian diplomats and other high-placed members of Danish society.

Standart was the largest and most elegant imperial yacht afloat at the time and an unusual feature was that her state rooms incorporated a Russian Orthodox chapel. Her bow was decorated with the double eagle emblem of Russia.

After such an unusual launch the ship went on to have an equally unusual and varied career; following her original design as a light cruiser, her launch and her first service as an imperial yacht, on the fall of the Romanov dynasty, she was stripped down and converted into a minelaying ship and served as such in the Second World War under the new name of *Marti*, and finally at the end of that war she was converted into a training ship.

Naming ceremony inside a hull

Unusual, but totally different, was the naming ceremony for the cruise ferry *Pride of Hull* which took place at King George Dock, Hull on 30 November 2001. This was the first naming ceremony ever to take place *inside* the ship being named on one of the ferry's immense car decks. The ship's sponsor, Cherie Blair, wife of the British Prime Minister, standing at a podium inside the ship, said: 'It is a particular thrill to be here for me as the granddaughter of a man who spent his whole working life at sea. I have never been invited to a ship naming before so I'm particularly delighted and honoured.'[16] She then pushed a red plunger; this released a rod to which was attached a magnum of champagne, causing it to smash outside against the ship's bow above the name *Pride of Hull*. Unlike the launch of *Orion* where the electric impulse to release the christening bottle needed to travel 12,000 miles, on the *Pride of Hull* it only needed to travel a few metres! Nonetheless, the 700 guests, including the author, assembled in the relative warmth of the car deck below, appreciated not having to stand outside on a dockside in Hull on a cold November day. The whole ceremony was relayed on two vast screens on the car deck for all to enjoy.

Bottle smashed by team of Royal Marine Commandos

Instead of simply pressing a button to send a bottle of champagne against the ship's side, how about the godmother commanding a crack team of Royal Marine Commandos to abseil down the ship's side and smash not one but two bottles of champagne? This was the dramatic 007-style solution chosen by P&O Cruises for the naming ceremony of its cruise vessel *Ventura* on 16 April 2008.

The background to this novel naming ceremony was the failure of the bottle to smash on two recent previous ceremonies for the naming of new cruise ships. In April 2000, as noted already, the bottle dropped off the lanyard at a naming ceremony for P&O's *Aurora*, where HRH Princess Royal was the godmother, and in December 2007, a few months prior to the launch of *Ventura*, there had been a technical glitch in the naming of the Cunard ship *Queen Victoria* by the Duchess of Cornwall when the bottle of champagne bounced off the bow and failed to break.

As described earlier,[17] for seafarers it is a bad omen if the baptising bottle fails to break and so P&O Cruises decided to take no chances when it came to the naming of *Ventura*.

Dame Helen Mirren, who won an Oscar for her role in the film *The Queen*, was to be the godmother, the first time she had performed this role. The P&O Cruises managing director, Nigel Esdale, said: 'Dame Helen embodies glamour, vitality and Britishness ... We are honoured that she has agreed to become the (ship's) Godmother.' He added: 'We are determined to get the bottle smashing right and are grateful for the co-ordinated assistance of the Royal Marines.'[18]

The guests were treated to a short 007 spoof film to set the scene, at the end of which Dame Helen said: 'I am honoured to name this ship. I hope you will all sail in her – I know I will.' She then gave the command for the Royal Marines to abseil down the ship's superstructure, which they did in true Royal Marine fashion.

Before the event the commanding officer of the Royal Marines Display team said: 'This is a rather unusual assignment for our lads, but well within their capabilities. They are very keen to assist Dame Helen with the launch – they will not let her down.'[19] They did not. Just to make sure, two bottles were smashed instead of one! It was a great success and certainly a break from the normal tradition.

While it was totally understandable that P&O Cruises wanted to avoid another failure to smash the bottle – by reason of the bad omen and adverse publicity – this was surely a case of taking a sledgehammer to crack a nut – or should the metaphor now be changed to refer to taking a squad of Royal Marines Commandos to crack a champagne bottle?

Christening of a ship constructed and launched in two halves

If a ship is constructed in two parts, launched on two different dates, *when* do you christen her? When the fore part is launched, or when the aft part is launched, or when the two parts have been joined together? This intriguing question arose in 1951 when John Crown & Sons, a yard on the river Wear in Sunderland, constructed a 23,000-dwt motor tanker for Norwegian owners, Olsen & Ugelstad of Oslo, in two parts. Some newspaper reports at the time said it was the first 'vessel' and others the first 'tanker' in the world to be constructed in two parts that were known locally as 'the two half crowns', a witty pun on the name of the builder and the British coin, the Crown.

The reason was that at the time of the placing of the contract this was the only way that the yard, one of the smallest on the Wear, could build a ship of such dimensions. The 290ft after end was launched first, without ceremony, on 9 April 1951 but with the name *Rondefjell* already painted on her stern (Illustration No. 35).

The fore part of 275ft was launched some six months later on 15 October 1951. Illustration No. 36 shows Mrs Erna Ugelstad, the wife of one of the owners, standing in front of the bow section of yard No. 233 smashing a bottle of champagne against the bow.

The intriguing question is what words did she actually use? With only half the tanker, the bow section, in front of her, did she say 'I name this ship *Rondefjell*' or what? We shall probably never know. A report in the *Sunderland Echo* for 15 October simply says: 'The fore end, 275 ft long was named by Mrs Erna Ugelstad,' and the *Newcastle Journal* on 16 October that 'she named the half vessel in her native Norwegian tongue'. The two sections were subsequently welded together at the Middle Docks & Engineering Company Ltd, South Shields, on the river Tyne to produce a ship of 602ft that is thought to have been the largest ship at that time ever constructed on the Wear. It may also be that it was the first deep sea vessel in the world to be constructed and launched in two separate parts.

It is a practice that has become quite common since then; and where a ship is being lengthened usually a new midsection is prefabricated and this is launched on its own, typically without ceremony. It is then inserted into the ship that is being lengthened in a dry dock by floating in the new midsection after the original ship has been 'cut' into two halves with one half, the bow section, already floated out of the dock to leave room for the new midsection. Finally, the bow section of the original ship is floated back into the dock to be joined to the other end of the new midsection to complete the lengthening. This was the precise engineering process for the stretching of the cruise ship *Windward* for Norwegian Cruise Line successfully completed by Lloyd Werft Gmbh. This unusual event was witnessed by the author and other guests standing on the dockside at the shipyard in Bremerhaven on a cold day in January 1998, where we were happily fortified by a welcome glass of *gluhwein* as we watched the three parts being brought together. At an early stage in the process a representative of one of the financiers present was heard to express some concern that 'his ship mortgage security was now in two halves'! It was a memorable event. The lengthened ship was renamed *Norwegian Wind*.

Night launch by torchlight

For obvious practical reasons, launches at night are rare. One such launch did, however, occur on 17 July 1855 at the shipyard of Messrs Bourne and Co. on the Clyde.

The iron screw steamer *Azof* of 700 grt had been ordered by local owner James Hartley and D. Hoyle of Greenock and had the further distinction of being the first ship built on the river Clyde under Lloyd's classification society's new rules for the construction of iron ships.

Poor tides at the place of launch during the day and better tides at night are one of the few reasons for contemplating a night-time launch. This was certainly the reason given in a report in the *Illustrated London News* on 11 August 1855 on the night launch of this ship: 'As the tides did not rise sufficiently during the day, the vessel had to be launched at night.'[20] No further information is available, however, as to the commercial pressures or other reasons underlying the decision that the shipyard could not wait until a suitable daytime tide to launch the ship but felt obliged to proceed with the much riskier course of a launch at night 'by torchlight'.[21] This unusual launch is portrayed in an etching at Illustration No. 38. The *Azof* was designed to carry 1,000 tons of cargo and with accommodation for forty first-class passengers. After delivery by the shipyard she was sold to The Peninsular and Oriental Steam Navigation Company.

A launch at night appears not to have been an everyday occurrence on the Clyde at that time since the *Illustrated London News* reports that 'a good deal of interest was excited by an event so unusual as a night launch'.[22] It was sufficiently unusual for the journal to add to the report, for the interest of its readers, an etching of the romantic torchlight scene showing the large crowd on the riverbank waving their top hats in the air in a ceremonial greeting as the hull was launched down the ways. The risks involved in such a night-time launch were evidently in the mind of the reporter when he added: 'The vessel entered the water beautifully and without mishap of any kind notwithstanding the impediments arising from the night.'[23]

There are a few other examples of night-time launches. In 1854 the frigate *Assange* was launched at midnight in Bombay Dockyard, no doubt by reason of it being cooler at that time of day for the guests to attend. On 23 December 1918 Short Brothers Ltd in Sunderland launched *War Seagull*, a 'B'-type standard cargo ship, on the Wear 'at 7.am in almost total darkness', which a local newspaper described as 'a circumstance well nigh unprecedented in the history of the River Wear'.[24] The prefix 'War' indicates that this ship was one of the wartime standardised ships ordered by the Controller of Shipping. This newspaper report does not give any reason for necessitating the launch in near darkness and one's first reaction is to imagine that the reason was once again a good tide in the Wear and no doubt also the desire to have the ship launched before the start of the Christmas holidays. These factors may well have been present but it appears that they are not the whole story. From a brochure produced by Short Brothers Ltd to celebrate 100 years of shipbuilding by the firm, it appears that the dominant factor may have been the keenness of the yard to establish a record for the time taken to build a standardised merchant ship and that this led them to undertake the early morning launch in near darkness.[25] The time taken from laying the first keel plate of this ship until launch was twenty-three weeks and four days including the Armistice holidays, and was believed to be a record in England and Scotland for the construction of a ship of this size at that time.

It might have been expected that launching at night under floodlights would have been practised at shipyards in the UK during the Second World War in order to avoid air raid damage; but this does not appear to have been undertaken, the thinking being that in a blackout the use of flares and other lighting to facilitate a night-time launch would only have served to attract greater attention from the air.

Chapter 15

Lifeboats and the Service of Dedication

Lifeboats not given a name until 1850s

In the first half of the nineteenth century it was the practice not to give new lifeboats a name, but by the 1850s this gradually became more established. The names chosen were frequently either to honour individuals who had given valuable service to the National Institution for the Preservation of Lives and Property from Shipwreck – founded in 1824 and which in 1854 became the Royal National Lifeboat Institution (RNLI) – or to acknowledge the generosity of individuals or associations who had provided funds to the RNLI for the establishment of a new lifeboat station or the construction of a new lifeboat. Since the establishment of a new station or the allocation of a new boat was a matter to be decided by the General Committee, they were frequently also asked to approve the giving of names to new lifeboats. The committee, in its efforts to encourage further giving so as to ensure that the coasts were adequately provided with serviceable boats for the purpose of saving life, readily adopted this practice, which has continued down the years. In recognition of their generosity, beautifully crafted models of lifeboats were also frequently given by the RNLI to major donors.

Lifeboats christened by ladies

The tradition of ships being christened by ladies, although not to the exclusion of gentlemen, which had begun during the Regency was soon extended to lifeboats. By the 1860s there are several reported examples of lifeboats being christened by a lady smashing a bottle of wine against the bow. For example we find the launch and christening of *Jessie Knowles* at Scarborough in 1861 by Miss Knowles, daughter of the donor[1], and *The Constance* named at Tynemouth on 13 November 1862 by the wife of the secretary of the local branch of the National Lifeboat Institution.[2] Since that time lifeboats have, in general, been named and christened in much the same way as other ships but with one significant difference: a lifeboat's purpose is to rescue those in peril on the sea and its 'dedication' by a member of the clergy for this noble purpose forms a solemn part of the ceremony.

Dedication by clergy

The word 'dedicate' is derived from the Latin verb *dedicare* and is often used in the context of something being set aside or devoted to a special purpose, for example a piece of land for a sacred use, such as a church. In a similar way a lifeboat at its service of naming and dedication is being solemnly devoted to the rescue of those in peril on the sea.

On 17 June 1975 the Right Reverend E.A.J. Mercer, Bishop of Exeter, at the naming ceremony and dedication of the Torbay Lifeboat *Edward Bridges* Civil Service and Post office No. 37, used these words of dedication:

> To the honour and glory of Almighty God and for the noble purpose of rescuing those in peril on the sea we dedicate this Life-boat, in the name of the Father and of the Son and of the Holy Ghost. Amen.

In the archives of the RNLI maintained at its headquarters in Poole there is a unique and fascinating collection of the programmes for the naming and dedication service for many of the new lifeboats launched at over 230 stations around the coasts of the UK and the Republic of Ireland over the last 100 years or so. The title of the ceremony has changed over time, being in the 1920s and 1930s usually called an 'inaugural ceremony', in the 1940s and 1950s a 'naming ceremony' or in the Republic of Ireland 'naming and blessing'. From the late 1950s until the present time it has been called the 'naming Ceremony and service of dedication'. Whatever the title given to the ceremony, its substance has largely remained the same for the last 100 years.

Typically it opens or ends with the appropriate National Anthem. A large proportion of new lifeboats have in the past been funded, and continue to be funded today, by legacies and private donations. For this reason the programme then usually proceeds with the presentation by the donor, or a representative of the donor, of the new lifeboat to the RNLI, which formally accepts it and then hands it over to the local lifeboat station, which formally accepts it.

There then follows a 'service of dedication' conducted by a member of the clergy. The new lifeboat is then named and launched. The dedication itself as well as the remainder of the ceremony has now been largely standardised but leaving open the possibility of regional variations in Wales, Scotland and Republic of Ireland. As Nathan Jones, Event Logistics Team Manager at the RNLI, has told the author: 'These range from having different National Anthems to slight differences in prayers, hymns and readings due to ceremonies being more commonly conducted by Catholic clergy as opposed to Anglican. We often have requests to ensure that our ceremonies are conducted in Welsh or Celtic and we have to prepare bilingual programmes.'

The standard dedication now reads:

In the faith of our Lord Jesus Christ, we dedicate this lifeboat for the noble purpose of rescuing those in danger on the sea. We commend to His care all those who serve in her, in the name of the Father and of the Son and of the Holy Ghost. Amen.

The dedication is usually followed by the 'Lifeboat Prayer', the wording of which has been revised from time to time but the opening words of which now read:

Merciful Father, all things in heaven and earth are held within your loving care, look with favour upon the Royal Lifeboat Institution.
Protect and bless the crews of all our lifeboats, our lifeguards and all who risk their own safety to bring help to others ...

The prayers are combined with hymns, among the favourites being 'Eternal Father strong to save', which has the appropriate refrain 'O hear us when we cry to thee for those in peril on the sea', 'Will your anchor hold' and 'O God our help in ages past'. Some prefer to end the service with the song 'Home from the sea'.

The dedication of a lifeboat to God for the purpose of saving life mirrors the sacred object of the institution, whose first priority, from the date when it was founded, is the preservation of human life from shipwreck. So how and when did the service of dedication originate?

Origin of the service of dedication

The period between 1853 and 1875 saw a rapid expansion of the number of lifeboats around the coasts of the British Isles from thirty-four in 1853 to 250 in 1875. Even by 1860, when the number of lifeboats managed by the RNLI amounted to 101 boats, it was described as 'the largest life saving fleet the world had ever seen'[3] and it continued to expand after that. Initially, some lifeboats were run locally by a trust or other organisation outside the management structure of the RNLI, but gradually even these came under its central umbrella. Much of this remarkably rapid expansion in a period of just over twenty years was funded by private donations made by philanthropic individuals or groups, this giving being actively promoted by the RNLI who emphasised the sacred object of saving life for which the institution was founded. By 1869 the generosity of the public was such that the RNLI no longer required the annual contributions to its funds that it had been receiving from the Board of Trade.

The religious element in the ceremony for the inauguration of new lifeboats was first seen in the 1860s and reflected the emphasis at that time on the sacred object of the institution to save life; there are examples of prayers and blessing being offered by the clergy in 1862 and in 1863: upon the launch of *The Constance* on 13 November 1862 at Tynemouth 'after quoting a few appropriate verses from the Psalms of David' Archdeacon Bland offered a prayer.[4] At the Launch of *The Hollon* at Filey in Yorkshire after reading verses from Psalm 117, the Rev. T.N. Jackson offered the following prayer of blessing: 'We implore thy favourable blessing on this instrument for saving life.'[5] In 1869 at the inauguration of the first lifeboat at Salcombe, Archdeacon Downall read a prayer, after which a choir sang the hymn 'These men see the works of our lord and the wonders in the deep'. The new lifeboat, gaily decorated with flags and drawn on its carriage by six horses, was then named by Miss Durant, daughter of the donor. She said: 'May this lifeboat realise the object of its institution. I send it forth on its mission of mercy before the tempest driven and shipwrecked mariners under the name of the "Rescue" and I ask you all to join in the prayer, "God bless the Rescue".' The boat was then launched.[6]

From these varied expressions of religious sentiment it was only a short step to the concept of a lifeboat being formally dedicated, by a member of the clergy, to God's service for the purpose of saving life. At the launch of *The Rescue* in Liverpool on 26 January 1863 the Rev. R. Funell was asked to offer up a prayer for the safety and success of the new lifeboat. He used the words:

> … mercifully grant, we beseech thee that the vessel which we this day dedicate to thy service may through thy help, be instrumental in saving many precious souls.[7]

When the new lifeboat *Clemency* was launched at Plymouth on 31 May 1873, the *Southern Reporter*[8] recorded 'the ceremony of dedication being performed by the Bishop of Exeter', but no further details of that ceremony were given by the newspaper. However, three years later there was a very clear example of a service of dedication.

On 24 May 1876 a new lifeboat, propelled by ten oars, double banked, which had been donated to Torquay by Mrs Mary Brundret of Manchester, was paraded through the town on a carriage drawn by six horses belonging to the local brewery. The procession was headed by a band from HMS *Britannia*. At the harbour slipway it is reported that the Venerable Archdeacon Earle conducted a 'Service of Dedication'.[9] The local archives of the lifeboat station record that 'in a short address [he] exhorted the crew of the lifeboat to be at all times ready to perform their duty' and then that 'he conducted a "Service of Dedication"'. He started with the words: 'Your Committee have wished that the life of this lifeboat be dedicated in prayer to Almighty God.' There followed a religious service that included the Lord's Prayer, Psalms, the Hymn 'Eternal Father Strong to Save' and a blessing of the lifeboat men and the new lifeboat 'May God bless you and the boat', most of these elements being included in today's standard form of service of dedication. After this religious service ended, Mrs Mary Brundret formally named the lifeboat *Mary Brundret*, as the boat was launched, sliding gracefully into the water.[10]

What can be safely concluded from these contemporaneous press reports is that the concept of 'dedication' of a new lifeboat for the purpose of saving life led by a member of the clergy, whether it took the form of a 'prayer', 'celebration' or a 'service', was by the 1860s to 1870s firmly established in the consciousness of lifeboat men and rapidly thereafter became a firm tradition. In the 1880s there are many further examples reported in the press of a 'dedication service', 'dedication prayer' or 'prayer of dedication' for new lifeboats.

While more research is needed to reach a final view, the evidence currently available suggests that the introduction of a service of dedication of a new lifeboat was not the result of any central decision by the RNLI General Committee. Like so many ship launching and naming traditions, it looks as if the ceremony of 'dedication' just evolved at local lifeboat stations and was gradually adopted more widely. A fairly thorough, but not exhaustive, review of the minutes of the General Committee between 1857 and 1877, which coincided with the period in which these early examples of 'dedication' of lifeboats occurred, has not found any circular being sent to local stations to require a service of dedication by a member of the clergy. Perhaps also of significance is the fact that the report on the launch of the *Mary Brundret* in 1876 tells us that Archdeacon Earle advised those attending that he was conducting the service of dedication because the local lifeboat committee wanted it: 'Your Committee have wished that the life of this lifeboat be dedicated in prayer to Almighty.' There was no suggestion from the Archdeacon or in the local reports that this wish was due to any directive of the General Committee of the RNLI.

It is also relevant to consider whether the introduction of the religious service upon the launch of naval ships in 1875[11] had any bearing on the introduction of the service of dedication of lifeboats. As we have noted, the earliest known examples of 'dedication' of lifeboats date back to the

1860s and so they predate, if only by a few years, the formal introduction of the religious service at the launch of naval ships in 1875. This appears to rule out any theory that the origin of the service of dedication for lifeboats was a direct result of the introduction in 1875 of the religious service upon the launch of naval ships. It seems, therefore, that it was a matter of coincidence that they both started at more or less the same time, the dedication of lifeboats evolving through the practise and tradition of local lifeboat stations and the religious service at the launch of naval ships as a result of an order issued by the First Lord of the Admiralty.

As we have seen from the account of *Mary Brundret*, at the end of the service of dedication the new lifeboat is then named and launched. The sponsor is typically selected not by the RNLI or local station but by the donor. In the same way that the tradition since the nineteenth century of ships being named by a lady did not exclude gentlemen as sponsors, so too, although the sponsor of a new lifeboat is frequently a lady, this is not the invariable rule. Apart from male members of the Royal family such as HRH the Duke of Kent, currently President of the RNLI, a position he has held since 1969, a male sponsor related to the donor is often chosen. A recent example of a man being the sponsor is the naming of *John D. Spicer* at Porthdinllaen in Wales on 28 September 2014 by the well-known broadcaster David Dimbleby, who was an executor of the estate of the donor, the John D. Spencer's estate, after whom the Tamar-class lifeboat was named. The hymns on this occasion were in Welsh.

A community event

In the nineteenth century shipping companies were, for understandable reasons, some of the earliest supporters of the lifeboats. This example was followed in a small way in 1989 when the maritime law firm Sinclair Roche & Temperley donated an inshore lifeboat [ILB] to the RNLI to mark the firm's jubilee. On 23 September 1989 several partners of the firm, including the author, attended the colourful naming ceremony and service of dedication of a new 'Atlantic 21'-class ILB at the small Yorkshire village of Staithes. After the service of dedication, Mrs Vera Morris, wife of the then senior partner, John Morris, poured champagne over the bow of the lifeboat, naming her *Ellis Sinclair* in honour of the firm's founder before passing the remainder of the bottle to the crew. After the ceremony and the ceremonial launch the new lifeboat was taken on a trip to demonstrate her capability and two of the donor's representatives (including the author) were privileged to be invited on board. The guests were then entertained to a traditional Staithes' teatime spread. Music was provided by the North Skelton Teesside BSC silver band. It was a memorable day with most of the village's inhabitants participating enthusiastically in the event. In such communities on the wild North Sea coast the lifeboat is a central and important part of village life.

On the subject of sharing of the ceremonial bottle, Nathan Jones has again added some colourful detail:

> Typically this sharing of the Champagne only occurs at the naming of ILBs, for All Weather Lifeboats we 'break' the entire bottle over the boat rendering it undrinkable, but the construction of ILBs means we cannot break bottles so adopt an open and pour approach which provides the crew with an opportunity to limit how much the boat gets!'

Champagne is not always the christening bottle and accounts of christenings of lifeboats in the annals include bottles of wine and port, while in Scotland they prefer to bless their lifeboats with whisky from a *Quaich*, Nathan Jones adding: 'This means that the boat will normally see a dram whilst the crew retain the bottle!' The drinking by the lifeboat crew from the ceremonial bottle at the service of dedication and naming of a lifeboat is in some respects resonant of the 'standing cup' ceremony where, it will be recalled, the sponsor drank from the ceremonial bottle before the name of the ship was called out.[12]

The same central importance of a lifeboat to the local community experienced in Staithes is also to be found in the little fishing ports and communities of Brittany in northern France. There are colourful accounts of the 'benediction' of new lifeboats to be found in the *Annales du Sauvetage* – Annals of Lifesaving – from local lifeboat stations. The ceremonies for the launch of ships in France, with features that are similar to a child's baptism have, in general, already been described[13] and it is sufficient to add here only a few further comments. In France the lifeboat to be launched is typically decorated with flowers and garlands of green foliage. A Roman Catholic priest, sometimes more than one, is always present. The priest often gives a *petit discours* – short address – before pronouncing a blessing on the lifeboat and the lifeboatmen. At the blessing of the lifeboat *Benoit Champy* at Cayeux on 3 March 1901 Abbe Roux's theme was that despite the progress of modern science, man is not the absolute master of the elements and man's strength is trifling against the wind of the storm. The lifeboatmen, therefore, look for reassurance in their dangerous work from the prayers that are offered in the religious service of benediction and the support of the local community.

After *ceremonies liturgiques* – a religious service – beside the new lifeboat, it is launched. The religious service for a lifeboat in France often includes the chant 'Ave Maris Stella' – Hail Star of the Ocean – a plain song Vespers chant to Mary, thought to date back to the ninth century. At some ceremonies the religious aspects are mixed with ancient pagan rites when *le ble* – corn – and *le sel* – salt – are sprinkled on the boat, as symbols of prosperity and preservation. It is not clear from reading these accounts whether giving the new lifeboat a name is part of this ceremony, the emphasis being rather on the religious element with the blessing by the clergy at the centre of the ceremony. It is usual for the godmother, after the benediction by the clergy, to distribute bags of sweet almonds (*dragees du bapteme*) to the lifeboatmen and any children present at the ceremony. This distribution recalls the similar tradition in France practised at the baptism of children.

The ceremony for the launch of a lifeboat in France, in typical French style, ends, with lunch or dinner, formal speeches and toasts of champagne to the lifeboat, their crew and the donors, and sometimes with dancing. In an account of the benediction of a new lifeboat *Ernest Crevant-Durant* for the fishing community at Trevignon in the Finistère Department of Brittany on 8 September 1926, the day's festivities ended with sailors, local men and women dancing *de joyeuses gavottes*, a local folk dance, in the port. Trevignon is on a dangerous stretch of coastline and, as in Staithes, the benediction of a new lifeboat in a small French port is very much a community event where the entire population of the village is involved, emphasising the importance of the lifeboat not only to the lives of the fishermen but to the whole community.

Although the naming and launch ceremony for any new ship is a special moment for all sailors, this moment at the launch of a new lifeboat has special poignance for lifeboatmen. They know only too well that they will be called upon to put their own lives at risk to save others and the harsh forces of nature to which their new lifeboat will be subjected. The essence of the service of dedication of a new lifeboat in the UK or the religious service at the blessing of a new lifeboat in France is the same: to ask for divine protection for their new lifeboat and themselves as they go about their selfless, but dangerous, work.

Chapter 16

Multiple Launches

Helen of Troy – myth or fact?

'Was this the face that launch'd a thousand ships and burnt the topless towers of Ilium.'

These famous and romantic lines from Christopher Marlowe's *Doctor Faustus* (1604) conjure in our minds an image of Helen, in Greek mythology said to be the most beautiful woman in the world, and the energy she inspired in Greek warriors to construct and launch the huge Achaean fleet that sailed to rescue her from Troy. Homer appears to add substance to the story with his colourful and impressively detailed description of the twenty-nine contingents from nearly 190 towns across the Hellenic world that made up the fleet. In total there were 1,186 ships and, if the Boeotian figure of 120 men per ship is taken, this means a total force of 142,320 men. There were squadrons of 'black ships' (being ships either painted or smeared in pitch), 'hollow ships', 'ships with crimson painted bows', 'trim ships', 'fast ships' and 'beaked sea going ships'.[1] The purpose of the catalogue was to represent the Trojan war as a pan-Hellenic exercise and to emphasize the large size of the squadrons involved in the expedition. Most commentators agree that the catalogue is myth; and doubts have been expressed as to whether a fleet remotely approaching the size of Homer's catalogue could ever in fact have been built at that time.[2] Nonetheless, the story remains a colourful introduction to the subject of multiple launches.

Ships, ships and more ships

Even if the Trojan War is myth, it does serve to remind us of the simple lesson from military history that if a nation wishes to fight a war against an enemy situated across the seas it will need ships, ships and more ships to transport its men and material to the battlefield. Most of the examples of multiple launches are, therefore, to be found in the context of war where, if there is a battle to be fought across the seas, mass production and multiple launching of ships becomes a necessity.

The launch of Caesar's fleet to invade Britain

Although we have occasional reports of large fleets being constructed in the ancient world, the early sources are largely silent on multiple launches. That said, in 54 BC, in order to mount his second incursion into Britain, Julius Caesar assembled a massive fleet in Gaul somewhere – the exact site is debated – near *Gesoriacum*, the Gallic name for the town later called *Bononia* that we now know as *Boulogne*. There were 200 or so ships left over from his earlier reconnaissance trip to Britain in 55 BC, which it is assumed were hauled ashore for the winter to prevent the timbers rotting.

Valuable lessons had been learnt from that earlier expedition. When Caesar left Gaul at the end of that campaign he gave detailed instructions on the design of a further 600 transport ships to be constructed over the winter. From Caesar's own journals[3] we know that, in order to simplify loading and beaching, these ships were to be of somewhat lower freeboard than was commonly used in the Mediterranean so as to allow for heavy cargoes including numerous pack animals, and to be broader in the beam. They were to be propelled by sail and oar. When Caesar returned to Gaul in the spring he went around all the winter quarters and learned that, as a result of the great efforts of his soldiers, about 600 ships of the type he had requested plus twenty-eight men-of-war had been constructed; and he found that 'they lacked but little to make them ready for launching in a few days'.[4] It was a remarkable achievement to have built so many ships in a period of some six months. Caesar himself warmly commended the achievement of his men and gave instructions that the ships assemble at *Portum Itium*. The reference in the text to winter quarters in the plural and the command that the fleet assemble at *Portum Itium* suggests that the ships were not built in one place but in a number of locations, probably in the rivers and creeks of Gaul as well as the Roman dockyard at *Gesoriacum*. Caesar's journals unfortunately do not describe the ship launch arrangements but, in order to have such a large number of vessels, which he described as 'lacked but little to make them ready for launching', assembled in one place at short notice, multiple launches at the shipbuilding sites would have been required and undoubtedly took place.

Scholars have debated where *Portum Itium* was located, the most likely choice being between the ancient lake of *Saint Omer*, which could have provided a basin for such a large fleet, and *Gesoriacum*. When the fleet finally set sail in early July, Caesar's journal tells us that it totalled over 800 ships consisting of the 200 ships left over from the previous year, the 600 new cargo ships, the twenty-eight new warships and some private vessels. They embarked five legions – about 27,000 men – 2,000 cavalry and all the support baggage and provisions that inevitably accompanies an invading army. For the Britons, standing on the cliffs opposite, the sight of a fleet of 800 ships, moving up the Channel under oar and sail, laden with the armour of Rome and, we can imagine, with their weapons glistening in the early morning summer sun, must indeed have been awesome. The whole fleet reached the shore of Britain about midday but no enemy was to be seen.[5]

Galley production in fifteenth- and sixteenth-century Venice

Fast forwarding, we turn to the galley assembly line of fifteenth century Venice for a concrete and well-documented example of multiple launching. Within a short distance of St Mark's square, at the very heart of Venice, is the *Arsenale*. The name is a corruption of the Arabic *dar as – sina a*, meaning a house of industry or manufacturing shop. This gives a good clue as its purpose: a factory to build, launch, arm and provision galleys in such quantity as was required from time to time by the Venetian state to meet the perceived threats of the day. Any visitor to the *Arsenale* today will be immediately struck by the immense 50ft high brick walls topped with imposing battlements that surround it. At the main gate, the so called *Porta Magna*, three stone lions stand guard. Apart from this land entrance the only other way in during medieval times was by water; the narrow water entrance that passes by the *Porta Magna* is guarded by a gate across the canal (see Illustration No. 39).

The wider entrance in the north-east corner at the *Canale Porta Nueva* was only created in the early nineteenth century; it is far away from the prying eyes in St Mark's square and is only accessible by boat. So, in the fifteenth and sixteenth centuries when galley production was at its height, the *Porta Magna* and canal entrance beside it were the only ways in and out. This made for a secure area of some 110 acres of workshops surrounded by water. Even today, when standing outside the high walls, there is an aura of secrecy and a certain foreboding as to what may be happening within.

In the early days, in the twelfth century, the Venetian state was mainly concerned to have a secure place for the storage of weapons and ships. However, in order for the Venetian merchants to prosper, it became essential that their trade routes should be made safe from the threats of pirates and the rising challenge from the Turkish fleet. This required the building of an increasingly large fleet of war galleys. This demand was met by the *Arsenale*, which by 1500 was the largest industrial complex in Europe responsible for manufacturing all the maritime apparatus of the Venetian state. It was considered to be the foundation of the power of Venice, the heart of the state, the secret source of its maritime power and was even mentioned in Dante's *Inferno* (Canto xxi).

There were two main sorts of galley, the 'great galleys' (*galea grosse*) and the 'light galleys' (*galea sottile*). The light galleys, being more manoeuvrable, were the main war galleys. Although primarily sailing ships, they used oars as their main means of propulsion.

The factory in the Arsenale

The factory behind the walls was gradually expanded to meet the demand from the state for more and more galleys. Soon not just storage but docks and covered sheds were needed to build and outfit the fleet, so that the work could continue regardless of the weather. Some galleys were built by private merchants but gradually the state took on itself all the galley building in Venice. This was facilitated by the construction in 1473 of the so-called New Arsenal, an additional factory and storage area behind the walls. This enabled the state to construct and store under cover a reserve fleet with which to meet, whenever needed, the increased threat to Venice from the Turks.

There were three stages of production of the galley: first, the frame was built by the carpenters; second, the planking was fastened into place and the cabin and superstructure built; and third, when called into service the galley's seams were filled with tar and pitch, the hull covered with tar or grease, the galley launched, the deck fittings fastened into place, rigging and mooring provided and oars and armament given out to the crew.[6]

In 1525 the state required '50 galleys – to be kept on land fully built-in readiness to be caulked, launched, rigged and armed. Their masts, spars, shrouds, sails, anchors, oars, thwarts, foot braces and all their deck furnishings and arms to be kept in readiness, each piece in the warehouse assigned to it.'[7]

Stored on land ready to be launched

The significant point to note from this and subsequent directives from the Senate was that the reserve galleys were to be kept *on land*. The innovation in naval strategic thinking was the concept that, in order to have a fleet in reserve, there was no need to caulk, launch and equip all the galleys that had been constructed. Wooden ships, once launched, inevitably deteriorate and then need to be repaired, recaulked and relaunched. The better solution was that after construction the hulls be dry stored on land under cover ready at short notice to be caulked, launched and equipped to meet the threat of the day. Giving each unlaunched galley a number and keeping its mast, oars and equipment stored in a separate shed with the same number speeded up the availability of these galleys for operational use. In this way the unlaunched galleys held in the reserve on land could nonetheless be treated as part of the available fleet at the disposal of the state, with the added advantage that such galleys stored on land would not be deteriorating in condition before they were needed.

Multiple launches and fit out in assembly line

A painted sign made in 1517 under the steward of carpenters of ships of the *Arsenale* (Illustration No. 40) shows various stages of galley construction in the *Arsenale*. Of particular interest is the completed galley in the top right-hand corner being dry stored under cover and held in reserve, illustrating that, with completed galleys kept in store ready to be launched at short notice, the Venetian state had a fleet in reserve. The maintenance of a permanent reserve fleet in this way gave Venice an edge over other naval powers of the day.

The rapid assembly line fit out and provisioning was the second stroke of genius. *The equipment was not brought to the galley, but the galley to the equipment.* From an eyewitness account of 1436 we know that each galley, once launched, was towed in the water along an arcade of stores and at each arch or window different items of equipment were installed or handed out, so that once the galley reached the end of the line it was fully equipped, crewed and provisioned.

Pero Tarfur, the Spanish traveller, in his *Travels 1435–1439*,[8] recorded:

> And as one enters the gate [of the Arsenale] there is a great street on either side with the sea in the middle, and on one side are windows opening out of the houses of the arsenal, and the same on the other side, and out came a galley towed by a boat and from the windows they handed out to them, from one the cordage, from another the bread, from another the arms, from another the balistas and mortar and so from all sides everything which was required, and when the galley had reached the end of the street and the men required were on board together with the complement of oars and she was equipped from end to end. In this manner came out ten galleys, fully armed, between the hours of three and nine.

The galley was ready then for action to be rowed out of the *Arsenale*, using the canal exit by the *Magna Porta* to join the Grand Canal. The key to the success of the rapid assembly line was specialisation and quality control. There were separate units for rope and sail makers, forges, gunpowder mills and store houses for every component in the process, each manned by its own team of specialist craftsmen. Quality inspection and control was exercised and poor workmanship by any craftsman resulted in dismissal.

At its peak some 1,500 to 2,000 men were employed in the *Arsenale*. The management of the work was under the control of a committee consisting of the Admiral of the Arsenal and four foremen in charge of the four main specialist skills: a carpenter, a caulker, a mast maker and an oar maker. The Admiral was less concerned with the production of hulls and more with the assemblage of the galleys. He took personal charge of the launching, stepping of the masts and outfitting.

Speed of the fit out

The speed of the process, launch followed by the outfitting and provisioning, amazed visitors. They were impressed too by the immensity of the industrial complex of the *Arsenale* and the orderly arrangement of war materials and building and out fitting gear. The story is told frequently that when Henry III, the King of France, visited Venice in 1574 a galley was assembled, launched and completely armed for his entertainment within one hour. Frederic Lane comments that: 'Since the exploit was designed as an entertainment it seems likely that the galley was launched in the royal presence but it may well be believed that many preparations, including practically all the caulking, had been performed before his arrival.'[9] This entertainment of the French King may well be the basis for the frequently made assertion that the Venetian *Arsenale* could build, launch, and arm a galley in a single day. What is nearer the mark is that a galley taken out of dry store in the *Arsenale* and, once caulked, could then be launched, rigged, armed and provisioned in one day.

Standardisation?

Although the outfitting was effected via an assembly line, it would be wrong to assume that the whole production of galleys was standardised. That was not in the minds of the state when the *Arsenale* was established. The initial concern was safe storage of arms and ships. The shipwrights and craftsmen continued to practise their skills individually in the design of the hulls. At the outset there was no thought of standardisation of the hull design. However, some standardisation did occur gradually: for example in 1516 'it was ordered that all stern posts of light galleys be built on the same design so that each rudder would not have to be especially fitted to its stern post but a single type of rudder would do for all the galleys'.[10] It was also suggested in the sixteenth century that all galleys should be built to one design selected by the foreman. Standardisation of masts, spars, benches and other deck fittings being part of the outfitting assembly line occurred earlier and, in order to achieve this, manufacture of these parts were not given to outside craftsmen but also concentrated inside the *Arsenale*.

Distribution of daily wine ration

The start and end of the day's work at the *Arsenale* were announced by the ringing of the *maragona*, the carpenter's bell from the *campanile* in St Mark's square. The half-day was the occasion for the distribution of a daily wine ration to the entire workforce. The *vino puro* was watered down but the wine ration *brevanda ordinaria* was intended to stimulate and nourish workers, and it was evidently safer than drinking water. However, on launch of a galley a stronger ration of wine was distributed: 'The launching of a new galley called for celebrations which included what the Patroni themselves referred to as "the good and ancient customs" of distributing twenty litres of wine (vino puro) to each work crew of ten masters – after which work was no doubt over for the rest of the day'![11] On days where there were multiple launches a great quantity of wine must have been consumed!

Galleys built in the *Arsenale* were launched bow first from the covered building where they were constructed or stored and were blessed in a simple ceremony as they went into the water; and at that moment they were also named. Galleys used as warships were 'public ships' and given names by the Senate. The names for merchant galleys were given by captains and private owners during peacetime but if they were used in war by the state they were then renamed using the feminine name of the captain or ship owner or the island where he came from – for example a galley owned by (say) Captain 'Gabrielli' would have been renamed *Gabriella*.[12]

Special status of the Arsenalotti

The workers in the *Arsenale*, the *Arsenalotti*, no doubt in recognition of their important contribution to the security and prosperity of Venice, enjoyed special status in Venetian society. They were a privileged group of workers. They rowed the *Bucintoro* carrying the Doge on Ascension Day for the special Marriage of the Sea ceremony.[13] After inauguration of a new Doge he was carried on their shoulders around the piazza. They had an honoured place in any processions. As trusted and loyal servants of the state they were also responsible, under the command of the *Paṭron di Guardia*, for the security of the *Arsenale* and the surrounding district and manned the watchtowers round the 2-mile perimeter wall. Nothing could be more central to Venice's safety than the security of the state's shipyard and this responsibility was entrusted to the *Arsenalotti*.

The Reserve Fleet

The greatest achievement of the *Arsenale* was the concept of the reserve fleet stored under cover but ready to be caulked, launched and fitted out at short notice. When the Senate gave the command to deploy, the speed of the process for multiple launching and assembly line fitting out was remarkable for a small medieval state and unique for its time. It was not to be repeated in any comparable fashion until the production of the 'Liberty ships' in the Second World War.

Hog Island – an assembly facility for mass production of merchant ships in the First World War

Before we examine the remarkable story of the multiple launches of the 'Liberty ship' we need to make a quick diversion to Hog Island, which in 1917 was a little-known desolate island on the River Delaware at Philadelphia. Here at the end of the First World War at a newly created shipyard there was conducted an experiment in standardised shipbuilding and mass production of merchant ships. It was here that the US learned how to build large ships quickly on a grand scale from prefabricated parts, a lesson that was to be so valuable two decades later.

When the US entered the First World War on 6 April 1917 it needed ships to transport men and material across the Atlantic to France. A shortage of merchant shipping was one of the factors that determined why the US remained neutral for so long. In order to maintain an army overseas it was not just the initial transportation for which ships were needed but a sufficient number to keep the army fed, clothed and supplied with arms and shells – and this to be achieved in the face of the mounting losses to shipping due to German U-boat activity. Ten days after entering the war the US Government created the Emergency Fleet Corporation to build, own and operate a merchant fleet. In addition to the requisition of existing shipbuilding facilities, a number of new shipyards were created. The largest of these new shipyards was at Hog Island, where in September 1917 American International Shipbuilding Corporation was hired to build and operate a facility for the mass construction of merchant ships.

Assembly Line Production

The concept behind Hog Island was a novel one; unlike a traditional shipyard it was to be an assembly facility with a large percentage of the parts of each ship being constructed elsewhere, which were then transported to Hog Island to be put together. There were two basic standard designs of ship: Type A was a cargo carrier and Type B was a troop transporter. It was the first shipyard to use the assembly line process on such a large scale. It was an enormous enterprise but those constructing the shipyard had the advantage that they were starting with a blank sheet, so they could design its layout in the best way to achieve an efficient assembly system. All ship parts and other material on arrival at Hog Island were carefully classified and located so as to systemise the assembly process. The shipyard was constructed in just ten months and occupied 846 acres. There were 250 buildings and by 10 June 1918 there were an impressive fifty slipways, stretching 1¼ miles along the Delaware, making Hog Island at that time the largest shipyard in the world. In order to appreciate the extent of the shipbuilding slips, it will be helpful to look at Illustration No. 42.

It shows in the foreground the extensive lunch arrangements, with tables decorated in stars and stripes and gentlemen dressed festively in boater hats and ladies in white dresses, upon the occasion of the launch of the first ship on 5 August 1918. It also clearly shows the extensive lines of building slips, fifty in total, so far as the eye can see, ready for multiple construction and launching.

Whilst Hog Island was gearing up to bring all its fifty launch ways into full production, shipbuilding was being carried out at other yards across America to meet the pressing demand. Edward N. Hurley, Chairman of the Shipping Board, was instructed by President Woodrow Wilson to 'Go to the limit' to ensure that there were sufficient ships to build a bridge to France to sustain the American and Allied armies.[14] On Independence Day, 4 July 1918 he encouraged the shipyards across America to make a special effort to celebrate that day not with fireworks but with the launch of as many ships as possible. His target was a round 100 but in the end ninety-five new ships were launched that day. That certainly was multiple launching!

Back to Hog Island: at its peak 35,000 workers were employed there, including 650 women. Most of the workers had no factory experience but were trained on the spot. The initial order from the US Government was for 180 ships but the Armistice, declared on 11 November 1918, took effect before the shipyard could reach its full production potential of fifty or more ships being constructed simultaneously and another twenty-eight being fitted out. Edith Bulling Wilson, the wife of US President Woodrow Wilson, was given the honour of providing names for the ships launched at Hog Island and she chose to give them native American names. The first ship to be completed, SS *Quistconck* – the local Lenape name for Hog Island – was christened and launched by the First Lady on 5 August 1918. Illustration No. 41 shows President Woodrow Wilson on the right of the launching platform waving his hat towards the ship as it enters the water with Mrs Wilson dressed in white next to him.

Within three minutes of that launch the keel for another ship had been laid in the same berth. In 1919 there was a frenzy of launches. To mark Memorial Day on 30 May 1919 five freighters, totalling 39,125 tons, were launched in just over forty-eight minutes. On 20 July 1920 seven Class 'A' cargo carriers were launched in one hour twenty-three minutes.

Out of the order of 180 ships a total of 122 ships, including twelve troop carriers, were built. They were ugly but well-built with good capacity and speed and became known as 'Hog Islanders'. None of the 122 ships built there were ready to take part in the First World War. By 1920 the 35,000 workforce had been reduced to 3,500, with shipbuilding ceasing on the site in 1921. In the meantime Hog Island had become an air force facility, the site subsequently being dedicated to Philadelphia Municipal Airport, which now covers much of the former shipyard.

Even if the ships built at Hog Island were completed too late to play an active part in the hostilities, the significance of the creation of a new fifty-slip shipyard would not have been lost on the Germans.[15] It would have been clear to the German high command that with increasing American shipbuilding capacity more and more ships and, therefore, more and more American reinforcements could be brought into the war. This was a factor in bringing about an early Armistice.

The expense of creating Hog Island was enormous. The initial estimate to build the shipyard was US $35 million but by the time of the launch of the first ship the total had escalated to US $65 million. This huge cost created controversy in the minds of the American public, especially when seen against the delivery of only 122 ships. Hindsight is so often a cruel judge in these matters. There were Congressional investigations. There were allegations of fraud or financial misdeeds but none were found, only waste.[16] The creation of Hog Island could not be justified in times of peace but in times of war against the background of the large losses of merchant tonnage due to enemy submarines and the urgent need for replacement ships, the creation at Hog Island of a facility for ship construction, using an assembly of prefabricated parts on such a huge scale, could be justified; and valuable lessons about mass production shipbuilding techniques were learned that were put to good use when in the Second World War the cry for 'ships, ships and more ships' was again heard.

The birth of the 'Liberty ship'

Among the many historic ships at the Maritime National Historical Park in San Francisco is the SS *Jeremiah O'Brien*. She is one of the 2,710 'Liberty ships' built in haste in the Second World War to support the Allied war effort and 'sent forth with the belief that if she completed even one voyage or delivered one cargo she would have already fulfilled her mission'.[17] In the event she not only survived the rigours of the North Atlantic convoys in winter but made over ten runs across the Channel to the D-Day beaches ferrying troops, equipment and explosives. She was the only ship from the D-Day armada to return to Normandy in June 1994 for the fiftieth anniversary of the invasion. Many of the 'Liberty ships' were altered after the war but she has the distinction of being 'the last unaltered Liberty in existence'.[18] What most struck the author on his visit to the ship was the immense size of her holds and, therefore, the size of the contribution that even one completed voyage would have made to the Allied cause.

Parentage of the 'Liberty ship'

SS *Jeremiah O'Brien* was launched in June 1943 at New England Shipbuilding Corporation at the very peak of 'Liberty ship' mass production at eighteen shipyards across America. By then three such ships were being completed every day. It is an extraordinary story. The true parentage of the 'Liberty ship' is not to be found in America but across the Atlantic in north-east England at Sunderland. It was largely due to the efforts of one man. Robert Cyril Thompson joined the family shipbuilding firm Joseph L. Thompson in 1930. During the depressed years of 1930–34, during which there were no launches at his yard, he led a team to develop a hull form that, with improved design of engine, would produce a more efficient and economic service using less power.[19] The first ship built to the new design was the *Embassage* ordered by Hall Brothers of Newcastle, launched in 1935 with a deadweight capacity of 9,100 tons at the comparatively modest cost of £95,000. The second prototype was the *Dorington Court*, 10ft longer and 18in wider than *Embassage*, built for Court Line of London in six months and delivered in May 1939, incorporating a new type of engine developed by North Eastern Marine Engineering Company.[20]

After the outbreak of war the characteristics of these prototypes, both of which were the subject of repeat orders, their low price and swiftness of construction caught the attention of the Admiralty in London, who were becoming concerned at the large losses of merchant shipping at the hands of the U-boats.[21] There was an immediate need for replacement merchant tonnage to be built in large volume at low cost to sustain the war effort. There was insufficient capacity in British yards for construction of such a volume of cargo ships in addition to the naval orders. Their thoughts turned to the possibility of having merchant ships built in the US; and they sent for Cyril Thompson.

On 11 September 1940 he received his letter of appointment from the Admiralty marked 'SECRET' to lead a Technical Merchant Shipbuilding Mission to the US 'to endeavour to obtain at the earliest possible moment the delivery of Merchant tonnage from USA shipyards at the rate per annum of about 60 vessels of the Tramp type each averaging about 10,000 deadweight and of 10.5 knots service speed …'[22] Financial perimeters for the order were also set, including the capital cost on new or extended yards, if necessary. Thompson was further instructed to ascertain what types, sizes and numbers of merchant ships could be built in American shipyards for delivery by 30 June 1941, 31 December 1941 and 30 June 1942 and to approve the various shipyards as suitable and capable of delivering this work. In other words what was needed from the US was an emergency supply of a large fleet of merchant ships. It was not stated that the ships were to be built to the British design, but Thompson did take with him a number of drawings of ships designed and built by his firm. He also took with him Harry Hunter of North-Eastern Marine Engineering Company, who had designed the engines for the prototypes.

Henry Kaiser's experience of production line techniques

On arrival Thompson and his team spent three weeks visiting shipyards across America. It rapidly became clear that there were no American ship designs suitable for Britain's requirements and that there was very little spare shipyard capacity for this huge order. Into this difficult situation stepped Henry J. Kaiser, head of a group of West Coast companies and working with the Bath Iron Works at Maine and the Todd Corporation, an established shipbuilder. What was key was Kaiser's experience of 'production line techniques and prefabrication methods' in major land construction projects and his enthusiasm to carry out the order.

An immediate decision for the Admiralty was the use of welding in the construction method, which at that time was being used widely in American shipyards and not riveting as provided in the British specification. The British design for the hull based on the specifications for Thompson's Hull 611, which was later to be named *Empire Liberty*, was adopted, as was the engine design of North-Eastern Marine Engineering Company. Permission was granted too by the US Government for the creation of two new shipyards, one at Portland, Maine, and the other at Richmond, California. These new sites had the space to accommodate mass production techniques. By 6 December it was time for Thompson to return to the Admiralty to report on progress. On the return voyage he had the misfortune that his ship was torpedoed – rather underlining the need for additional tonnage – but he managed to rescue his briefcase containing all the mission's valuable papers and to scramble into a lifeboat. After rowing for nine hours, he and his fellow passengers were fortunately rescued by a passing freighter.

Thompson's conclusion was that there were insufficient building ways in existence in the US to meet the demand for a high volume of merchant tonnage in addition to naval ships. New shipyards would need to be created. Churchill had not forgotten the lessons learned at Hog Island in the First World War and it is significant that on 8 December 1940 he wrote to President Roosevelt: 'Looking into the future it would seem that production on a scale comparable to the Hog Island scheme of the last war ought to be faced for 1942.'[23] In other words, what was needed was mass production of ships based on a standard design.

The result was that on 20 December 1940, only three months after Cyril Thompson had first set out to America, the contracts with the Kaiser–Todd-Bath consortium were signed and the huge 'Liberty ship' production programme was under way. The construction of both shipyards was completed in a very short time and the keel of the first Richmond ship was laid on 14 April 1941. The initial order for the British using Cyril Thompson's design was for sixty ships at a cost of $96 million, these ships to be purchased by the British Government in cash and not leased.

Mass production using a standard design

The US Maritime Commission initially hesitated over whether to adopt the same British design for the construction of its own emergency fleet. The oversupply of the Hog Islanders at the end of the last war was remembered. There was concern that at the end of the conflict they could be left with a large fleet of slow, unsophisticated ships that, while suitable for emergency wartime use, had no long-term economic purpose in peacetime. In the end the argument based on the need for mass production using a standard design prevailed and on 29 January 1941 the decision was made to use the British design for the American emergency fleet as well but with some modifications. This decision was based on the realisation that the British had given much thought to the need for a design that made quick construction possible and the need for a standard ship that could be built quickly, cheaply and simply in a mass production system. The initial order was for 200 ships in the American emergency ship programme, which were to be constructed and delivered before the end of 1942, in addition to the sixty ships already ordered by the British.

By the autumn of 1941 work began on another seven shipyards to build 'Liberty ships', the peak of production being reached in 1943 when eighteen shipyards were involved in the work, 'containing 210 slipways with a workforce which swelled to over 650,000 people by mid-1943 ...'

'By training each worker in one or two tasks, using sub-assembly methods to the utmost, applying mass production technology, and building a series of identical vessels, enormous savings in slipway building times were achieved.'[24]

Origin of the name 'Liberty ship' and 'Liberty Fleet Day'

Like its predecessor the Hog Islander, the new ship was no beauty. When in 1941 President Roosevelt first saw the profile plan of these ships it is said that he commented: 'Admiral, I think this ship will do us very well. She'll carry a good load. She isn't much to look at though, is she? A real ugly duckling.'[25] Whether or not he actually used these words, this is said to be the origin of the 'Ugly Duckling' epithet frequently applied. Over time the reliability of these ships was appreciated and they became the workhorse of the Allied fleet. They were literally the ships that won the war. The origin of the name 'Liberty ship' is more definitely sourced to a letter dated 19 July 1941 which Cyril Thompson wrote to the Admiralty seeking their approval to the name of Hull 611 then ready for launch at Thompson's yard:

> In view of the fact that this vessel is the parent type for those building in Canada and USA, we think that special consideration should be given to its name.
>
> As ships building in America are known as the Liberty fleet, we suggest that an appropriate name would be Empire Liberty.[26]

This name was approved. The first Liberty named in the USA was the *Patrick Henry*, named after a lawyer who at the time of the American War of Independence famously said 'Give me liberty or give me death'. She was launched on 27 September 1941. The day had been designated 'Liberty Fleet Day' and during the ceremonies across America fourteen 'Emergency' ships including the *Patrick Henry*, which was the first of the 'Liberty ships', and thirteen other types were launched. President Roosevelt used the occasion to send a special message to shipyard workers urging them to build more cargo ships and referred to *Patrick Henry* as 'the first Liberty ship'.[27] Illustration No. 43 shows the launching ceremony of SS *Patrick Henry*, which was christened by Ilo Browne Wallace, wife of Vice President Henry A. Wallace.

Victory Fleet Day

27 September was celebrated in shipyards across America in subsequent years, being sometimes also known as 'Victory Fleet Day'. On 27 September 1943 shipyard workers across America made a pledge of even greater productivity. Since the launch of *Patrick Henry* just two years earlier some 2,100 merchant ships of various types had been launched in what President Roosevelt termed 'the world's most outstanding accomplishment in shipbuilding. Nothing in maritime history approaches that achievement.'[28]. At the Wainwright Yard, Panama City, Florida, 27 September 1943 was celebrated with the launch of its fourteenth ship and the account of the day in the yard's magazine, appropriately titled *Wainwright Liberator*, speaks of the workers' pride in what they had achieved. As soon as the ways were cleared, sections for the keel

for another ship were laid immediately. There can be no doubt that the high morale in the workforce as well as the mass production techniques contributed to the rapid multiple launchings of 'Liberty ships' that were achieved at this time.

The *Patrick Henry* was built in 150 days from keel laying to launching and this was bettered regularly as more identical ships were built. Some yards achieved a rate of about seventeen days from keel laying to launching. At Kaiser's Richmond yard on 12 November 1942 when the '*Robert E. Peary* slid down the ways a large placard on her bow proclaimed the incredible fact it had taken only four days, 15 hours and 29 seconds from keel laying to launching'.[29] It should be added that, although this was clearly intended as a propaganda stunt in much the same way as the galley in the *Arsenale* in 1576 was assembled, launched and completed within one hour to impress King Henry III of France, the *Robert E. Peary* was soundly built and survived the war!

Names chosen

The same enthusiasm for the project was demonstrated when it came to naming of the 'Liberty ships'. In early 1941 the US Maritime Commission set up a Ship Naming Committee, the policy being to name the vessels after persons who had made a significant contribution to American life and history. Despite the need to get started on the construction of the next ship, launching ceremonies for 'Liberty ships' were almost invariably held and well attended, with the sponsor usually a lady who had some family connection to the person after whom the ship was being named or the shipbuilder that built her. Sponsoring was regarded as being a great honour and the launch celebration was also a great opportunity for morale boosting and publicity. Any group who raised $2 million in War Bonds could suggest a name. If new 'Liberty ships' were handed over to Britain the American names were replaced with a name beginning with 'Sam'. There is the suggestion that this was a direct reference to 'Uncle Sam', the owner of the ships, but this is not proven. These ships were nicknamed 'Samboats' by British sailors.[30] Notwithstanding the enthusiasm for naming these ships, for security reasons, their names were painted out before their maiden voyage.

Cost of launching ceremonies

On 12 December 1941, due to the war, the US Maritime Commission was invited to revise peacetime procedure and to adopt three recommendations with regard to the launching ceremonies for the American emergency vessels designated EC2 being constructed for the Commission's account:

1. The cost of ceremonies be limited to $100, subject to reimbursement by Commission to shipyards.
2. Sponsors to be chosen by yards. In special cases they may be nominated by the Commission, with appropriate advance notice.
3. Informal christenings. No stoppage of work.

These recommendations were adopted unanimously by the Commission, with the modification that no reimbursement was to be made by the Commission to the shipyards with respect to the cost of launching ceremonies.[31]

However, this financial rigour from the Commission does not appear to have dampened the enthusiasm for the sponsoring ceremonies and launches which 'were always treated as exercises in morale boosting and publicity'.[32]

Permanente Metals Corporation, a company in the Kaiser group, even went to the trouble of adopting in 1943 an 'Official Launching Song' with words and music composed by Stephen McNeil, a well-known San Francisco Bay Area composer of the day. It is appropriately called 'Smooth Sailing' and was sung by local choirs at its 'Liberty ship' launch ceremonies.

Prefabrication procedure

Kaiser's great contribution to the multiple launching of 'Liberty ships' was in prefabrication procedure and its application to shipbuilding. Following the example of Hog Island, components were built all across America and transported to shipyards where the ships could be assembled in record time. In the assembly line method of ship construction whole sections were prefabricated as completely as possible so that the whole superstructure built in the workshop could then be lifted by gigantic crane and lowered into place on the already launched hull. As in the Venetian *Arsenale* some four centuries earlier and at Hog Island some twenty years before, all work processes and materials in the mass assembly line had to be well co-ordinated. In the fifteenth-century *Arsenale* multiple launches of galleys was made possible by the rapid assembly line fitting out of completed hulls; the hulls, however, in the early days in Venice were not of uniform design. In the case of the 'Liberty ships' it was standardisation of hull and ship design, prefabrication of sections and the rapid assembly line production of the entire ship from prefabricated parts that made rapid multiple launches possible. Over 2,700 'Liberty ships' were built in the American yards using J.L. Thompson's original design.

Construction of 'Empire' ships in UK shipyards

Back in the UK the yards in Sunderland led the way in the production of merchant ships of similar design to the 'Liberty ships', all named with the prefix *Empire*. Construction was carried out not only by J.L. Thompson but also by other famous yards on the Wear including Short Bros, Sir James Laing & Sons, George Bartram & Sons, Austin Pickersgill, J. Crown & Sons and William Doxford & Sons. Between September 1939 and the end of 1944 Sunderland launched 'a total of 249 ships aggregating 1,534,981 gross tons equal to 27 per cent of the total output of 5,722,532 gross tons from UK shipyards in that period of five years and four months'[33] – a comparatively small number when compared to the total output of 'Liberty ships' from the American shipyards over the same period, but an impressive figure nonetheless for one town on a narrow tidal river in wartime conditions.

Further merchant ships were also built in the shipyards along the Tyne during this period. Illustration No. 32 shows the launch in the Tyne in July 1941 of one such ship, *Empire Scott*, built at John Readhead & Sons Ltd. Of note are the use of outline for camouflage paint on the hull, the barrage balloons for protection from air attacks and that the ship's name has the prefix 'Empire'.

An increasing number of women were employed in the shipyards and, by agreement between employers and the unions, there was an absence of labour troubles.

Compared to the UK yards, those in America had the advantage of starting from scratch in being able to lay out spacious yards with unlimited room for handling and prefabricating parts and identical slipways. The yards in the UK had to do their best with existing premises not laid out for mass production methods on any large scale and little room to extend their workplace for prefabrication techniques. The historical layout of shipyards and the varying size of slipways in the UK yards, therefore, made mass production more difficult.

The American yards could also work free of the anxieties of bombing raids, air raid precautions and blackouts, which was a day-to-day concern for the British yards. J.L. Thompson's yard in Sunderland was bombed heavily on two successive weekends in May 1943, wrecking the boardroom and offices, burning the joiners' shop, sinking one ship and causing damage to another; but perhaps surprisingly, few British shipyards and engine works were put totally out of action by bombs. If the British yards had worked at night using floodlights it is likely that this would have resulted in even greater bombing damage from the Luftwaffe.

The ability to build merchant shipping at a rate faster than it was lost, while maintaining a steady stream of supplies to the front, was one of the keys to winning the war. This was the great contribution of the 'Liberty ship' fleet – for which Sunderland is rightly proud that it produced the prototype – and, of course, it is also another great example, if not *the* example, of multiple launching!

Multiple launches out of the context of war

Outside of war, multiple launches of merchant ships are comparatively rare; but on 15 August 1863 there is to be found a colourful example of multiple launching, not this time in order to fight a war, but organised by a shipyard to self-promote its shipbuilding capability on the Tyne. It was an event that was described at the time as being 'entirely unprecedented in the annals of Iron shipbuilding'.[34] Palmer Brothers in Jarrow arranged for the simultaneous launch of four merchant ships into the Tyne, two from their Jarrow yard on the south bank between Hebburn and South Shields and two from their Howdon yard a little way upstream on the opposite bank. The multiple launches, all in very close proximity to one another, appear to have been intended by Charles and his brother George Palmer as a well-co-ordinated promotional spectacle, with a gun being fired to signal the start of the simultaneous launching of the four ships, dressed overall with flags, and another gun to mark its successful completion two minutes later. It was reported that there were a 'goodly number of spectators' and that:

> The scene during these two minutes was a most exciting one. As ship after ship breasted the water the sullen river leapt up in a mountain of spray ... but by far the most pleasing circumstance in connection with the proceeding was the fact that not the slightest accident of any description occurred during the launches and that all the vessels were brought up in perfect safety.[35]

The four ships became known as the 'Palmer Quartet'.[36]

Chapter 17

Ship Launches and Politics

Wider significance

Down the ages a ship launch has not only been a public spectacle attended by thousands but on occasions has had a far wider significance than the mere physical transfer of a newly constructed hull into water.

Public relations opportunity

The launch of a new commercial ship, especially if it is innovative or is the start of a new trade, is a great public relations opportunity for the owner and is often taken as the moment for a major promotional speech and public relations campaign.

Expression of patriotism

In the case of naval ships, the launch of a new ship arouses different and more powerful sentiments in terms of patriotism and national identity and these sentiments on occasion need to be expressed. They are events of national significance.

The launch days of the nine Dreadnought battleships at Portsmouth Dockyard in the early 1900s have been described as 'collective events when thousands of participants renewed their affinity and belief in Britannia's continued ability to "Rule the Waves"'.[1]

Such national sentiments and values were pre-dominantly collective experiences or as 'quasi-magical moments of grandeur; a time to express and articulate deeply held imperial values'.[2]

In the event of war or imminent hostilities, ship launches of naval ships have often been used as a stage for giving a wider political or patriotic message.

Hitler's speech at launch of *Bismarck*

The launch of the German battleship *Bismarck* at Blohm+Voss, Gmbh in Hamburg on 14 February 1939 was one such occasion. To the sound of salutes being fired from the guns of a 'pocket' battleship, a cruiser and three destroyers, Adolf Hitler arrived down the Norder Elbe in brilliant sunshine on board the yacht *Hamburg*. Both banks of the river were covered in bunting and a cheering crowd of 60,000 was there to welcome the Führer and to witness this historic launch. The ship known during construction simply as 'F' was appropriately to be named by Frau Dorothee von Loewenfeld, granddaughter of Chancellor Otto von Bismarck. On his way to Hamburg the previous day, Hitler had stopped his special train at the Bismarck estate to place a wreath on the grave of the man who had founded the Empire of Hohenzollerns in 1871 and unified the different states into a powerful German empire.[3]

In his speech Hitler began with an emotional commemorative reference to Germany's last fleet, a large part of which was scuttled by its officers in Scapa Flow in June 1919, following the signing of the Armistice treaty, which brought the First World War to a close. The loss of these ships was, he said, a blow still felt by the German people. The new battleship to be launched that day was the third ship of a new squadron to be built under the Anglo-German Naval Agreement of 1935 that limited the German naval fleet to 35 per cent of the Royal Navy. The choice of *Bismarck* as the name of this first new battleship, which was built to the maximum size permitted and which marked an important step in renewal of the German fleet, was therefore hugely significant and an opportunity for Hitler to appeal to wider patriotic sentiment.

Appealing not just to those attending the launch but to a wider audience he said, in summary, that he could think of no better name for this ship than the name of the former Chancellor who had done so much to restore the country from despair.

He called upon the officers and men who would in the future have the honour to command the ship to prove themselves worthy of *Bismarck*'s name and for the spirit of the Iron Chancellor to suffuse them in their actions.

He ended: 'With this fervent wish the German *Volk* now greets its new battleship.'

Frau von Loewenfeld then broke a bottle of German sparkling wine on the bows, decorated with garlands, declaring the ship to be named *Bismarck*. The hull did not move immediately and there was an anxious pause for more than three minutes before the ship slid slowly away from the launching platform. As the giant ship started to move, in accordance with local Hamburg tradition and so as not to flout the superstition – that the name of a new ship should remain a secret until after it has been called out by the sponsor, workmen then immediately let down a name plaque on each side of the bow on which the single word 'Bismarck' was inscribed. This movement down the slip was greeted spontaneously with the loud singing of the German national anthem and the applause of the 60,000 spectators.

The battleship *Bismarck* of displacing 41,700 tons was the largest ever constructed in Germany. A magnificent large-scale model of the ship remains proudly displayed to this day in the Hamburg offices of her constructor, Blohm+Voss Gmbh. It is said that during the Second World War this model was hidden underground so as to save it from Allied bombing.

American President's speech at launch of 'Liberty ships'

Some two and a half years after the launch of *Bismarck*, on 26 September 1941 US President Franklin D. Roosevelt used the launch on the same day of fourteen emergency cargo ships across America – on the Atlantic, Pacific and Gulf – to deliver a totally different, but equally political, and patriotic, speech. His speech, pre-recorded on 26 September, was transmitted by loudspeaker at each shipyard as the chief event in the programme at each of the fourteen launchings. He used as the basis for his speech the launch of the first 'Emergency' ship in Baltimore, the SS *Patrick Henry* (Illustration No. 43). She was named after a lawyer who at the time of the American War of Independence gained immortality by enunciating the words 'Give me liberty or give me death!' These words were the inspiration to name the merchant ships being constructed under the Emergency programme as 'Liberty ships'. These stirring words also very much reflected the mood in 1941 when America was striving with

Great Britain to construct as rapidly as possible enough replacement merchant tonnage under the emergency fleet programme to make good the losses sustained as a result of the menace of the U-boats:

> My fellow Americans.
> This is a memorable day in the history of American shipbuilding – a memorable day in the emergency defense of the nation. Today from dawn to dark, fourteen ships are being launched – on the Atlantic, on the Pacific and on the Gulf and among them is the first Liberty ship, the *Patrick Henry*.
> Whilst we are proud of what we are doing, this is certainly no time to be content. We must build more cargo ships and still more cargo ships – and we must speed the program until we achieve a launching each day then two ships a day, fulfilling the program undertaken by the Maritime Commission …
> The ship workers of America are doing a great job. They have made a commendable record for efficiency and speed. With every new ship they are striking a telling blow at the menace to our nation and the liberty of the free people of the world. They have struck fourteen such blows today …
> The *Patrick Henry* as one of the Liberty ships launched today renews that great patriot's stirring demand 'Give me liberty or give me death'.
> There shall be no death for America, for democracy, for freedom. There must be liberty, worldwide and eternal. That is our prayer and our pledge to all mankind.[4]

The significance of the fourteen launches in one day across America on 27 September resulted in the day becoming known as 'Liberty Fleet Day' and later as 'Victory Fleet Day'.

Mrs Henry Wallace, wife of the Vice President, led the fourteen prominent women who sponsored the launching of the fourteen ships across America. She christened the *Patrick Henry* at the Bethlehem-Fairfield yard at Baltimore (see Illustration No. 43). As the vessel gathered speed down the ways, an overhead crane with the keel plate for the next ship swung into place and lowered it onto the vacated keel blocks of the *Patrick Henry*. No time was being lost in the determination to keep the ships coming.

Launch of Le France – French national pride

After the end of hostilities it was time to rebuild nations and build new commercial ships. On 26 July 1956 a new transatlantic liner was ordered by Compagnie Generale Transatlantique from the famous shipyard Chantiers de L'Atlantique at Saint Nazaire. At that time the only remaining liners that France had were *Ile de France* and *Liberte*, both of which were old fashioned and over twenty-five years old. There was a need to build new ships fit for the modern post-war era.

The initial concept was to build two liners to replace *Ile de France* and *Liberte* and then there was the question how the project would be financed. General Charles de Gaulle favoured one superliner that could be seen as a bold statement of France's revival and recovery after defeat, occupation and liberation. The idea of public funds being used to support such a project was the subject of much debate in the French parliament, but in the end de Gaulle's vision of one grand ocean liner to restore national pride prevailed, with the project being underwritten by the French Government.

The liner would be the longest ever built and needed to be something special for the sake of the nation and the fact that it would replace not one but two *grande dames* of the ocean; it had to be an ocean-going symbol of France of which the nation could be proud. She had a unique funnel design with side fins that became a marketing feature. She was one of the last great purpose-built ocean liners.

Against this background it also easy to see why Madame Charles de Gaulle was the right choice of godmother for *Le France* and why General de Gaulle, who in the meantime had become President of his country, wanted to use the occasion to make a keynote patriotic speech about the great French engineering achievement that the ship represented and to restore in the citizens of France a feeling of *la grandeur* of their country after the disappointment of the war years. Before launch the liner was blessed by the Bishop of Nantes, Monseigneur Villepelet.

General de Gaulle is seen in Illustration No. 44 immediately after the launch of the liner, making his speech, standing alone and aloft on the official launching platform, which is decorated with the French Tricolour.

A ship is masculine in the French language, unlike most other countries where it is always a 'she'. This gave de Gaulle the opportunity to make a clever play on words between *Le France* and La France, with only the gender of the definite article marking the difference between the ship and the nation.

He finished with the words, which will be quoted in French, since the original expresses more clearly the emotion and patriotic fervour he intended:

Dans ce vaisseau, nous salutons L'une des grandes reussites, dont presentement la technique francaise fait hommage a la patrie ...
La ceremonie d'aujourd'hui ajoute a la fierte que nous avons de la France ...
Vive le *'France'*, vive la France![5]

Of which a rough translation by the author is:

In this vessel we salute one of the great success stories, whose demonstration of French technology honours our country ...
Today's ceremony strengthens the pride that we have in France.
Long live *Le France* [the ship], long live La France [the country]!

For a politician as proud of his country as General de Gaulle, the launch of this super new liner provided the ideal platform for his patriotic fervour and a strong political statement that what was being launched was not just a new liner but a new ship of state. He had the grand design for his country and what better public occasion on which to express it.

Chapter 18

Launch Day Gifts and Launch Cards

Launch day gifts

Ship model

S hip launches of a new liner in the early twentieth century and in more modern times of a new cruise ship were then, and continue to be, carefully staged 'showpiece' events attended by hundreds of honoured guests. These launch ceremonies often include a centrepiece display at the shipyard of a large-scale model of the ship so as to give guests at the launch an early impression of what the new ship would look like when completed. The practice of making these beautifully crafted builder's models of new ships was begun in the nineteenth century. A builder's model was often not a gift from the shipbuilder but an item included in the technical specification and factored into the contract price. They were manufactured by professional model makers and were used not only as promotional tools but, in case of a technical problem arising on the ship, to inform and educate. These models were then proudly displayed in the ship owner's boardroom or in the front hall of its head office to be admired by visitors. A builder's model has always been cherished and if the ship is later sold a buyer will frequently wish to acquire it along with the ship; but, since the models are part of the original owner's heritage there is, understandably, often a reluctance to part with them. In contrast, smaller-scale miniature models are often given to guests attending a ship launch as a memento of the occasion and as promotion of the new ship.

Launch box

We have already learned of the tradition in Royal Dockyards in the UK of the sponsor of a naval ship being presented with a wooden launch box containing a mallet and chisel after they had been used by the sponsor to symbolically sever the last rope that released the dog shores, setting the ship free to move down the ways.[1] This tradition started in the nineteenth century and continued until the onset of the Second World War. After the war the tradition in the UK and in other countries has been for the lady sponsor of a naval ship or godmother of a merchant ship to be presented by the shipbuilder with a commemorative gift to mark the occasion but, instead of a launch box, a gift of jewellery is often made. A quite popular alternative gift is the presentation to the sponsor or godmother of the head of the champagne bottle she has just used to christen the ship, mounted on a special commemorative wooden plaque inscribed with the name of the ship, the date, the shipbuilder and the name of the sponsor or godmother.

Special jewellery

At the launch of HMS *Gurka* at Cammell Laird in July 1940 the sponsor was Mary Soames, granddaughter of Winston Churchill:

> I had watched my mother at the launch of the *Indomitable* earlier in the year, so I knew the form and also the emotion … It was at that time customary for the shipbuilder to give the sponsor of a ship a present: my 'prize' was a lovely Victorian diamond necklace.[2]

Another good example is the launch of the battleship HMS *Vanguard* on 30 November 1944 at John Brown shipyard on Clydebank by Queen Elizabeth II, then Princess Elizabeth. The shipyard presented the Princess as the ship's sponsor with a piece of diamond-studded jewellery that has come to be known as the 'Vanguard Rose Brooch'. It takes the form of a wild rose with three leaves in a sprig with a small bow at the base and was worn frequently by the Queen.

Gift of speedboat

Although jewellery is now the most common gift to the sponsor, this tradition is not followed without exception. Of interest is the gift of a speedboat for the royal yacht *Britannia* that was jointly given to Queen Elizabeth II by John Brown shipyard and Cunard on the occasion of the launch of *QE2* on 20 September 1967. This unusual gift, however, all makes sense when it is recalled that the royal yacht had also been built by John Brown's yard.

Crystal glass bowl

At the naming ceremony of the new aircraft carrier HMS *Queen Elizabeth* at Rosyth Dockyard on 4 July 2014 Queen Elizabeth II, as sponsor, was presented by the builder with a hand-engraved sixty-year-old Webb Corbett crystal glass bowl. The engraving on the bowl depicts the previous HMS *Queen Elizabeth*, a dreadnought battleship that served from 1913 to 1948, as well as an impression of the new aircraft carrier.

Gifts to guests

Other guests at ship christening and launch ceremonies also frequently receive commemorative gifts such as silver armada dishes, china plates, miniature propellers made of bronze, model engine order telegraphs, glass ship decanters and goblets as well as miniature models of the new ship, all usually inscribed or engraved with the name of the ship, the launch date, shipyard, etc. They all serve to remind the recipients of the special day on which they were privileged to witness the launch of the new ship and, of course, help to promote it.

Launch cards

Launch cards are frequently issued to official guests at launching ceremonies. They are often colourful and informative souvenirs with an artist's impression of the ship that is to be launched, brief particulars of the ship, the name of the dignitary performing the ceremony and the programme of events. They are, as ephemera, a rich source of detail produced for the guests at the launch and then frequently thrown away; but fortunately some have survived.

The artwork in these cards has often been of the highest standard. There is a colourful collection in the Tyne and Wear Archives[3] of some fifteen of these beautiful launch cards from Elswick shipyard on the river Tyne at Newcastle, which belonged to Sir W.G. Armstrong, Whitworth & Co. Ltd. This shipyard constructed many battleships for foreign navies as well as the Royal Navy between 1885 and 1918 and the collection of artistic launch cards in the archives covers the period 1897 to 1911.

An interesting example from the Elswick collection is the launch card for the Chinese training cruiser *Chao Ho*, launched on 23 October 1911 by Miss Amy Lew, daughter of 'His Excellency Yuk Lin Lew, Envoy Extraordinary and Minister Plenipotentiary to the Court of St James'. There is in the card a beautiful coloured engraving giving an artist's impression of the ship under way at sea, with two funnels and a square-rigged sailing ship in the background. The ship was probably the last built on the Tyne for Imperial China. Illustration No. 45 is a beautiful example of the launch card for this Chinese training ship with Chinese motif dragon. The artwork is of the highest standard.

It is reported that, unusually, the *Chao Ho* entered the water with machinery and boilers on board, funnels fitted and other work in an advanced stage. After the ceremony, as might be expected for the launch of a Chinese ship, tea was served to the guests!

Elswick yard constructed a large number of battleships for the Imperial Japanese Navy during the period covered by the collection and the launch cards for these ships were illustrated with increasingly elaborate Japanese motifs and symbols.

Launch cards were also prepared for some launches of naval ships at Royal Dockyards. An early example was a souvenir card produced for the prestigious launch of HMS *Prince Consort*, the first ironclad built at Pembroke Dock, which was launched on 26 June 1862.[4] This gives a pen and ink impression of the ship as it would appear after launch from the covered construction yard, which is shown in the background. Launch cards usually contain the name of the sponsor. Of special interest in the case of the launch card for HMS *Prince Consort* is that the name of the sponsor is left blank to be written in later. The reason appears to be that at the time of production of the card the name of the sponsor was not finally determined. It had been hoped that Prince Alfred, the second son of Queen Victoria and who was then serving in the navy, would have the honour but in the event he decided not to attend and the christening was conducted by Miss Jones, daughter of David Jones, MP for Carmarthenshire.

The author has also seen examples of launch cards for other naval ships: HMS *Warrior* and HMS *Defence,* also launched at Pembroke Dock in 1905 and 1907, and various submarines constructed at Chatham. On the front cover was typically given the date of the launch, the names of the sponsor, the Superintendent and the Chief Constructor. On the inside or on folding flaps were sometimes: the programme for the launch, an artist's impression of the outline of the ship or how it was expected she would look when completed, the main particulars of the ship and, if applicable, a list of the sister ships of the same class. Where the spectators were being entertained by a military band, the musical programme was sometimes also added.

For security reasons such launch cards were not produced at any time where the disclosure of particulars of the ship would be contrary to the national interest.

The author has attended a number of launches where launch cards have been handed to the guests but, while these have been informative about the particulars of the ship and the programme for the launch ceremony, they have tended to have a rather simpler silhouette of the ship on the front of the card and not the impressive artwork that was given to guests attending the *Chao Ho* or the *Prince Consort* launch. Nonetheless, launch cards remain a fine tradition of some ship launches even today and a lovely memento of the event.

At other ceremonies, for example at the naming by HM Queen Elizabeth II of the new aircraft carrier HMS *Queen Elizabeth* on 4 July 2014 at Rosyth Dockyard, as already mentioned, a special event programme for the naming ceremony was produced. This included the order of the day and the form of religious service conducted by the Chaplain of the Fleet.

Commemorative menu cards

Launch day celebrations traditionally end with a lunch or dinner for the principal guests with speeches and toasts to the godmother/sponsor and the new ship. Special commemorative menu cards are often produced for such an occasion. At the launch for P&O's new liner *Canberra*, named and launched by Dame Pattie Menzies on 16 March 1960 at Harland &

Wolff Ltd, Belfast, the guests enjoyed a meal that appropriately included Ulster salmon mayonnaise and roast Co. Down lamb and other courses listed in a special menu card.[5] At Jacobs Pill, a private yard 1½ miles from Pembroke Dock, on 11 June 1877 a three-masted barque rigged ship, the *Hei-Yei*, was launched for the Imperial Japanese Navy in the presence of His Excellency Jushie Wooyeno Kagenori, Imperial Minister of Japan. At the banquet held in his honour that evening there was an elaborate feast of six or seven courses and nine toasts![6] Quite a celebration, featured again in a unique menu card specially printed for the occasion.

Chapter 19

Launch Miscellany

D uring the research for this book the author has come across a number of ship launch stories or other information related to launches or naming ceremonies that, while they do not fit readily into any of the chapters, are of sufficient interest not to be forgotten.

1. Athenian Liturgy of 'Trierarchy' and the threat of imprisonment if your trireme was not launched in time

In an earlier chapter[1] mention has been made of the shipsheds of the fifth century BC in Piraeus for storing triremes, the Athenian warships that belonged to the state. The shipsheds were not the only remarkable invention of the Athenians at this time. They also invented the system of 'trierarchy', an extraordinary public service, called a 'liturgy', by which wealthy citizens of Athens known as 'trierarchs' (meaning one who fitted out a trireme for public service), were obliged to provide for the launch initial equipment and provision of one trireme each for a period of one year, at the end of which they had the obligation to return the equipment in good order. It was then passed to another wealthy citizen as successor trierarch. The state was obliged to provide the hull and the triremes were allocated by lot to wealthy citizens. The giving of names to the triremes[2] would have facilitated the allocation process. No citizen of sufficient wealth could claim exemption from this public service unless he was a chief magistrate. Having completed his twelve-month term, a trierarch could not be compelled to serve a second term within two years after his former service. The expenses of running a trireme for twelve months could be considerable, depending on the duration of the military campaign and the initial condition of the trireme, so trierarchy was probably one of, if not, the most onerous, of the 'liturgies' or public services undertaken by wealthy Athenians. But it was clearly an effective means by which the wealthiest citizens financed the Athenian state and provided for its fleet.

When the Athenians voted in assembly that the trierarchs should launch their ships, they were required to launch and get them fitted out as quickly as possible and bring them round to the jetty in the main harbour of Piraeus. There they underwent trials and inspection and received the last of the equipment and provisions. In theory the state provided all the gear, as a public supply as well as the crews, but in practice the trierarchs frequently provided both. There were prizes, a sort of turn out prize, given to the first three trierarchs to bring their ships round properly equipped. This prize took the form of the honour of wearing a crown usually made of gold or ivy, which symbolised excellence in the execution of an official duty. These prizes were intended to express the gratitude of the state to those who did their duty well.

Demosthenes, the famous orator, made a speech in about 330 BC to his fellow Athenians putting the case why he, rather than some of his fellow trierarchs, deserved the crown.[3] He criticised his fellow trierarchs who hired out deputies to do the work for them, who he said were acting in their own interests and were not serving the state.

What mattered to the state was the recovery of the hull and equipment in good condition for future use. The trierarchs had the absolute responsibility to return the equipment in good seaworthy order at the end of their twelve-month service. As well as prizes there were sanctions too. If a trierarch did not launch his allocated trireme by the end of a set period he faced censure from his fellow Athenians for failing in his duty to the state. This lever for compliance was usually enough but, if he continued to default, the dockyard officials could bring an action against him before the magistrates' courts. The usual sanction was a punitive fine, double the amount of the original debt, but potentially and as a last resort, which was rarely used, a defaulter could be sent to prison and lose his civic rights. What other state has ever imposed a prison sentence on any of its citizens for failure to launch a ship for the state or to return it in good condition?

When the scheme first started it was usual for the trierarch to be the captain but this changed over time. By the fifth century BC two trierarchs could share a trireme and substitute captains could be hired. Hence, many trierarchs never set foot in their ship, so that they became in effect financial backers not captains.[4]

2. Launch in a hole in the ice

Peter the Great, in striving to achieve non-stop work at his shipyards in Imperial Russia throughout the year, proposed to launch ships even in the winter in a specially prepared hole in the ice.[5]

3. A 21-gun salute from a naval ship while still on launching stocks

A 74-gun ship, *HMS Illustrious*, was ready for a royal launching from Buckler's Hard in 1789 when the following unusual event occurred:

> In July of that year His Majesty King George III and his Queen … on their way from Windsor to Plymouth … paid a state visit to Beaulieu, where they were royally entertained by John Duke of Montagu. The *Illustrious* was then on the stocks at Buckler's Hard, and strange to say, fired a salute of 21 guns, in honour of their Majesties' visit, whilst still on dry land, a circumstance probably without parallel in our naval annals …[6]

The explanation is that John Adams had made preparations for a royal launching of *Illustrious* and had the cannon fitted on board in readiness for the event but when the royal party did not go to Buckler's Hard the 21-gun salute was still fired in honour of the King while the ship was still on the stocks.

It is thought that this may be the only occasion in British naval history on which a 21-gun salute has been fired from a naval ship in honour of the monarch while the ship was still on its launching stocks.

4. The Royal Prayer and how it has evolved

The words used by HM Queen Elizabeth II to christen the new aircraft carrier HMS *Queen Elizabeth* in Rosyth on 4 July 2014, 'I name this ship Elizabeth. May God bless her and all who sail in her', take the form of a royal prayer. The same words have been used by the Queen in naming both naval and merchant ships on many occasions. They were first used by the Queen on 30 November 1944 when, as HRH Princess Elizabeth, she launched the battleship HMS *Vanguard* at the yard of John Brown & Company on the Clyde. This was the first time that HRH Princess Elizabeth had performed a principal role in such an event. Of interest too is that, although at the moment of launch she actually named the ship 'Vanguard', in the film made by Pathé News to record the event the wartime censors shortened her speech to omit the name of the ship and also stated vaguely that 'the event had taken place somewhere in a Northern port'. The only recorded words of the Princess in the published film were 'May God bless her and all who sail in her', so omitting for security reasons both the name of the ship as well as the identity of the shipyard.

Princess Elizabeth's next launch of a naval ship was after the end of the Second World War at Harland & Wolff in Belfast, when on 19 March 1946 she christened the aircraft carrier HMS *Eagle* (originally designated *Audacious*). On this occasion she also made a royal prayer but used the slightly different words 'I name this ship *Eagle*. May God *protect* her and all who sail in her' (emphasis added).

After her accession to the throne Queen Elizabeth II, in general, reverted to the same language of the Royal Prayer she had used to launch HMS *Vanguard*, asking for God's blessing on the ship and those who sail in her. If the royal yacht *Britannia* is excluded (see below), the first naval ship she launched as Queen was on Trafalgar Day 1960 when she christened the Royal Navy's first nuclear submarine HMS *Dreadnought* at Vickers yard in Barrow-in-Furness using the same prayer asking for God's blessing on the ship and those who sail in her. It is interesting to note that the same words of the Royal Prayer have subsequently been used by HRH The Duchess of Cornwall to name the submarine HMS *Astute* on 8 June 2007, again in Barrow-in-Furness, indicating that these words are not the exclusive prerogative of the Sovereign.

The wording used in England at the christening of royal naval ships has evolved from the purely secular to the current Royal Prayer. As we have seen at launches of naval ships between the Reformation and the introduction of the standard Religious Service in 1875,[7] there was no religious sentiment but only the secular formula of wishing 'success' or 'good luck' to the new ship. Even the introduction of the religious service for the launching of naval ships did not result in any immediate change to the words used at the moment of christening but, on occasion, there were added good wishes 'to all who would sail in her'. For example, the traditional words used by the sponsor for the launch of most, but not all, of the fifty-one dreadnought battleships launched at British shipyards between 1906 and 1918 were 'I wish success' or 'I wish good luck' to the ship, often adding 'and all who sail in her'.[8]

Of greater significance is the launch of one dreadnought, the giant cruiser HMS *Lion* at Devonport by Viscountess Clifden on 6 August 1910, when she christened the ship with the words: 'I name you *Lion*, God bless you and those who sail in you'. This wording marks a change to the standard secular wish for 'success' and comes very close to the prayer for God's blessing that, as we have noted, was subsequently adopted by Queen Elizabeth II, then Princess Elizabeth, in 1944 and was frequently used by her thereafter.

There have been other words used as well and we find the following examples:

Naming without any wish or prayer

On 10 February 1906, at the launch of HMS *Dreadnought* by King Edward VII, he did not follow the traditional wording but he said simply: 'I christen you *Dreadnought*.'

Similarly, on 26 September 1934 at the launch by Queen Mary at John Brown shipyard, not of a naval ship this time but of the ocean liner *Queen Mary*, she said: 'I am very happy to name this ship *Queen Mary*.'

Wish for success or good luck for the new ship and her crew

The British practice, inevitably with some variations, was followed in the Commonwealth. When the torpedo boat destroyer *Torrens* was launched at Cockatoo Island Dockyard in Sydney on 28 August 1915 by Lady Helen Munro Ferguson, wife of the Governor General Sir Ronald Munro Ferguson, she did so with a bottle of the best Australian wine, saying: 'I name you *Torrens*. May you play a distinguished part in the defence of the country and may the blessing of God rest on those who sail in you.'

On 7 December 1934, at the launch of another ocean liner, RMS *Orion*, by HRH The Duke of Gloucester, he used his own rather different but elegant words: 'I name you *Orion*. Good fortune attend you always and those whom you bear across the world to their brothers overseas.'

On 16 April 1953, at the launch of the royal yacht *Britannia* at John Brown shipyard by Queen Elizabeth II, she said: 'I name this ship *Britannia*. I wish success to her and all who sail in her.' This wording is of interest since, as noted earlier, RY *Britannia* was designed not only to be a royal yacht but in time of war to be a naval hospital ship. At her launch she was treated as a naval ship flying the White Ensign. The Queen might, therefore, have been expected to use the words of the Royal Prayer seeking God's blessing on the ship and all who would sail in her, which she had introduced for naval ships when launching HMS *Vanguard* in 1944. But it is, on reflection, understandable that since the yacht would primarily be used by Queen Elizabeth II and her family and be a home to them when on board, she did not on this occasion think it appropriate to make her usual prayer for God's blessing on the ship and those who would sail in her.

5. Launch day customs on the Tyne in the 1860s

In April 1860 'The launch of the barque *Vencedora* was the occasion of great rejoicing': 'The apprentices followed the ancient custom and went through the ceremony of ducking and plunging in the water as soon as the ship was safely launched ...'[9]

The act of ducking in the water was to symbolise that the ship would not sink.

6. Fire risk when two ships are launched on the same berth

Southwick yard of Austin & Pickersgill

Rawson & Watson partners built two ships on the same berth and when the day came for launch, men lined both sides of the ways to throw buckets of water onto the ship as she went down to stop any fires caused by friction.

7. Dockyard worker as the ship's godmother

'I remember I had to go home and change into Sunday suit for the ceremony. When I tried to go back into the yard they did not recognise me at first because I was usually dressed in a boiler suit.'

Launch of *Heathergate* on 14 November 1956 christened by Annabelle Jenkin, a worker at the yard of Clelands Shipbuilding Co. Ltd on the Tyne.

8. Union representatives do not attend launch parties

'Asked about Launch parties and were they invited. Representatives of the Union are always invited but the Shop Stewards Committee refuses because they believe it to be a soft form of corruption. "They wouldn't drink with us socially, so why should we do it for that occasion ..."'[10]

9. Admiralty flag at launching of Royal Navy ships

In 1936 an officer of the Signals School wrote that some shipyards flew only the White Ensign and Union Jack on a naval ship when it was launched, but that a few others flew the Admiralty flag as well. In the eighteenth century it had been customary to fly the flag of the Lord High Admiral on men-of-war during the launching ceremony, but the tradition died as more ships were built by contractors in commercial shipyards. The Admiralty owned a ship when it was launched in a Royal Dockyard but not when it was launched in a contractor's yard. It was decided that the custom should be revived as the flag had been flown as decoration and not to signify the presence of authorities.

An Admiralty Fleet Order of 1938 announced the revival of a 200-year-old tradition: 'At all launches of HM ships, whether dockyard or contract built, White Ensign is to be flown at ensign staff, Union Jack at jack staff and Admiralty flag at main masthead or equivalent position.'

The practice came to an end in 1964 when the Admiralty flag became solely the flag and prerogative of Queen Elizabeth II, as Lord High Admiral.[11]

On the occasion of the ninetieth birthday of HRH the Duke of Edinburgh, the Queen conferred on him the title of Lord High Admiral and in the Admiralty Boardroom on 24 November 2011 the Duke received Letters of Patent conferring on him the title and the Lord High Admiral flag. Following the death of Queen Elizabeth II, the title and the flag have, it is thought, now been vested in the new Sovereign, King Charles III.

Chapter 20

Some Conclusions

Each ship launch is unique, bringing new challenges. For the builder making the launch arrangements, there can be no complacency. His experience and know-how must be applied individually to each launch, even if he has just launched a sister ship. As we have seen, the launch conditions, the launch weight, the declivity and condition of the launch ways, the weather, the wind, the height and the strength of the tide will all play their part.

A successful launch is the first – but crucial – step in the life of a ship. Completion of the construction and fit out follow, then sea trials and the determination of speed along the measured mile before handover or, in the case of a naval ship, commissioning. During the construction process there are opportunities for ceremonies at keel laying, launch, naming, handover and, in the case of a naval ship, at commissioning but the launching ceremony, the ceremony that marks the moment the ship enters the water for the first time, when the hull ceases to be an 'it' and becomes a 'her', remains the most important of them all.

The moment that the new ship enters the water for the first time is *the* critical moment: Will she run true down the slipway? Will she have initial stability? How will she move through the water? As we have seen, these characteristics are readily apparent in the few seconds it takes the hull to move down the slipway. The ceremonies for keel laying or handover or commissioning, colourful as they may be with a band playing and a patriotically decorated dais for dignitaries, do not have the same emotive or immediate significance as the launch ceremony. There is no real emotion at keel laying, even if a coin is, by tradition, symbolically placed underneath the keel, and by the time handover or commissioning arrive any technical problems, more often than not, have been addressed; so the ceremony is more of a formality. Launch is different because the hull is being put into water for the first time and even today the element of anxiety remains. It is true that the commissioning ceremony has important patriotic significance when a new naval ship is accepted for service into the national fleet – and for the first time the national flag is hoisted on board and the National Anthem played – but this is more like a graduation ceremony after the newly born is fully grown, has been tested and is ready for adult life. No moment can be more important or emotive or risky than birth; and certainly there is no event in the course of construction of a ship that appeals more to the imagination than launch.

As we have learned, the sentiment that lies behind all launching ceremonies is fear. A feeling of fear or awe has been experienced by sailors down the ages. The recognition by seafarers, even today, that, in the face of the strength of wind and waves, man is insignificant, however large or strong his ship. His immediate physical security is his ship but ultimately even this is at the mercy of the elements. Although he will not always acknowledge it, man is afraid. Fear motivates the seafarer to seek to propitiate the unseen powers or to pray for protection. So, at the moment of launch of a new ship the seafarer is alert to any sign or omen that his ship is not sound but he also needs and seeks reassurance from the divine or the supernatural that he and his new ship will be protected and any evil spirits driven away. The form of reassurance provided by the ceremony varies according to local religion, superstition and tradition, but the underlying sentiments are the same.

Sacrifice or the making of gifts to the gods in return for seeking reassurance of protection from the dangers of the deep was, historically, in the pre-Christian era, at the centre of the ceremonies of the ancient seafarers from Babylon, Phoenicia, and Greece; and certain of these elements are to be found too in the *puja* practised today by Hindus prior to a ship launch. Although we have seen an example of animal sacrifice at a ship launch in the Ottoman Empire as late as 1885, this was exceptional. In general, sometime before that date sacrifice of animals through 'bloodletting' to appease the gods was replaced by the rite of pouring of red wine over the stern into the sea or onto the deck and then replaced again by the custom of the breaking of a bottle of wine against the bow, but still retaining symbolically the element of sacrifice. Even in Christian countries where the religious ceremony at ship launches is based on religious faith and prayers for the ship's safety and of those who will sail in her, there is still, by long-standing tradition, retention in some countries of elements of superstition and belief in the supernatural.

Symbolism has been and continues to be a common feature of ship launch ceremonies. If we recall, for example, the release of doves at the launch of a Japanese Imperial warship as a symbol of safe homecoming or the breaking of a coconut in India as a symbol of success or the painting of the eyes of *Horus* on a Portuguese fishing boat as a symbol of protection, they all reflect the underlying anxiety of sailors at the moment of launch of a new ship and their wish for reassurance. They help to explain why in some countries both the mystical and the religious elements continue to co-exist: here we can we recall France, where blessing by a Catholic priest has been an invariable feature of ship launches down the centuries and yet the pagan customs of sprinkling of salt and blessed corn as symbols of preservation and prosperity are still performed. The continuing practice of these quite different rituals, side by side, appears to be a matter of tradition.

Excitement, anxiety, fear, joy, pride and relief: the whirlpool of emotions that in a few seconds is a ship launch. Any reader who has never attended a launch, especially one down a slipway or a sideways launch, will, it is hoped, feel inspired to do so and come to appreciate for himself or herself the special atmosphere, the rituals and the mixture of emotions that this unique event invariably engenders.

Appendix I

Ships Launched/Named by HRH Princess Elizabeth/HM Queen Elizabeth II

As Princess Elizabeth

Date	Ship	Place
30.11.44	HMS *Vanguard*	Clydebank
19.3.46	HMS *Eagle*	N. Ireland
30.4.46	MV *British Princess* (oil tanker)	Sunderland
30.10.47	SS *Caronia* (Cunard)	Clydebank

As Queen

Date	Ship	Place
16.4.53	RY *Britannia*	Clydebank
17.8.54	SS *Southern Cross*	Belfast
22.6.55	SS *Empress Of Britain* (Canadian Pacific Railway)	Govan
21.10.60	HMS *Dreadnought*	Barrow-in-Furness
17.3.65	MV *British Admiral* (oil tanker)	Barrow-in-Furness
20.9.67	*Queen Elizabeth 2* (Cunard)	Clydebank
10.6.71	HMS *Sheffield*	Barrow-in-Furness
17.7.72	*The Royal British Legion Jubilee* (RNLI Lifeboat)	Henley-on-Thames
27.6.73	*Training Ship Playfair* (naming)	Toronto

Date	Ship	Place
3.5.77	HMS *Invincible*	Barrow-in-Furness
14.7.77	*The Scout* (RNLI Waveney Class lifeboat)	Hartlepool
24.5.90	HMS *Lancaster*	Yarrow, Strathclyde
1.12.90	*James Clark Ross* (Royal Research Ship)	Swan Hunter, Newcastle upon Tyne
11.12.92	MV *Pharos* (Northern Lighthouse Board Lightship)	Ferguson, Glasgow
16.7.93	*Her Majesty The Queen* (RNLI lifeboat: naming)	Ramsgate
7.10.93	MT *Jo Selje* (Selje Shipping)	Kvaerner Govan
6.4.95	MV *Oriana* (P&O: naming)	Southampton
20.2.98	HMS *Ocean* (VSEL, GEC Marine)	Barrow-in-Furness
14.3.00	*Team Philips* (naming)	Tower Bridge
2.8.00	MV *Hebrides* (Caledonian MacBrayne car ferry)	Ferguson, Glasgow
1.5.02	*Richard Cox Scott* (RNLI lifeboat: naming)	Falmouth Museum
23.7.03	*Sybil Mullen Glover* (RNLI lifeboat: naming)	Plymouth
8.1.04	*Queen Mary 2* (Cunard: naming)	Southampton
17.10.07	*Galatea* (Trinity House: naming)	Pool of London
11.10.10	*Queen Elizabeth* (Cunard: naming)	Southampton
4.7.14	HMS *Queen Elizabeth* (naming)	Rosyth
10.3.15	*Britannia* (P&O cruises: naming)	Southampton

Appendix II

Religious Service at the Launch of
Naval Ships

The copy of the form D-10 shown here was used at the launch ceremony of HMS *Leopard* named by Princess Marie Louise on 23 May 1955 at Her Majesty's Dockyard, Portsmouth. Courtesy of the National Museum of the Royal Navy, Portsmouth.

D. 10

SERVICE

for the

LAUNCHING OF SHIPS

of

HER MAJESTY'S NAVY

2

* PSALM CVII.   *Confitemini Domino.*

VERSE 23.   THEY that go down to the sea in ships : and occupy their business in great waters ;

24.   These men see the works of the Lord : and His wonders in the deep.

25.   For at His word the stormy wind ariseth : which lifteth up the waves thereof.

26.   They are carried up to the Heaven, and down again to the deep : their soul melteth away because of the trouble.

27.   They reel to and fro, and stagger like a drunken man : and are at their wits' end.

28.   So when they cry unto the Lord in their trouble : He delivereth them out of their distress.

29.   For He maketh the storm to cease : so that the waves thereof are still.

30.   Then are they glad, because they are at rest : and so He bringeth them unto the haven where they would be.

31.   O that men would therefore praise the Lord for His goodness : and declare the wonders that He doeth for the children of men !

43.   Whoso is wise will ponder these things : and they shall understand the loving-kindness of the Lord.

Glory be to the Father, and to the Son : and to the Holy Ghost ;

As it was in the beginning, is now, and ever shall be : world without end.

Amen.

---

* NOTE.—*When the Service is conducted by a Presbyterian Minister, these verses of Psalm C V I I may be read from the Authorized Version of the Bible.*

3

Let us Pray.

O THOU that sittest above the water floods, and stillest the raging of the sea, accept, we beseech Thee, the supplications of Thy servants for all who in this ship, now and hereafter, shall commit their lives unto the perils of the deep.   In all their ways enable them, truly and godly to serve Thee, and by their Christian lives to set forth Thy glory throughout the earth.   Watch over them in their going forth and in their coming in, that no evil befall them, nor mischief come nigh to hurt their souls.   And so through the waves of this troublesome world, and through all the changes and chances of this mortal life, bring them of Thy mercy to the sure Haven of Thine everlasting Kingdom, through Jesus Christ our Lord.   *Amen.*

The Minister and People shall say,

OUR FATHER, which art in Heaven, Hallowed be Thy Name.   Thy kingdom come.   Thy will be done, in earth as it is in Heaven.   Give us this day our daily bread.   And forgive us our trespasses, As we forgive them that trespass against us.   And lead us not into temptation ; But deliver us from evil : For thine is the kingdom, The power, and the glory, For ever and ever.   Amen.

A Hymn may here be sung.

THE LORD bless us and keep us ; the Lord lift up the light of His countenance upon us, and give us peace, now and for evermore.   *Amen.*

After this, the ceremony of launching shall proceed with the usual formalities.

4

* HYMN for *optional* use.

1.

Eternal Father, strong to save,
Whose arm hath bound the restless wave,
Who bidd'st the mighty ocean deep
Its own appointed limits keep :
    O hear us when we cry to Thee
    For those in peril on the sea.

2.

O Christ, whose voice the waters heard
And hushed their raging at Thy word,
Who walkedst on the foaming deep,
And calm amid the storm didst sleep ;
    O hear us when we cry to Thee
    For those in peril on the sea.

3.

O Holy Spirit, who didst brood
Upon the waters dark and rude,
And bid their angry tumult cease,
And give, for wild confusion, peace ;
    O hear us when we cry to Thee
    For those in peril on the sea.

4.

O Trinity of love and power,
Our brethren shield in danger's hour ;
From rock and tempest, fire and foe,
Protect them wheresoe'er they go ;
    Thus evermore shall rise to Thee
    Glad hymns of praise from land and sea.

                         AMEN.

---

* No. 370, *Ancient and Modern ;* No. 626, *Church Hymnary ;*
No. 540, *English Hymnal.*

FORM D-10   (Sta. 28/35)
(AMENDED, MARCH, 1953).

(8O 5089) Wt 19017—D7735 10M 8/53 H & S Ltd. **Gp. 399**

Acknowledgements

I could not have written this book without a great deal of assistance from many people and I am grateful to you all. If I have inadvertently omitted to mention the names of anyone who has so kindly helped me on my way, please forgive me. Any errors in or omissions from this book are mine and mine alone.

As with all research of this nature it has not always been possible to pinpoint the original historical source. There is much myth surrounding ship launch ceremonies and some traditions do not appear to have any clearly identifiable start, but have just evolved. So there remain unanswered questions. When studying the writings of others, I have, on occasion found it frustrating where sources have not been named. In order not to commit this sin myself I have included my sources to the fullest extent possible in the end notes at the back of the book.

Very early on, Gina Bardi, the Reference Librarian at Fort Mason, the Maritime National Historical Park in San Francisco, helpfully drew my attention to the relevance of superstition in shaping ship launch ceremonies. My subsequent research has confirmed that superstition and sailors' need for reassurance is indeed at the heart of many ship launch rituals. I am grateful to her for that valuable lead.

In addition to ship launch ceremonies in England, my intention from the very beginning was to include an account of some of the diverse ship launch ceremonies performed in countries outside of England.

I am grateful to Henning Morgan of Maersk for guidance on Denmark and for the use of her research.

Vladamir Krestyaninov and Yuri Basilov, both of St Petersburg, kindly delved into nineteenth-century Russian sources for examples of launches of ships of the Imperial Russian navy. My thanks go to them, and to Jenny Antill, who has so ably translated old Russian texts into English.

On early ship launch ceremonies of the Ottoman Empire I have relied heavily on the scholarship of Tuncay Zorlu, who has generously permitted me to prepare a summary of his research, which he has authorised me to include in this book.

The Hindu Institute in Oxford provided me with material that gave me a better understanding of the importance of *puja* in Indian ship launches.

On the unique ring ceremony performed at the stern of Italian naval ships built in the *Arsenale* in Venice at the end of the nineteenth century, Retired Admiral Lorenzo Sferra kindly permitted me to take photographs of the collection of ceremonial rings that are exhibited in the *Museo Storico Navale*. I am grateful also to *Biblioteca Nazionale Marciana* in Venice, who kindly provided me with copies of reports in the newspaper *Il Gazzettino* for 29 and 30 April 1897 describing the launch on 29 April 1897 of the cruiser *Ammiraglio di Saint Bon*, and to Renata Cibin, formerly of the Bodleian Library in Oxford, for her translations into English of these Italian texts.

Frederic Cornette has generously allowed me to use the research in his recent book *85 ans de lancements a Dunkerque* to inform my section on France and to refer to some colourful traditions followed in Dunkerque.

Henry Zhang, of Shandong Nanhai Airbag Engineering Co. Ltd, has kindly explained the modern technique of using vulcanised airbags for ship launches and allowed me to use his explanations and photograph in this book.

Guido Ercole, a naval historian and writer in Venice, gave me the benefit of his great knowledge on the launches of galleys in the *Arsenale*; my thanks also to Valeria Cafe for her guidance on the *Museo Correr*'s collection of pictures of the *Arsenale*.

The Atwater Kent Collection, Drexel University in Philadelphia, have kindly provided me with illustrations of multiple ship launches at Hog Island.

The National Archives and Records Administration of the US has given me information related to launches of 'Liberty ships'.

Dr Joacquim, of the *Manso Museum* in Nazare, is to be thanked for valuable information on the customs and traditions for the launch of fishing boats in Portugal.

Janet Gehman, Historian at the Society of Sponsors of the US Navy, has given me great insight into the role of lady sponsors of naval ships of the US Navy, and the society's president has kindly authorised me to quote from its website. The Venerable Ian Wheatley, Deputy Chaplain of the Fleet and Archdeacon for the Royal Navy, has guided me on religious services at the launch of naval ships.

Nathan Jones, Event Logistics Team Manager at the RNLI head-quarters in Poole, kindly answered my many questions on the ceremonies for naming and dedicating of lifeboats, and Caroline Young permitted me to explore the RNLI archives.

At the SS *Great Britain* Trust in Bristol, Eleni Papavasileiou, Head of Curatorial and Library Services, helpfully drew my attention to the many 'inventions' proposed by the general public to I.K. Brunel as he struggled to solve the problem of how to launch his *Great Eastern* sideways into the Thames.

The Royal Archives at Windsor Castle kindly allowed me to read the private diary of Queen Mary of 1934 and to study papers held by the Royal Archives relating to the launches of RMS *Queen Mary* and RMS *Queen Elizabeth*.

Ian Friel, Author of *The Good Ship, Ships, Shipbuilding and Technology in England 1220–1520*, helped me with source information on the launch of King Henry VIII's *Katherine Pleasaunce* in 1519.

Rodney Towers has kindly permitted me to include the story told by his father, George Towers, Managing Director of Tyne shipbuilder John Readhead & Sons, about a ship launched in 1940 in the middle of an air raid.

BAE Systems kindly sent me a copy of the event programme for the naming ceremony at Rosyth for the new aircraft carrier HMS *Queen Elizabeth*.

Michael Nield used his knowledge of the Classics to alert me to a useful passage in Horace's *Odes*.

Up and down the country many libraries and archives have generously allowed me to use their resources and given me guidance. At the head of a long list must come the Caird Library at the National

Maritime Museum in Greenwich, London with its unique collection of maritime books and archives and the Bodleian and Sackler libraries of Oxford University, all of whom have been most helpful throughout. I should not, however, forget the British Library; the National Archives; the City Library Newcastle upon Tyne; Tyne and Wear Archives and Museums; Glasgow City Archives, Mitchell Library; Hull History Centre; the British Newspaper Archives; Heather Johnson of the Library and Information Service Royal Navy Portsmouth; Stuart Berry of Heritage Centre, Pembroke Dock; the Dock Museum, Barrow-in-Furness; Cumbria Archive Service; the Library of University of Bath, Hollingworth Collection; University of Bristol, Special Collections; Brunel Institute, a collaborative venture of the University of Bristol, and the SS Great Britain Trust; Sunderland Local Studies Library, Special Collections, the Ulster Transport and Folk Museum; Southampton Central Library and the Musée portuaire Dunkerque, all of whom have given me valuable assistance.

On the illustrations I am grateful for the support and co-operation of Defence Historical Service, Vincennes; Detroit Historical Society; Meyer Werft GmbH & Co. KG, Papenburg; Musée portuaire Dunkerque; National Museums Northern Ireland Picture Library; British Pathe Ltd; Tyne and Wear Archives & Museums/Bridgman Images; Newcastle City Library, Local Studies and Family History Centre; Hulton Archives/Getty Images; Glasshouse Images/Alamy; the Picture Art Collection/Alamy; Glasgow Museums and Libraries Collection, Mitchell Library Special Collections; Brunel University London Archives and Special Collections; George Eastman Museum, New York; National Maritime Museum, Greenwich, London; Naval History and Heritage Command, Washington; Mary Evans Picture Library; Ufficio Storico Marina Militare (The Italian Navy Historical Office); Bibliotheque municipale de Rouen; Musée national de la Marine, Paris; the Dock Museum, Barrow-in-Furness; Central State Archives of Cinematic, Phonographic and Photographic Documents St Petersburg; Trustees of the National Museum of the Royal Navy; Photo Archive-Fondazione Musei Civici di Venezia; and Collection Saint-Nazaire Agglomeration Tourisme-Ecomusee.

My brother-in-law, Kenneth Usher, and Christopher Barstow both kindly read an earlier draft and gave me valuable comments and encouragement.

Finally, my thanks go to both Iain Atkins of Computer Solutions and to Rachael and Nat Ravenlock of The Book Typesetters for their vital help on digital challenges and book setting respectively.

Glossary

B

Ballast: heavy substance, solid or liquid, stowed as low as possible in the bottom of a ship to improve its stability or to alter its trim; larger ships in the modern era use sea water in a ballast tank, which can be easily pumped in and out to alter the trim as required.

Beakhead: a small platform immediately above the bows on a large sailing ship.

Blocks: heavy blocks of wood that support the keel of a ship during its construction and need to be removed prior to its launch.

Booth: a stall or other specified area in a dockyard set aside for visitors to view an event such as a ship launch.

Broadside: side of a ship or the battery of cannon on one side of a warship; and, from this, firing of all the guns on one side of a warship became known as a 'broadside'.

Bulbous bow: protruding bulb at bow of a ship just below the waterline used to smooth out the bow wave and to improve progress of the ship through the water.

Bulkhead: an upright wall within the hull of a ship, built across the ship from one side to the other and which may also be used to create a watertight compartment within the hull.

C

Caisson: the floating part of a dock that opens and closes, acting as a gate.

Camels: a method of reducing the draught of a ship that has stuck on the ways: a pair of watertight boxes, 'the camels', are filled with water so they sink and are then secured one on each side of the ship on the ways that, when the water is pumped out of the boxes, may, through their additional buoyancy, reduce the draught of the ship in the middle in order to facilitate its launch.

Capstan: a revolving cylinder for winding rope, cable or hawser, powered by motor or pushed round by levers. It is mounted vertically, whereas a windlass is mounted horizontally.

Carrack: three- or four-masted sailing ship, characterised by high superstructure fore and aft, originally a type of merchantman constructed in the Mediterranean between the fifteenth and seventeenth centuries.

Caulk: process of making seams in wooden boats watertight, usually by driving in oakum with a caulking iron and then pouring in hot pitch or resin in the crack to protect the oakum.

Caulker: a shipyard worker who caulks a ship.

Caulking iron: a chisel-shaped iron used for hammering oakum into a ship's seams.

Coffer: strong chest for storing valuables.

Colours: flags, for example 'launching colours'.

Cordage: rigging, cords, and ropes attached to masts and sails of a ship.

Cradle: a device, originally in timber, made up and fastened to either side of the hull of a ship as it is launched to keep it upright as it descends the launch ways.

Curve of stability: graphic representation of the successive leverages with which the buoyancy of a ship tends to force her either back into the upright position or further from it, when she has by force been inclined from that position.

Cutwater: the forward curve of the stem of a ship.

D

Daggers: a steel bar that plays an essential part in the launching mechanism of a ship: when the dog shores are knocked out (in the old days with a sledgehammer and today using power) the dagger acts as a trigger that releases the hull of a ship and starts it down the launching ways.

Deadweight or dwt: the measure of the cargo-carrying capacity of a ship.

Declivity: the downward inclination of the slope of launch ways.

Displacement: weight of water displaced by the immersed volume of a ship's hull exactly equivalent to the weight of the whole ship.

Dog shores: each of a pair of blocks of timber positioned on each side of a ship on a slipway to prevent it sliding down the ways before launching.

Draft or draught: depth of a ship's keel below the waterline and 'launching draught' is the depth of the ship's keel below the waterline at the time of its launch.

Drag chains: bundles of heavy chains attached to the hull that are used to exert a frictional force to slow the velocity of the hull in the water resulting from its launch. They are mostly used when the launch way is in a narrow waterway or river where there is not enough room for the ship to be launched without stopping her for fear of her running ashore on the opposite bank.

F

Fore poppet: when a ship is launched stern first, a temporary structure, originally made of wood, which supports the bow of a hull on the ways, especially at the moment when the stern becomes waterborne and the weight of the forward part of the hull is still carried on the ways.

Freeboard: the height of the deck of a ship over its waterline.

Fulcrum: the point against which a lever is placed to get a purchase.

G

Galley: a warship propelled by oars and lying low in the water, typically constructed in the Mediterranean.

Graving dock: a narrow basin closed by gates or caisson into which a ship may be floated and water then pumped out, leaving the ship supported on blocks, so that it may then be 'graved' – that is have the weeds and barnacles that have grown on its bottom burnt off – or it may be repaired.

Gross registered tons or grt: a ship's total internal volume expressed in 'register tons', each equal to 100 cubic feet.

Ground-ways: the large blocks and thick planks that support the cradle on which a ship is launched.

Gunwale: upper edge or planking running along the top of the side of a ship.

H

Hawser: a thick rope or cable used in mooring or towing a ship.

Hog-backed: a ship that is supported in the middle by, say, a wave but not at the ends is subject to hogging stress, tending to cause arching in the middle section.

Hydraulic press: a device using a hydraulic cylinder to generate compressive force.

Hydraulic pump: a mechanical device that converts mechanical power into hydraulic energy.

I

Inclining experiment: a test performed on a ship to determine its stability and the co-ordinates of its centre of gravity, involving the ship being caused to heel to small angles by moving known weights known distances transversely across the deck and observing the angles of inclination.

Initial stability: stability of a ship when it is upright or very nearly so, that is having a zero list.

Ironclad: an early name given to a mid-nineteenth-century warship with a hull that was either built with or protected by iron plate.

K

Keel: (in a wooden ship) the principal timber at the bottom of the hull and running the length of the ship or (in a metal ship) the lowest continuous line of plates.

L

Launch way: a sloping path or track into the water over which the hull of a ship slides, supported by its cradle and fore poppet, and which is usually coated with special launching grease.

Longitudinal: running lengthwise.

M

Metacentre: midway point between ship's centre of buoyancy when upright and her centre of buoyancy when tilted.

O

Oakum: material used for caulking seams in hulls, often hemp or fibres from old untwisted ropes treated with resin and pitch.

Ordinary: ships laid up at a dockyard.

P

Pennant or pendant: a long tapering flag generally flown from the masthead of a warship denoting that the warship is in commission or actual service.

Pitch: tar used with oakum for caulking.

Poop deck: usually the highest deck built over the after end of the quarter deck. This was the deck on which the ancient Greeks placed an ornamental image of the ship's guardian deity and on which in Stuart England the gilt cup was placed prior to the 'standing cup' naming ceremony.

Poppet: timbers, often in the shape of a cradle, used to support a hull on its launching ways, a fore poppet (see separate definition) being used to support the bow in a stern-first launch and a stern poppet being used to support the stern in a bow-first launch.

Prow: another word for bow, frequently used in poetry or literature, derived from the ancient Greek word *proira*.

R

Ram: An underwater prolongation of the bow, usually made in bronze, which was used by the ancient Greeks and Romans to rupture the hull of an enemy ship. The ramming ship after the initial contact needed to disentangle itself quickly from the rammed ship to avoid sinking along with it and to prevent the crew of the rammed ship from boarding.

Rate: formal system of dividing warships of Navy Board into groups, first rate down to sixth rate, originally according to number of men required to man the ship at sea, in 1660 altered to the number of carriage guns on board and in 1677 further modified by Samuel Pepys.

Reciprocating engine: an engine in which one or more pistons move up and down in a cylinder.

Restraints: ropes, often the last ropes, which hold a hull on its launch way that, when severed, will cause it to move down the ways into the water.

Rigger: workman who rigs a sailing ship.

S

Sagging stress: the straining of a ship that tends to make the middle portion of a ship lower than the bow or stern.

Screw windlass: a windlass is an apparatus for moving heavy weights; a screw windlass was the invention attributed to Archimedes 287–212 BC.

Shore: a temporary timber prop used to keep the hull of a ship upright during its construction before launching or when stored or beached on land before relaunching.

Side lever engine: first type of steam engine adapted for marine use in driving a paddle wheel, having two side levers and two side rods.

Slamming: the impact, especially if heavy, of the bottom of the ship onto the surface of the sea that occurs especially when sailing into large waves in heavy seas, causing stress to the hull.

Slide ways: that part of the launching ways which moves with the ship.

Slipway: ramp on the shore by which a ship can be moved to and from water and which is used for building or repairing a ship.

Stem: a timber rising from the keel and forming the centre of the bow.

Step: a socket built into the keel of a ship in which the base of the mast rests; a mast is said to be *'stepped'* when its heel is fitted into the step and it is raised.

Stocks: another name for 'keel blocks', the line of blocks in a building berth on which the keel of a ship is laid when being built, sloping down to the water. A ship that is said to be 'on the stocks' is one in the course of construction.

T

Tallow: wax used for waterproofing along with tar and pitch.

Thole pin: peg set in the gunwale of an oar-propelled ship that served as a fulcrum for an oar.

Trierarch: a wealthy citizen of ancient Athens who launched and fitted out a trireme for public service.

Trireme: from ancient Greek word *triere*, literally a three-rower, being a type of fighting galley with three banks of oars used by the Phoenicians, ancient Greeks and Romans.

Trigger: the letting fall of the catch on the cradle, as a result of which the dog shores offer no further resistance to the hull of a ship sliding down the ways.

Trigger rope: the rope that releases the catch on the cradle.

Trim (of a ship): inclination of its keel in a fore and aft direction.

Tort: an actionable civil wrong.

Twart: structural cross piece forming a seat for a rower.

V

Vulcanised rubber: vulcanisation is a chemical process for converting natural rubber into a more durable and stronger material by the addition of a curing agent such as sulphur followed by heating under pressure, *'vulcanised rubber'* being rubber that has been subject to this process.

W

Ways, also known as 'launch ways': timbers laid down at a shipyard that slope into the water and along which a ship is launched; 'way' also means, in the correct context, the movement of a ship through the water.

Select Bibliography

Act for Further Increase and Encouragement of Shipping 1786.

Admiralty Manual of Seamanship 1951.

Admiralty Manual of Seamanship 1966 Volume IV.

T.W. Allen, *The Homeric Hymns*, Oxford Clarendon Press, 1936.

Athenaus, *The Deipnosophists (The Philosophers at dinner or the learned banqueters) Book 5.*

Evgenii Anisimov, *The Reforms of Peter the Great*, 1993.

David Baldwin, *Royal Prayer: A Surprising History*, Continuum International Publishing Group, 2009.

Richard Barker, *Cradles of Navigation*, VIII Reuniao Internacional de Historia da Nautica e da Hidrografia, Viana, 1994.

Patrick Beaver, *The Big Ship: Brunel's Great Eastern: a Pictorial History*, Bibliophile Books, first published 1969 and then 1987.

Horace Beck, *Folklore and the Sea*, published for the Marine Historical Association by Wesleyan University Press, Middletown, Connecticut.

Gus Bourneuf Jr, *A Workhorse of the fleet: A History of the Liberty Ships*, American Bureau of Shipping © 1990, 2008.

Steven Brindle, *Brunel: The Man Who Built The World*, Weidenfeld & Nicolson, 2005, paperback 2006.

Richard Johnstone Bryden, *The Royal Yacht: Britannia*, Conway Maritime Press, 2003.

John Gurley Bunker, *Liberty Ships: the ugly ducklings of World War II*, 1972.

Bye-Laws and Regulations enacted by the Trustees of the Clyde Navigation 1903.

Caesar, *De Bello Gallico Book V.*

Phil Carradice, *The Ships of Pembroke Dockyard*, Amberley Publishing, 2013.

Lionel Casson, *Ships and Seamanship in Ancient World*, Princeton University Press, 1971.

Frederic Cornette, *Ateliers et Chantiers de France 85 ans de lancements a Dunkerque*, Volume 1 1902–1950, Volume II 1950–1987, Societe Dunkerquoise d'Histoire et d'Archeologie, 2017.

J.D. Crawshaw, *The History of Chatham Dockyard*, Newcastle upon Tyne, 1999.

Roger Crowley, *City of Fortune: How Venice Won and Lost a Naval Empire*, Faber and Faber Ltd, 2011.

Robert Crowley, *Conquerors: How Portugal Seized the Indian Ocean and Forged the First Global Empire*, Faber & Faber Ltd, 2015.

Jim Cuthbert and Ken Smith, *Palmers of Jarrow 1851–1933*.

Tony Dalton, *British royal yachts*, Halsgrove, 2002.

Richard Davis, *Shipbuilders of the Venetian Arsenal*, Longman, 1991.

Demosthenes, *On the Crown*, Harvey E. Yunis (ed.), Cambridge University Press, 2001.

Helen Doe, *The First Atlantic Liner*, Amberley Publishing, 2017.

V.A. Dygalo, *The Fleet of the State of Russia and Origin of the Russian Navy*.

Peter Elphick, *Liberty: The Ships that Won the War*, Chatham Publishing, 2001.

Guido Ercole, *Galeazze*, Gruppo Modellistico Trentino, 2010.

Antonia Fraser, *King Charles II*, Weidenfeld and Nicolson, 1979.

Edward Fraser, *'The Londons' of the British Fleet*, Bodley Head, 1908.

Ian Friel, *The Good Ship: Ships, Shipbuilding and Technology in England 1220–1520*, Johns Hopkins University Press, 1995.

C.M. Gavin, *Royal Yachts*, Rich & Cowan, 1932.

A.G. George, *The Babylonian Gilgamesh Epic*, Oxford University Press, 2003.

Jim and Cherie Gibbs, *Unusual side of the Sea*, Windward Publishing.

Ann Martin Hall and Edith Wallace Benham, *The Ships of The United States Navy and Their Sponsors 1913–1923*, privately printed, 1925.

Alec Harrison, *Superstitions*, Kenneth Mason Publications Ltd, 1972.

Edward Heath, *Sailing: A Course of My life*, Sidgwick and Jackson Ltd, 1975.

A.J. Holland, *Buckler's Hard: a rural shipbuilding centre*, Kenneth Mason, 1985.

Home Dockyard Regulations 1925.

Horace, *Odes Book 1*.

Stephen Howarth, *Morning Glory: A History of the Imperial Japanese Navy*, Hamish Hamilton, 1983.

Edward N. Hurley, *The Bridge to France*, Kessinger Publishing.

Bettany Hughes, *Helen of Troy, Goddess, Princess, Whore*, London Pimlico, 2006.

David T. Hughes, *Chatham Naval Dockyard & Barracks*, The History Press, 2004, reprinted 2006.

Iliad, Chapter 2.

International Standard Organisation (ISO)-14409.2011, *Ships and marine technology: Methodology for ship launching utilizing air bags*.

Capt. Walter W. Jaffee, *SS Jeremiah O'Brien: The History of a Liberty Ship from the Battle of the Atlantic to the 21st Century*, The Glencannon Press Palo Alto, 2008.

Fred Jane, *The Imperial Russian Navy*, Conway Maritime Press, reprinted 1899.

Judith Jesch, *Ships and Men in the Late Viking Age*, Woodbridge Boydell & Brewer, 2001.

William Jones, *Credulities Past and Present*, London, 1880.

Don H. Kennedy, *Ship Names*, 1974.

G.S. Kirk, *The Annual of the British School of Athens XLIV*, 1949.

Vladimir Krestjaninov, *Imperial Russian Navy 1890s–1916*, Uniform Press, 2013.

Andrew Lambert, *Trincomallee*, Chatham Publishing, 2002.

Frederic Chapin Lane, *Venetian Ships and Shipbuilders of the Renaissance*, Johns Hopkins Press, Baltimore, 1934 edition reprint.

Malcolm Letts (translated and edited), *Broadway Travellers* series, George Routledge & Sons, 1926.

Bjorn Loven, *The Ancient Harbours of the Piraeus: The Zea Shipsheds and Slipways*, Danish Institute at Athens, 2011.

Charles Rathbone Low, *History of the Indian Navy 1613–1863*, London, R. Bentley and Son, 1877.

Colin Maggs, *Isambard Kingdom Brunel: The Life of an engineering Genius*, Amberley Publishing, 2016.

Alan P. Major, *Royal Yachts*, Amberley Publishing, 2011.

Rob McAuley, *The Liners: A Voyage of Discovery*, Boxtree, an imprint of Macmillan Publishers Ltd, 1997.

Merchant Shipping Act 1873.

John Second Lord Montagu, *Buckler's Hard and its Ships*, London, 1909.

J.C. Morrison and R.T. Williams, *Greek Oared Ships 900–322 BC*, Cambridge University Press, 1968.

Roger Morriss, *The Royal Dockyards during the Revolutionary and Napoleonic Wars*, Leicester, University Press, 1983.

Peter Munday, *Travels of Peter Munday in Europe and Asia 1608–1667*, Cradles of Navigation note 37 ed. R.C. Temple Hakluyt Society.

A.J. Murray editor, *New English Dictionary on Historical Principles*, Oxford Clarendon Press, 1903, Volume VI L to N.

Naval History Division Department of the Navy Washington DC, *Ships of the United States Navy: Christening, Launching and Commissioning*, second edition, 1975.

Naval Intelligence Division, Admiralty, *German Battleship Bismarck: Interrogation of Survivors*, August 1941 CB 4051 (24) p.10, Para IV Early History and Trials.

R. Nisbet and M. Hubbard – *A Commentary on Horace Odes Book I*.

Odyssey Book 15.

John Peter Olseson, *Oxford Handbook of Engineering and Technology in the Classical World*, Oxford University Press, 2009.

Tom Packard, *We Make Ships*, Secker & Warburg, 1989.

B.H. Patterson, *'Giv'er a cheer Boys': The Great Docks of Portsmouth Dockyard 1830–1914*, Portsmouth Royal Dockyard Historical Society.

Samuel Pepys, *Diary: volume 5 1664*, Harper Collins, 1971.

Mrs Elizabeth E. Peters, *The History of Pembroke Dock*, London, 1905.

Phineas Pett, *The Autobiography of Phineas Pett 1570–1647*, HardPress Publishing.

Lieutenant Commander Lawrie Phillips, *Pembroke Dockyard and the Old Navy: A Bicentennial History*, The History Press, 2014.

Plutarch, *The Rise of Rome: Twelve Lives by Plutarch*, Penguin Classics, 2013.

Plutarch's Lives: translation Bernadotte Perrin 1914–1926, Cambridge Mass, Heinemann Harvard University Press.

Sharon Poole and Andrew Sassoli-Walker, *Oriana & Aurora: Taking UK cruising into a new millennium*, Amberley Publishing Plc, 2012.

Ian Rae and Ken Smith, *Swan Hunter: The Pride and the Tears*, Tyne Bridge Publishing, 2001.

Sir Edward Reed, *A Treatise on the Stability of Ships*, Charles Griffin & Co., London, 1885.

Sir Edward James Reed, *Report on the 'Daphne' Disaster*, Nabu Public Domain Reprints.

Alessandro Renier, *Feste E Varo Di Navi All'Arsenale Di Venezia 1866–1914 Circumnavigazioni del Mondo*, La Toletta edizioni, 2013.

Report given to Annual General Meeting of RNLI 15 March 1860.

Dr Silvia Rodgers, *Feminine Power at Sea*, Royal Anthropological Institute News 64 (1984).

L.T.C. Rolt – *Isambard Kingdom Brunel* – Longmans, 1957.

President Franklin D. Roosevelt, 'The Queen with a Fighting Heart', Article in *Sea Breezes*, 1936.

Paul Sebillot, *le folk-lore des pecheurs*, Paris J. Maisonneuve, 1901.

Andrew N. Sherwood, Milorad Nickolic, John W. Humphrey and John P. Oleson, *Greek and Roman Technology: a Sourcebook of Translated Greek and Roman Texts*, Routledge Taylor and Francis Group, 2020 second edition.

Short Brothers Ltd, '*Mowbray Quay to Pallion Yard 1850–1950*' (brochure), Sunderland Library.

Alexander Stephen, *Diary 1883*, Archives of Glasgow University ref UGD 4/8/25.

Patrick Stephens, *Ocean Liners of the Past No. 6*, reprint from *The Shipbuilder and Marine Engine Builder*, 1972.

William Shawcross, *Queen Elizabeth The Queen Mother The Official Biography*, Macmillan, 2009.

J.W. Smith and T.S. Holding, *Where Ships are Born Sunderland 1346–1946: a history of shipbuilding on the River Wear*, Thomas Reed and Company Ltd.

Ken Smith, *Queens of the Tyne*, Tyne Bridge Publishing, 2007.

Ken Smith, *Turbinia: The story of Charles Parsons and his ocean Greyhound*, Tyne Bridge Publishing, 1996, revised second edition 2009.

Taylor, *Notes and Queries* 9th series volume 1.

Henry Teonge, *Diary 1675–1691*, transcribed G.E. Manwaring, George Routledge & Sons, 1927, Routledge Curzon, 2005.

The Lessons of the Liberties, © 1974 American Bureau of Shipping.

The Naval Chronicle 1799–1818.

The Society of Sponsors of the United States Navy, https://societyofsponsorsofusn.org.

Roger D. Thomas and Brian Patterson, *Dreadnoughts: A Photographic History*, The History Press, 1998.

J.L. Thompson and Sons Centenary Brochure 1946.

Thucydides, *History of the Peloponnesian War Book 6*.

Cecil Torr, *Ancient Ships*, Cambridge University Press, 1894.

John Tredrea and Eduard Sozaev, *Russian Warships in the Age of sail 1696–1860*, Seaforth Publishing, 2010.

United States Supreme court decision 1902 Tucker v Alexandroff 183 US 424,438.

University of Bath Archives Hollingworth Collection: Material re the *Great Eastern* steamship.

University of Bristol Library, Special Collection, material relating to Brunel and launch of *Great Eastern*.

Valerius Maximus, volume II.

A.R. Wadia, *The Bombay Dockyard and the Wadia Master Builders*, Godrej Memorial Press, 1955.

Fred M. Walker, *Song of the Clyde*, John Donald Publishers, Edinburgh, revised edition 2001.

Clarence Winchester, *The Queen Elizabeth: The World's Greatest Ship*, Winchester Publications Ltd, 1947.

Robert Woodcock, *Side Launch: The Collingwood Shipyard Spectacle*, Summerhill Press, Toronto, 1983.

Richard Wortman, *Scenarios of Power: myth and ceremony in Russian monarchy from Peter the Great to the abdication of Nicholas II*, Princeton Press, 1995.

Powell F. York, *Edith Corpus Poeticum Boreale: the poetry of the old northern tongue from the earliest times to the thirteenth century*, Oxford University Press, 1883.

Dr Tuncay Zorlu, 'Ottoman Ship Launching Ceremonies: a Practice between Symbols and Rites', *International Review of Turkology*, Vol. 1, 2008.

The Author

George Hodgkinson, a graduate of St John's College, Oxford, spent thirty years practising as a solicitor in the City of London in the field of international ship finance. In this capacity he was privileged to be invited to some fifty naming and launch ceremonies in nine different countries. These included P&O's cruise ship *Aurora* named by HRH The Princess Royal and North Sea ferry *Pride of Hull* named by Cherie Blair, wife of the British Prime Minister, the latter being the first ship-naming ceremony to take place inside a ship. He has witnessed side launches and stern launches down slipways and 'float ups' in construction docks. The ships named and launched or just named have ranged from river coastal ships to supply ships, from suction dredgers to container ships, from ferries to cruise ships and a semi-submersible drilling ship.

As a partner in the maritime law firm Sinclair Roche & Temperley, he attended in 1989 the naming ceremony and service of dedication of the 'Atlantic 21' lifeboat *Ellis Sinclair*; this was donated by the partners of the firm to the Staithes and Runswick lifeboat station on the North Yorkshire coast in order to commemorate the firm's jubilee.

He has been a Liveryman of the Worshipful Company of Shipwrights in the City of London since 1998.

Notes

In these notes, the following abbreviations shall have the following meanings:

Caird   The Caird Library at The National Maritime Museum, Greenwich
NMM   The National Maritime Museum, Greenwich
OGL   The Open Government Licence
RA   Royal Archives
TNA   The National Archive

1. A Ship is Born

1. In March 2022 Lloyd's List, the chronicler of the maritime industry for over 250 years, decided to abandon 'she' for 'it' but the Royal Navy decided that it would continue the long-standing tradition of referring to ships as feminine.
2. See further under 'Greece' in Chapter 13.3.
3. Dr Silvia Rodgers 'Feminine Power at Sea' Royal Anthropological Institute News 64 (1984), extract reprinted by kind permission of John Wiley & Sons Inc. RAIN© 1984 Royal Anthropological Institute of Great Britain and Ireland.
4. Bodleian Libraries, Johnson e.740(1) with their kind permission.
5. United States Supreme Court decision of 1902 in Tucker v Alexandroff 183 US 424, 438.
6. *A New English Dictionary on Historical Principles* Edited by Dr James A.H. Murray, Oxford Clarendon Press 1903 Vol. VI L to N, p.106. See also ISO's definition of 'ship launching' in Chapter 2 in the modern context of launching a ship using vulcanised air bags.

2. A Ship's Shortest Trip – Launching methods

1. The title to this chapter has been derived from *ABS Surveyor Quarterly*, the Quarterly Publication of the American Bureau of Shipping, August 1974, p.22, and is used here with their kind permission.

2. The translation is based on standard Arkadian edition *The Babylonian Gilgamesh Epic* by A.G. George, 2003, Oxford University Press, ISBN 0-19-814922-0.
3. See *The Ancient Harbours of the Piraeus: The Zea Shipsheds and Slipways* by Bjorn Loven, Danish Institute at Athens, 2011, ISBN 9788771240078.
4. *Iliad* Chapter 2 151–4.
5. *Greek and Roman Technology: a Source book of translated Greek and Roman texts* by Andrew N. Sherwood, Milorad Nikolic, John W. Humphrey and John P. Oleson, Second Edition, 2020, Routledge Taylor and Francis Group, ISBN 978-1-138-92789-6, p.556, under 'Apollonius of Rhodes Argonautica 1.367.90'.
6. *Oxford Handbook of Engineering and Technology in the Classical World*, Oxford University Press, p.657.
7. See Chapter 19.
8. *Athenaeus, The Deipnosophists* (*The Philosophers at Dinner*) with English translation by Charles Burton Gulick, Book 5 verse 207, London William Heinimann Ltd and Cambridge University Press, 1928, and see also *Plutarch Lives Marcellus* 14.8, p.473, with English translation by Bernadette Perrin, Book 5, published London William Heinimann Ltd and Cambridge Massachusetts Harvard University Press, 1917. Plutarch refers to use of 'compound pulleys' rather than a screw windlass. Some sources give length of *Syracusia* as 110m.
9. *Athenaeus The Philosophers at Dinner* 5.207.
10. *Horace Odes* 1.4.
11. *Nisbet and Hubbard Commentary on Horace Odes Book 1*, Oxford University Press, 1970, ISBN 0-19-814914X, p.63.
12. TNA. PRO Exchequer LTR E 364/364/57.
13. TNA. PRO E36/11 f84r and f85v.
14. *Autobiography of Phineas Pett 1570–1647*, HardPress Publishing, p.75.
15. *Illustrated London News*, 6.4.1884.
16. R.C. Temple ed., *Travels of Peter Mundy in Europe and Asia 1608–1667*, Hakluyt Society 2nd series Vol. XLV, Cambridge 1919, p.59.
17. *Athenaeus Book* verse 204 translated into English by Charles Burton Gulick, William Heiniman Ltd and Harvard University Press, 1928, reprinted 1957.
18. Navires Ports et Chantiers, May 1968, No. 216.
19. 85 ans de lancements a Dunkerque by Frederic Cornette, Societe Dunkerquoise d'Histoire et d' Archeologie 2017 vol. II, p.151, with his kind permission.

20. Fred Jane, *The Imperial Russian Navy 1899,* Chapter XVII, pp.340–341.
21. See Chapter 14, 'Sideways launch using elephants'.
22. *Side Launch – The Collingwood Shipyard Spectacle 1983,* by Robert Woodcock, Summerhill Press Ltd, Toronto, ISBN 0-920197-00-0 (*Collingwood Shipyard*), p.72, by kind permission of the author Robert Woodcock.
23. Ibid.
24. Ibid.
25. *Buffalo Courier,* 31 July 1919.
26. Ibid.
27. *Collingwood Shipyard,* p.59, by kind permission of the author Robert Woodcock.
28. Meyerwerft website, extracts as downloaded by the author on 3 January 2015, with kind permission of Meyer Werft GmbH & Co.KG.
29. Courtesy Henry Zhang, Shandong Nanhai Airbag Engineering Co. Ltd, 5608 Shuangshan North Road, Shuangshan Street, Zhangqiu District, Jinan City, Shandong Province, China.
30. ISO 14409.2011 issued on 2011.09.01. Ships and marine technology – Ship launching air bags and ISO 17682.2013(E) issued on 2013.5.01. Ships and marine technology – Methodology for ship launching utilizing air bags. For definition of 'ship launching' see ISO 17682. 2013(E) para 3.1 quoted here with kind permission of the International Organisation for Standardisation (ISO).

3. The Superstition of Sailors

1. *Superstitions* by Alec Harrison, 1972.
2. *Ships of the United States Navy Christening, Launching and Commissioning* Second Edition Naval History Division Department of the Navy Washington, DC, 1975.
3. *Odyssey* 15.222.
4. *Thucydides History of the Poloponnesian War,* 6.32 translated by Rex Warner, 1954, Penguin Classics revised with new introduction and appendices, 1972, with kind permission of Penguin Books.
5. Drinking undiluted wine was not regarded as being good practice in ancient Greece.
6. *Greek Oared Ships 900–322 BC* by J.C. Morrison and R.T. Williams, Cambridge University Press, Arch 34, pp.85–6.

7. *The Aeneid Book 5 Text, Translation and Commentary*, edited by Lee M. Fratantuono and R. Alder Smith Brill, Leiden/Boston, ISBN 978-90-04-30124-5, p.108. Line 774 ff. 'Eryx' in Greek mythology is said to have been the son of Poseidon, god of the sea. With kind permission of Brill.

8. Aeneid 4. 418, Georgics 1.304.

9. Taylor in *Notes and Queries*, 9th series Vol. 1.

10. The word hlunn means roller. See also *Ships and Men in the Late Viking Age* by Judith Jesch, 2001.

11. Eddas Corpus Poeticum Boreale I, p.410.

12. VALERIUS MAXIMUS: Vol. II, translated by D.R. Shackleton Bailey, Loeb Classical Library Vol. 493, Cambridge, Mass.: Harvard University Press, Copyright © 2000 by the President and Fellows of Harvard College. Loeb Classical Library is a registered trademark of the President and Fellows of Harvard College. Used by permission. All rights reserved.

13. See France and Japan in Chapter 13.

14. But note that the ritual of sacrifice of sheep continued to be a traditional feature of ship launches in the Ottoman Empire until at least 1885. See Chapter 13.7.

15. *The 'Londons' of the British Fleet*, Edward Fraser, The Bodley Head, 1908, p.68.

16. *Autobiography of Phineas Pett 1570–1647*, HardPress Publishing, pp.81–82.

17. *The 'Londons' of the British Fleet*, Edward Fraser, The Bodley Head, 1908, p.68.

18. Caird PBC 1787/1-3, *Admiralty Manual of Seamanship* 1951 Vol. 1, p.264, under *Some Naval Customs and Ceremonies*, © Crown copyright licensed under OGL.

19. See launch of the *Prince Royal* at Deptford 1610, described in the *Autobiography of Phineas Pett 1570–1647*, HardPress Publishing, pp.83–84. 'His Highness ... with many gracious words to me [Phineas Pett] gave the standing cup into mine own hands ...'

20. The name was chosen by President Washington himself. She was one of six (later reduced to three) warships that he was authorised to purchase in an Act of 1794 'to provide a naval armament' to protect the country against the depredations of the Algerine Corsairs; and it was the legislative start of the United States Navy.

21. *Naval Chronicle*, Vol. 33, p.398.

22. *Illustrated London News* 29.5.1852, with kind permission of Mary Evans Picture Library.

23. Credulities Past and Present, 1880, Chapter 1.

24. Extract from *Sailing: A Course of my life* by Edward Heath p.142, re-printed by permission of Peters Fraser & Dunlop (www.petersfraserdunlop.com) on behalf of the Estate of Edward Heath.

25. *Folklore and the Sea* by Horace Beck, published for The Marine Historical Association by Wesleyan University Press, Middletown, Connecticut.

26. 'Oriana & Aurora', Sharon Poole and Andrew Sassoli-Walker, Amberley Publishing, 2012, p.95, reproduced with kind permission.

27. 'Oriana & Aurora', Sharon Poole and Andrew Sassoli-Walker, Amberley Publishing, 2012, pp.94–95, reproduced with kind permission.

28. See Chapter 14 for a more detailed description of this unusual ceremony.

29. Sebillot writing in *Le Folklore des Pecheurs* in 1901 at p.141 said that in Brittany it would be difficult to find a crew for a vessel that has not been blessed by a priest; it was sure to be unlucky.

30. *The Doncaster Gazette*, 1841.

31. See, for example, Denmark in Chapter 13.1.

4. Things do not Always go to Plan

1. 'How HMS *Victory* nearly never made it to the Battle of Trafalgar' by Maev Kennedy, published in *The Guardian*, 22 February 2015.

2. A similar but different problem occurred in 1843 in Bristol in respect of Brunel's 'Great Britain', which although launched successfully was too large to fit through the gates of the Floating Harbour, where it was consequently marooned for eighteen months. See Chapter 6.

3. *The Daily Telegraph*, 27 June 2017, p.1, quoted with their kind permission.

4. See Chapter 9.

5. See Chapter 6.

6. *Illustrated London News*, Vol. 38, 1861.

7. Ibid.

8. See Chapter 10.

9. *Illustrated London News*, 15.8.1874.

10. *Illustrated London News*, 24.3.1866, 14.4.1866 and 28.4.1866.

11. *Independenzia* was fully insured and the failure of its launch, although it may have looked like the cause of failure of the business at J. and W. Dudgeon, this was not necessarily the case.

12. *Swan Hunter The Pride and the Tears* by Ian Rae and Ken Smith, 2001, ISBN.9781857951066 with kind permission of Tyne Bridge Publishing.
13. See Chapter 5.
14. *Doncaster Gazette*, 1841.
15. *The Times*, 8 August 2009.
16. See Chapter 7.
17. Tyne and Wear Archives TWCMS 2009.4950.
18. At the naval review held at Spithead on 26 June 1897 in honour of Queen Victoria's Diamond Jubilee, 160 warships were on display drawn up in four lines. After the formal inspection, in an unscheduled but sensational exhibition of her speed, *Turbinia* went up and down the lines at 30 knots.
19. *Sunderland Echo & Shipping Gazette*, 7 March 1947.
20. *Side Launch* by Robert Woodcock, 1983, Summerhill Press Ltd, p.96, with kind permission of the author Robert Woodcock.
21. See Chapter 6.
22. See Chapter 3.
23. *Illustrated London News*, 9 July 1898.
24. *The Times*, 22 June 1898.
25. *Home Dockyard Regulations*, 1925 para 609.2.

5. The *Daphne* Tragedy 1883

1. *Engineer*, 6 July 1883.
2. Based on evidence of Alexander Stephen at the subsequent Inquiry, see Notes of Proceedings at Inquiry, p.22, attached to Report on the 'Daphne Disaster' by Sir Edward J. Reed, 1883, presented to both Houses of Parliament by Command of Her Majesty, and reprinted by Nabu Public Domain Reprints ('Daphne Inquiry Report').
3. Notes to Daphne Inquiry Report, p.23.
4. Archived under ref UGD 4/8/25.
5. See Chapter 10.
6. Charles Griffin & Co. London, 1885.
7. Diary of Alexander Stephen, Glasgow University Archives, archived under ref UGD 4/8/25.
8. Ibid.
9. Cf the stability problems at launch of SS *Principessa Jolanda* in 1907, the largest passenger ship built in Italy at that time, referred to in Chapter 4.
10. Daphne Inquiry Report Appendix, pp.54–5.

11. Daphne Inquiry Report Appendix, p.63.
12. *Byelaws and Regulations Enacted* by the Trustees of the Clyde Navigation, published 1903 and archived by Glasgow City Archives under ref T–CN5/10. This record does not specify the exact date when the new by-law relating to launches came into effect but sometime between 1883 and 1903 is the best estimate.

6. The Launch of Brunel's Three Great Ships

1. *Brunel: The Man Who Built the World*, Steven Brindle, Weidenfeld & Nicolson.
2. *Bristol Mirror*, 22 July 1837.
3. Reproduced from Appendix 2 of *The First Atlantic Liner*, Helen Doe, 2017 (with kind permission of Amberley Publishing).
4. Helen Doe op. cit., p.111, with kind permission of Amberley Publishing.
5. Helen Doe op. cit., p.119, with kind permission of Amberley Publishing. Concorde, like *Great Western*, had a single class of mainly wealthy passengers, was a supersonic aircraft with maximum of 92 to 128 passengers, crossing the Atlantic in three and a half hours at twice the speed of sound and, like *Great Western*, which traded for seventeen years, was in operation only for a short time between 1976 and 2003.
6. *Illustrated London News*, 29 July 1843.
7. *Isambard Kingdom Brunel* by Colin Maggs, 2016, Amberley Publishing ('Colin Maggs'), p.188.
8. *Isambard Kingdom Brunel* by L.T.C. Rolt, Longmans, 1957, p.236.
9. *Brunel: The Man Who Built the World*, Steven Brindle, Weidenfeld & Nicolson, 2006, p.133.
10. Hollingworth Collection 2, The Library, University of Bath.
11. Hollingworth Collection 4, The Library, University of Bath.
12. Ibid.
13. University of Bristol Library Special Collections reference DM162/10/12 folios 262,263,265, courtesy of the Brunel Institute, a collaborative venture of the University and of the SS Great Britain Trust.
14. See R.A. Buchanan, The Great Eastern controversy, a comment, *Technology and Culture*, The Johns Hopkins University Press, January 1983.
15. *The Big Ship* by Patrick Beaver, 1969, Bibliophile Books, p.33.
16. University of Bristol Library, Special Collections ('UBSC') reference DM1306/11/23/64, courtesy of the Brunel Institute, a collaborative

venture of the University and of the SS Great Britain Trust ('Brunel Institute').

17. UBSC reference DM 1306/11/23/133 courtesy of Brunel Institute.
18. UBSC reference DM1306/11/23/292 courtesy of Brunel Institute.
19. UBSC reference DM1306/11/23/155 courtesy of Brunel Institute.
20. UBSC reference DM1306/11/23/130 courtesy of Brunel Institute.
21. UBSC reference DM1306/11/23/163 courtesy of Brunel Institute.
22. *Mechanics Magazine*, 15 December 1857, see also Colin Maggs, p.257.
23. Hollingworth Collection 6, The Library, University of Bath.
24. See Chapter 2.

7. Largest Liner Launched

1. *Liners*, Bob McAuley 1997, pp.40–1.
2. Ibid., p.42.
3. See Chapter 4.
4. *The Evening Chronicle*, 21.9.1906.
5. The name is that of the ancient Roman province of north-west Africa.
6. *The Evening Chronicle*, 21.9.1906.
7. Tyne and Wear Archives Service note on *Mauretania*.
8. Tyne and Wear Archives Service note on *Mauretania*.
9. Tyne and Wear Archives Service note on *Mauretania*.
10. See Chapter 4.
11. *The Newcastle Daily Journal*, 21.9.1906.
12. Article by President Franklin D. Roosevelt, 'The Queen with a Fighting Heart', 1936, published in 'Sea Breezes', quoted with kind permission of Sea Breezes Publications Ltd, Isle of Man.

8. 'Ladies Who Launch'

1. *King Charles II*, Antonia Fraser, 1979, Weidenfeld and Nicolson Ltd, p.224.
2. Dr G. Conceicao Silva, *Mariner's Mirror*, Vol. 93, p.362.
3. Whitehall April 21 1670 to Williamson, Keeper of Archives.
4. *The Times* (of London), 10 January 1803, p.2 column 4.
5. *The Times* (of London), 10 January 1803, p.2 column 4.
6. Caird PCB 1787/1-3 *Admiralty Manual of Seamanship*, 1951, Vol. 1, p.264. © Crown Copyright licensed under OGL.
7. *Naval Chronicle*, Vol. 26, p.322.

8. *Naval Chronicle,* Vol. 26, p.325.
9. TNA ADM 106/3336. © Crown Copyright licensed under OGL.
10. Forward edge of the ship's prow.
11. *Naval Chronicle,* Vol. 33, p.398.
12. *The Unusual Side of the Sea*, Jim Gibbs, Windward Publishing Co.
13. Caird 1787/1-3. *Admiralty Manual of Seamanship,* 1951. © Crown Copyright Vol. 1, p.264, under 'Naval Customs and Ceremonies' see under 'Launching Ceremony' the following: 'It is interesting to note that on one subsequent occasion a certain lady missed her aim with the bottle, which struck and injured a spectator who sued the Admiralty for damages, and this resulted in the Admiralty directing that in future the bottle should be secured to the ship with a lanyard.' No source or date for this incident or date of the direction from the Admiralty is given in the *Admiralty Manual of Seamanship*.
14. Ibid.
15. Viscount Sydney was a courtier of the royal household and held various senior Cabinet positions in the late eighteenth century.
16. *Naval Chronicle,* Vol. 40, p.362.
17. *Mariner's Mirror,* Vol. 70, August 1984, p.329, Hugh Moffat.
18. *Suffolk Chronicle,* 4 August 1821.
19. *Ipswich Journal,* 29 September 1821.
20. *Ships of the United States Navy* 'Christening, Launching and Commissioning', 2nd Edition, Naval History Division Department of the Navy Washington DC, 1975, p.9.
21. Website of the Society of Sponsors of the United States Navy, https://societyofsponsorsofusn.org, with their kind permission.
22. Ibid.
23. See Chapter 10.

9. Launches at Royal Dockyards

1. *The Royal Dockyards during the Revolutionary and Napoleonic Wars* by Roger Morriss, 1983, Leicester University Press, p.26. 'With refitting and repairs taking priority there was never enough labour to devote to new construction especially at the yards most accessible from the sea.'
2. *Buckler's Hard: a rural shipbuilding centre*, A.J. Holland, 1985, Kenneth Mason ('Holland, *Buckler's Hard*'), p.120.
3. *Buckler's Hard and its Ships 1909*, John Second Lord Montagu ('Lord Montagu, *Buckler's Hard*'), p.39.

4. Lord Montagu, *Buckler's Hard*, p.39.

5. For the letters sent by the Naval Overseer on launch of 28-gun *Greyhound* on 20 July 1773 and 32-gun *Thetis* on 2 November 1773 see TNA PRO 1218. © Crown Copyright Licensed under OGL.

6. Holland, *Buckler's Hard*, p.74.

7. Until 1832 when the Admiralty assumed this role.

8. TNA PRO ADM 174/226. © Crown Copyright Licensed under OGL. Compare *Daphne* tragedy in July 1883, where there was no such regulation as to numbers of workmen remaining on board at launch of this merchant ship.

9. Based on correspondence between Navy Board and Commissioners at various Royal Dockyards archived at TNA PRO under ADM 106.

10. See Chapter 19 for changes to the practice of flying the Admiralty Flag at launch of naval ships.

11. See Chapter 3 for description.

12. Memorandum from papers of 4th Earl of Sandwich reproduced in *Mariner's Mirror*, Vol. XXIV, p.355.

13. National Maritime Museum Margarette Lincoln, *Mariner's Mirror*, Vol. 83 No. 1, 1997.

14. *Naval Chronicle*, Vol. 24, p.35.

15. *United Service Journal*, May 1883.

16. *Pembroke Dockyard and the Old Navy* Lawrie Phillips 2014 ('Phillips Pembroke Dockyard') p.26, The History Press.

17. *The Pembrokeshire Herald*, 29 July 1853.

18. *The History of Pembroke Dock*, Elizabeth Peters, London, 1905, p.18.

19. *Pembroke Dock and Tenby Gazette*, 30 April 1885, reporting on launch of HMS *Howe*.

20. TNA: PRO ADM 106/406/209. © Crown Copyright licensed under OGL.

21. TNA: PRO ADM 106/459/255. © Crown Copyright licensed under OGL; a 'firkin' was another name for a barrel.

22. Holland, *Buckler's Hard*, p.122.

23. *Autobiography of Phineas Pett*, ed. W.G. Perrin, HardPress Publishing ('Pett *Autobiography*') Introduction p.xviii and following pages.

24. Ibid., p.82.

25. Ibid., p.84.

26. 'hansel' means to inaugurate the use of, Ibid., note on p.84.

27. R.D. Merriman, *Mariner's Mirror*, Vol. 43, 1956, p.231.

28. *Diary of Samuel Pepys*, Vol. V, 1664, Harper Collins, p.306.
29. TNA: PRO ADM 106/3520. © Crown Copyright licensed under OGL.
30. *The History of Chatham Dockyard*, 1999, J.D. Crawshaw.
31. TNA: PRO ADM 106/520/174. © Crown Copyright licensed under OGL.
32. TNA: PRO ADM 106/10389. © Crown Copyright licensed under OGL.
33. TNA: PRO ADM 106/2664. © Crown Copyright licensed under OGL.
34. Caird ADM/BP 25A. © Crown Copyright licensed under OGL.
35. Caird ADM/BP 35A. © Crown Copyright licensed under OGL.
36. *Illustrated Times*, 11 September 1858.
37. Dockyard Instructions 1875 'Gratuities to be allowed to the Chief Constructor for the safe launching of Her Majesty's ships or floating them out of dock after building in dock', Chapter XXXVIII. Courtesy of the National Museum of the Royal Navy, Portsmouth.
38. *Dreadnoughts – A Photographic History*, Roger Thomas and Brian Patterson, 1998, The History Press ('The Dreadnoughts Photographic History'), p.52, with kind permission.
39. Ibid., pp.80–81.
40. Ibid., p.53.
41. National Maritime Museum OBJ 0227.
42. Home Dockyard Regulations 1925, Regulation 609.14 TNA ADM 275/24 TNA. © Crown Copyright licensed under OGL.
43. Home Dockyard Regulations 1925, Regulation 609.11. TNA ADM 275/24 TNA. © Crown Copyright licensed under OGL.
44. Home Dockyard Regulations 1925 Addendum TNA ADM 275/25 TNA. © Crown Copyright licensed under OGL.

10. Religious Service at the Launch of Naval Ships

1. Pell Rolls, 16 July 1418.
2. TNA ADL/A/7.
3. Silk cloth.
4. *The Autobiography of Phineas Pett* 1570–1647, pp.79–80, HardPress Publishing.
5. Ibid., p.81.
6. See Chapter 3.
7. Ibid.
8. The Diary of Henry Teonge Chaplain on board HM's ships *Assistance*, *Bristol* and *Royal Oak* 1675–1691, transcribed from the original manuscript and

edited with introduction and notes by G.E. Manwaring, Welcome Collection, Public Domain Mark. Henry Teonge was born on 18 March 1621, became rector at Alcester 1648 and took additional living at Spernall in 1670. He resigned the living at Alcester in 1675. By this time he had three sons and one daughter. It was almost certainly debt that made him take the surprising decision at the age of 55 to look for a chaplaincy post in the Royal Navy.

9. George Hunt was appointed Chancellor of the Exchequer by Prime Minister Disraeli in 1868. When he presented his one and only budget speech he discovered he had left the ministerial 'Red Box' containing it at home. This is said to be the start of the tradition that when a Chancellor leaves for the House of Commons on Budget Day he shows the assembled crowd the box by holding it aloft. Hunt was a 'very heavy set person' and an uncorroborated story about him is that he was the origin of the semicircle cut into the end of the table in the Admiralty boardroom that enabled him to sit more comfortably at that table!

10. Dockyard Instructions 1875, Chapter LXX, Chaplain para 7. Courtesy of the National Museum of the Royal Navy, Portsmouth ('Dockyard Instructions 1875').

11. *Mariner's Mirror,* Vol. 35, pp.43–46.

12. Hansard 1875, Vol. 222, cc393–4.

13. See Chapter 4.

14. In the Dockyard Instructions 1875, Chapter LXX, Chaplain para 7, it is stated that: 'On the occasion of the launching from the dockyard of any ship or vessel which may be added to the list of Her Majesty's Navy,' the Chaplain 'is preliminary to the launch to read the Form of Service (drawn up by His Grace the Primate) to be used at the launching of Ships of Her Majesty's Navy.' See also Regulation 59 in Regulations for Government of His Majesty's Dockyards at Home 1925: 'Before the launch from the Dockyard of any ship or vessel of His Majesty's Navy, he [the Chaplain] is to read the service authorised for use on such occasions.'

15. See format in Appendix II to this book that consisted of part of Psalm 107: 'They that go down to the sea in ships; and occupy their business in great waters,' a special prayer appropriate to the occasion and other prayers. The form exhibited in Appendix II, amended since the original form introduced in 1875, was used at the launch of HMS *Leopard* by Princess Marie Louise on 23 May 1955 at Her Majesty's Dockyard Portsmouth. Courtesy of the National Museum of the Royal Navy, Portsmouth.

16. *Admiralty Orders and Instructions for building and fitting of ships*, 4th edition, 1892, ADM 7/957, p.9.
17. Letter dated 8 March 1875 from First Lord of Admiralty to Archbishop Tait.
18. *Pembroke Dock and Tenby Gazette*, 11 March 1875.
19. Admiral Sir Herbert King-Hall, *Naval Memories and Traditions*, Hutchinson, 1926, pp.10–11. King-Hall was Superintendent 1871–75. See also *Mariner's Mirror* Vol. XII, 1926, p.350.
20. Launch of HMS *Fearless* on 12 June 1919. *Pembroke Dock and the Old Navy*, Lieutenant Commander Lawrie Phillips, The History Press, 2014, p.300.
21. *Pembroke Dock and Pembroke Gazette*, June 1904.
22. Launch of HMCS *Ojibwa* 25 February 1964 by Lady Miers.
23. *Pembroke Dock and the Old Navy*, Lieutenant Commander Lawrie Phillips, 2014, The History Press, p.295 and p.300, accounts of launches of HMS *Blanche*, 25 November 1909, and HMS *Fearless* on 14 March 1911.
24. *History of Pembroke Dock*, London, Eliot Stock, 1905.
25. *Chatham in Old Photographs*, Philip MacDougall, 1994, p.47.
26. *Ships of the United States Navy and their Sponsors 1787–1913*, p.152. 'This is the single instance found in examined records of any religious service at the launching of a US Navy Ship.'
27. See Chapter 8 for the origin of the society.
28. *NY Times*, 24.3.1914.

11. Royal Launching and Christening of Ships

1. See Chapter 9.
2. *The Autobiography of Phineas Pett 1570–1647*, HardPress Publishing, ISBN 9781290996013 ('Pett, *Autobiography*'), p.21.
3. Ibid., p.23.
4. See Chapter 9. Memorandum in papers of 4th Earl of Sandwich reproduced in *Mariner's Mirror* XXIV, p.355.
5. *Naval Chronicle*, 1804, Vol. XI, p.407.
6. *Naval Chronicle*, Vol. 38, p.113.
7. *Pembroke Dockyard and the Old Navy*, Lt Commander Lawrie Phillips, The History Press 2014, p.101 ('*Pembroke Dockyard and the Old Navy*').
8. See Chapter 14.
9. This list excludes the first small yacht *Tsarevna* built in Hull whose launch in 1873 the Grand Duke Alexander Alexandrovich, the 4th son of Tsar Alexander II, attended. See Chapter 14.

10. Meaning orb, referring to the orb that appears clutched in the talons of the double-headed eagle in the Russian State seal.

11. Meaning Polar Star.

12. See Chapter 13.5.

13. Richard Wortman, in *Scenarios of Power*, 1995, Princeton Press, Vol. 2, p.4, writes 'the failure of the ruler [tsar] to make appearances at ceremonies and festivals ... appeared as derelictions of his symbolic obligations. Such lapses cast doubt on the monarch's superhuman capacities and portended a broader loss of authority and control over the political order.'

14. *Pembroke Dockyard and the Old Navy*, op. cit., p.264.

15. *Royal Yacht – Britannia*, Richard Johnstone Bryden, 2003, Conway Maritime Press ('*Royal Yacht*, Bryden'), p.20.

16. Ibid., op. cit., p.20.

17. Copyright David Baldwin, 2009, Royal Prayer, Continuum, an imprint of Bloomsbury Publishing Plc, p.16, with their kind permission.

18. See correspondence at RA PS/PSO/GV/PS/MAIN/55153.

19. Fred Walker, *Song of the Clyde*, Patrick Stephens Ltd, 1984, and revised 2001, p.149.

20. *The Times*, 27 September 1934.

21. Ibid.

22. The Diary of Queen Mary RA QM/PRIV/QMD/1934: 26 September 1934, with kind permission of His Majesty King Charles III.

23. Announcement from Buckingham Palace, 26 September 1938, given to Press Agencies, RA PS/PSO/GVI/PS/MAIN/2721.

24. *Queen Elizabeth the Queen Mother The Official Biography*, William Shawcross, Macmillan, 2009, pp.440–1.

25. See correspondence at RA PS/PSO/GVI/PS/MAIN/2721.

26. *The Liners*, Rob McAuley, 1997, Boxtree copyright (text) The Liners Pty Ltd, p.84.

27. *Glasgow Herald*, 17.10.1947.

28. The Daily Telegraph 5.7.2014 p8. The Royal Communications Dept at Buckingham Palace has confirmed that it has no objection to these words of The Late Queen being cited here.

12. Venice's Unique Ring Ceremony

1. The origin of this word is obscure but it is thought to derive from the Venetian *burcio*, a traditional term for a lagoon boat, and *in oro*, meaning covered in gold.

2. See Feste E Varo di Navi All'Arsenale di Venezia 1866–1914, Alessandro Renier, 2013, p.73.
3. This account is based on contemporaneous press reports in Venice published in *Il Gazzettino* on 29 and 30 April 1897, kindly supplied by Biblioteca Nazionale Marciana, Venice, and in Alessandro Renier's book referred to in note 2. The press reports have been translated into English by R. Cibin, formerly of Bodleian library, University of Oxford, and her translated words are reproduced here with her kind permission.
4. Richly decorated boats with eight oars.
5. Marcia Reale d'Ordinanza or Fanfara Reale, the Royal March of Ordinance, the official national anthem of Italy in 1861–1946.

13. Different Traditions in Different Countries

1. See Chapter 14 for a more detailed description of the launch.
2. Based on Article in *Maersk Post* by Dr Henning Morgen, Group History Documentation, AP Moller Maersk, and used in the writing of this section with kind permission of Dr Henning Morgen.
3. Alternative wording is: '*Seigneur-Dieu, du ciel, daignez ecouter nos priers et benir ce navire et touts qui vont y embarquer*' – Lord God of heaven deign to listen to our prayers and bless this ship and all who will embark on her.
4. See Chapter 17.
5. See Chapter 19.4.
6. The origin of the Te deum is ascribed by some to the baptism of St Augustine by Saint Ambrose in AD 387 and can, therefore, be seen to be appropriate for this occasion.
7. See Chapter 3.
8. Exhibit 2008.23.3.
9. See Chapter 9.
10. For the history of launches at ACF, see 'Ateliers et Chantiers 85 ans de lancements a Dunkerque', Frederic Cornette, 2017, ISBN 979-10-94763-08-7. With his kind permission, material from this book has been reproduced here.
11. The words frequently used by *La Marraine* to name the ship are '*Je te nomme … et je souhaite bonne fortune et bon vent*' – I name you … and wish you good fortune and fair wind.
12. For examples of the names chosen by the ancient Greeks see *Ships and Seamanship in the Ancient World*, L. Casson, pp.350–353.
13. Ibid., p.345 note 5.

14. Herodotus 8.88.
15. Casson, op. cit., p.345 note 5.
16. *Ancient Ships*, Cecil Torr, Cambridge University Press, 1894, p.67.
17. 1786 Cap 60 'An Act for the Further Increase and Encouragement of Shipping' Section XIX. 'the owner shall ... paint or cause to be painted in white or yellow letters the name by which such ship ... shall have been registered and the port to which it belongs on some conspicuous part of the stern.'
18. Merchant Shipping Act 1873 36 and 37 Victoria C85 applicable to every British ship registered after the passing of this Act. 'Her name shall be marked on each of her bows and the name of her port of registry shall be marked on her stern.'
19. See Chapter 3 note 8.
20. *Greek Religion*, Walter Burkett, Blackwell Publishing, 1987, p.284.
21. *The Homeric Hymns*, T.W. Allen, Oxford Clarendon Press, 1936.
22. A guardian or protector.
23. *Credulities Past and Present*, William Jones, 1880, Chapter 1 'The Sea and Seamen', p.65.
24. Apuleius, 'The Golden Ass' 11.16, translated by P.G. Walsh, Clarendon Press, Oxford, 199,4 pp.228–9.
25. See also *Iliad* 16 228–32, where Achilles used sulphur to fumigate, and then water to wash, a special cup before a libation to Zeus was offered from it.
26. See Chapter 3.
27. Virgil, *Aeneid* 5.774.
28. Book V, pp. 482–483 para c, translated by S. Douglas Olson, Harvard University Press, 2006 ISBN -3: 978-0-674-99621-2.
29. British Museum, London, 1899, 0219.1.
30. G.S. Kirk, *The Annual of the British School of Athens*, XLIV, 1949, p.93 ff.
31. See Chapter 3.
32. Ibid.
33. *Morning Glory: a history of the Imperial Japanese Navy*, Stephen Howarth, 1983, Hamish Hamilton, p.1.
34. Camellias in Japan symbolise the divine and are often used in religious and sacred ceremonies.
35. *The Times*, March 1877.
36. *Melusine*, Vol. III 1886–7, p.23.
37. *Barrow News*, 10 July 1905, by kind permission of *Northwest Evening Mail*.

38. This name is an old poetical name for Japan.

39. *Illustrated Sporting and Dramatic News*, 12.11.1898, p.24.

40. *Daily Telegraph & Courier*, 2.11.1898, p.10.

41. Preface to Russian Naval Statute 1720.

42. Courtesy Vladimir Krestjaninov, St Petersburg, author of *Imperial Russian Navy 1890s–1916*, published by Uniform Press, 2013.

43. The name connotes greater Russia including its empire.

44. See image on p.220 in *Russian Warships in the Age of Sail 1696–1860*, John Tredrea and Eduard Sozaev, Seaforth Publishing, 2010.

45. See Chapter 11.

46. Princess Dagmar of Denmark, who on becoming a member of the Russian Orthodox Church assumed the name Marie Feodorovna.

47. The base of the Baltic fleet on Kotlin Island founded by Peter the Great that guards the approach to St Petersburg.

48. The first permanent bridge across the River Neva.

49. Based on report in the *Government Herald* repeated in *Niva Magazine*, 1890, Issue No. 22, p.579, and translated from the Russian by Jenny Antill, her translation being reproduced here with her kind permission.

50. See note above.

51. Issue No. 42, p.817.

52. Translation from the Russian by Jenny Antill, reproduced here with her kind permission.

53. The yacht's name is a reference to the imperial family's retreat on the coast of Crimea, where they went frequently to escape from the court in St Petersburg.

54. *Glasgow Herald*, 8 July 1880.

55. *Illustrated London News*, 17 July 1880, includes a lithograph of the launch showing its unusual shape.

56. Report in *Niva Magazine*, 1902, Issue No. 41, translated from the Russian by Jenny Antill, her translation being reproduced here with her kind permission.

57. *The Fleet of the State of Russia. The Roots and Origin of the Russian Navy*, V.A. Dygalo.

58. *Glasgow Herald*, 8 July 1880.

59. Zoroastrianism is one of the world's oldest religions and is based on the teachings of the Iranian-speaking prophet Zoroaster and founded before

the sixth century BC. Parsees are descended from Persian Zoroastrians who relocated to India to escape from Moslem persecution.

60. *Asiatic Journal*, January 1820, quoted in *The Bombay Dockyard and the Wadia Master Builders*, Godrej Memorial Press, 1955, pp.197–198. See also *The Mariner's Mirror* MMLXII, 1976, p.95, para 14, referring to *Illustrated London News*, 6 January 1849, which describes the silver nail ceremony for battleship *Meanee* at Bombay Dockyard in 1848.

61. *The Bombay Dockyard and the Wadia Master Builders*, Godrej Memorial Press, 1955.

62. *The Bombay Courier*, 23 June 1810.

63. Ibid.

64. Museum of London. The gift of Robes of Honour were also a feature of ship launches under the Ottoman Empire, see Chap 13.7.

65. *The Bombay Dockyard and the Wadia Master Builders*, op. cit., p.209.

66. *Trincomallee*, Andrew Lambert, Chatham Publishing, 2002.

67. *History of the Indian Navy*, Charles Rathbone Low, 1877, Vol. 1, p.29.

68. *American Bureau of Shipping ABS Surveyor Quarterly*, August 1974, edition p.25.

69. Sanscrit for 'killer of enemies'.

70. See also under India in Chapter 13.6, where under the Zoroastrian ritual of the silver nail ceremony at Bombay Dockyard, robes of honour were traditionally presented to the Master Builder.

71. The above paragraphs are based on research by Professor Dr Tuncay Zorlu of Istanbul Technical University in an Article titled 'Ottoman Ship launching ceremonies: a Practice between Symbols and Rites' published in *International Review of Turkology*, Vol. 1 No. 1 (Winter 2008), pp.55–63, and reproduced here with his kind permission.

72. *London Evening Standard*, 5.1.1855.

73. See launch of two-decker *Fechinje* reported in *Leeds Times*, 27.12.1856.

74. *London Evening Standard*, 29 October 1874, reporting on the launch at Thames Ironworks and Shipbuilding of *Mesudiye*, which means 'fortunate', where the christening was performed by Miss Minsurus, the fourth daughter of the Turkish Ambassador.

75. *Conquerors*, Roger Crowley, 2015, Faber and Faber Ltd, pp.52–53.

76. Ibid.

77. Roger Crowley, op. cit., p.51.

78. Cradles of Navigation note 37, R.C. Temple ed., *Travels of Peter Mundy in Europe and Asia 1608–1667*.
79. *Gazeta de Lisboa*, 21 November 1721.
80. *Daily Post*, 24 July 1733.
81. *Wide and Beautiful Port of Lisbon*, Pedro Castro Henriques.
82. *Ancient Ships,* Cecil Torr, Cambridge University Press, 1894, p.69 and illustrations 12, 13, 15, 19 and 40 showing vases of *c*.500 and 600 BC with images of ships with an 'eye' painted on the bow and which are explained further in the index to the Illustrations to Torr's book.

14. Unusual Launches and Naming Ceremonies

1. *History of Indian Navy*, C.R. Low 1613–1863, Vol. 1, 1877, p.182.
2. See Chapter 6.
3. See Chapter 10.
4. See Chapter 5.
5. *Eastern Morning News*, 7 July 1873.
6. *Eastern Morning News*, 2 September 1874.
7. See Chapter 16 on Multiple Launches and the contribution to this standard design of another Tyne shipbuilder, Cyril Thompson.
8. *Shields Gazette*, 21 September 1940 with kind permission.
9. Ibid.
10. Ibid.
11. See Chapter 16 on Multiple Launches.
12. Based on reports in *Vickers News*, pp.255–256.
13. Article in *Glasgow Herald*, 20 August 1947, p.6, headed 'Liner launched by radio', with kind permission.
14. Harald Hendriksen, webmaster@yachtstandart.com
15. See Chapter 13.6.
16. *Yorkshire Post*, 1 December 2001.
17. See Chapter 3.
18. Emily Garnham, *Express*, 16 April 2008.
19. bbcnews.co.uk 2.4.2008: *Southend Echo* 3.2.2008.
20. *Illustrated London News*, 11 August 1855 p.172.
21. Ibid.
22. Ibid.
23. Ibid.

24. Short Brothers Ltd brochure 'Mowbray Quay to Pallion Yard 1850–1950', pp.15–16, Sunderland Library.
25. Ibid.

15. Lifeboats and the Service of Dedication

1. *Morning Chronicle,* 12 September 1861, p.3.
2. *Newcastle Chronicle,* 15 November 1862, p.8.
3. Report given to Annual General Meeting on 15 March 1860.
4. *Newcastle Chronicle,* 15 November 1862.
5. *York Herald,* 28 November 1863, p.5.
6. *Kingsbridge Journal,* 25 September 1869.
7. *Liverpool Mercury,* 26 January 1863, p.3.
8. 12 June 1873, p.3.
9. *Exeter & Plymouth Gazette,* 25 May 1876, p.3.
10. *Torquay Times and South Devon Advertiser,* 27 May 1876, p.5.
11. See Chapter 10.
12. See Chapter 3.
13. See Chapter 13.2.

16. Multiple Launches

1. See Homer's *Iliad* Book II for Catalogue of Ships.
2. *Helen of Troy, Goddess, Princess, Whore*, Bettany Hughes, Jonathan Cape, 2005, p.198.
3. *De Bello Gallico* Book V.1.
4. Based on translation into English by H.J. Edwards, Harvard University Press, 1917, of *De Bello Gallico* Book V.2.
5. Op. cit. Chapter V. 9. The Britons had, as Caesar learned later from prisoners, assembled on the shore in large companies but, alarmed at the host of ships, they had withdrawn from the shore and concealed themselves on the high ground.
6. *Venetian Ships and Shipbuilders in the Renaissance*, Frederic Chapin Lane, 1934 ('Lane'), p.143.
7. Lane, op. cit., p.141, by kind permission of Johns Hopkins University Press.
8. The Broadway Travellers series translated and edited by Malcolm Letts, Chap XX, p.170, George Routledge & Sons, 1926.

9. Lane, op. cit., p.144, by kind permission of Johns Hopkins University Press.

10. Ibid., p.212.

11. *Shipbuilders of the Venetian Arsenal*, Richard Davis, 1991, Johns Hopkins University Press, p.24.

12. Based on information kindly provided to the author by Guido Ercole, author of 'Galeazze', Gruppo Modellistico Trentino di studio e ricerca storica, Trento, 2010, ISBN 978-88-902511-7-70.

13. See Chapter 12.

14. *The Bridge to France*, Edward N. Hurley, reprinted by Kessinger Publishing, ISBN 9781419155338, p.94.

15. Hurley, op. cit., p.97.

16. See cartoon in the *New York Herald*, 10 February 1918, a clear pun on a 'piggy bank', which is normally used for saving money!

17. *SS Jeremiah O'Brien: The history of a Liberty Ship*, Capt. Walter W. Jaffee, The Glencannon Press, Palo Alto, 2008.

18. Ibid.

19. *Liberty: The Ships that Won the War*, Peter Elphick, 2001, Chatham Publishing, p.26, (Peter Elphick), with kind permission.

20. Peter Elphick, op. cit., p.27, with kind permission.

21. Within four months of the start of the war more than 215 merchant ships had been sent to the bottom. *ABS Workhorse of the Fleet: A History of the Liberty Ships*, Gus Bourneuf Jr, published by American Bureau of Shipping, 1990, p.7.

22. TNA reference PRO ADM 1/10278. © Crown Copyright published here under OGL.

23. *The Lessons of the Liberties*, Robert T. Young, Chairman and President of the American Bureau of Shipping, 1974.

24. Ibid.

25. Peter Elphick, op. cit., pp.18–19, with kind permission.

26. Tyne and Wear Archives DS JLT/6/1/1, Peter Elphick, op. cit., p.68, with kind permission.

27. See Chapter 17 for speech of President Franklin D. Roosevelt.

28. Statement of President Roosevelt released to the Press on 25 September 1943 prior to Victory Fleet Day on 27 September 1943. See also *New York Times*, 26 September 1943.

29. Peter Elphick op. cit., p.80, with kind permission.

30. Ibid., p.106.

31. National Archives Building, Washington DC-Record Group (RG) 178, Entry NC-51, Minutes of Commission Meetings 29 September 1936–23 May 1950 Vol. 46, pp.20100–20101.
32. Peter Elphick, op. cit. p.105, with kind permission.
33. *Where Ships are Born 1346–1946*, J.W. Smith and T.S. Holder, 1947, Thomas Reed and Company Ltd, p.2.
34. Ibid.
35. *Newcastle Daily Journal*, 17 August 1863.
36. *Palmers of Jarrow*, Jim Cuthbert and Ken Smith, 1964, ISBN 185795.

17. Ship Launches and Politics

1. *Mariner's Mirror*, Vol. 88, p.202, 'Empire, Naval Pageantry and Public Spectacles', R.D. Thomas.
2. *Dreadnoughts – A Photographic History*, Roger D. Thomas and Brian Patterson, The History Press, ISBN 978 0 7524 5695 9, p.53.
3. Naval Intelligence Division, Admiralty – German Battleship *Bismarck* – Interrogation of Survivors, August 1941, CB 4051 (24), p.10, Part IV Early History and Trials.
4. Courtesy FDR Presidential Library's Collections.
5. Discours du General de Gaulle pour le lancement de France le 11 Mai 1960.

18. Launch Day Gifts and Launch Cards

1. See Chapter 9.
2. *A Daughter's Tale*, Mary Soames, 2011 ISBN 9780812 993332.
3. Tyne and Wear Archives DX1454.
4. *Pembroke Dockyard and the Old Navy*, Lieutenant Commander Lawrie Phillips, 2014, The History Press, p.175.
5. National Maritime Museum Archives P&O/91/19.
6. *The Ships of Pembroke Dock*, Phil Carradice, Amberley Press, 2013, p.142.

19. Launch Miscellany

1. See Chapter 2.
2. See Chapter 13.3.
3. *On the Crown*, Demosthenes, ed. Harvey E. Yunis, 2001.
4. See *Greek Oared Ships*, J.S. Morrison and R.T. Williams, 1968, Cambridge University Press, p.183, and *Financing the Athenian Fleet*, Vincent Gabrielsen, 1994, Johns Hopkins University Press.

5. *The Reforms of Peter the Great*, Evgenii Anisimov, 1993.
6. *Buckler's Hard and its Ships*, John Second Lord Montagu of Beaulieu, 1909, pp.29–30.
7. See Chapter 10.
8. See the launch of the dreadnought battleship HMS *Iron Duke* at Portsmouth on 12 October 1912 by the Duchess of Wellington, when the traditional words for the launch of Dreadnoughts were used: 'I wish good luck to the *Iron Duke* and all those who sail in her.'
9. J.L. Thompson and Sons Centenary Brochure, 1946.
10. 'We make ships', Tom Packard Secker & Warburg, 1989, ISBN 0436369605.
11. *Admiralty Manual of Seamanship*, August 1966 Vol. IV Chapter 14, under Naval Ceremonial 'When in 1964 the Board of Admiralty was integrated into the Defence Council, the office of Lord High Admiral reverted to the Sovereign.'

Index

rituals performed at ship launch
ceremonies by seafarer
seeking supernatural or divine
protection for his new ship and
those who will sail in her, general
comments, 8, 275
rollers:
launch of Argonauts ship over rollers
described by Apollonius, 21
hlunn-rod, Viking folklore, 39
'roller reddening' at ship launch
by Carthaginians over captured
Roman soldiers, 40
rollers, vulcanized air bags modern
use of, to launch ship, 33
Rondefjell, oil tanker, launched 1951 in
two halves, naming, 219
Roosevelt, John Franklin, President of
United States of America (USA):
admiration for RMS *Mauretania,* 96
speech on Victory Fleet Day (launch
of Liberty Ships) 26 September
1943, 249
'ugly duckling' epithet, Liberty
Ship, 248
Rossiia, 120/128 gun ship of Russian
Imperial navy, launch 1839 from
covered yard, 187
Royal Albert HMS, launch Woolwich
1854, named by Queen Victoria,
launch casket symbolically made
with timber from HMS *Victory,*
128
Royal Dockyards:
closure of, 130
establishment and location of, 111
gun signal to announce launch,
safety of spectators, 116
launching caskets (mallet and chisel)
tradition at, 126-8
launching casket ceremony
described, 127
gradual end of tradition, 128-9
timber from HMS *Victory* used, 127

Master Shipwrights (from 1875
known as 'Chief Constructors')
tradition of gratuity of silver plate
on successful launch, 121
attempts to abolish custom, 124
cash alternative, 125
disputes as to entitlement, 124
Home Dockyard Instructions
1875/Home Dockyard
Regulations of various dates,
regulating expenditure on
launch caskets, 128-9
origin of plate gratuity custom, 121
permission to launch from Navy
Board, and from 1832 Admiralty
Board in lieu, 113, 128
Refreshment for dockyard workers, 120
Royal booths, 115
wine product of British Empire to
be used, 129
Royal George, royal sailing yacht, 1817
launch, 145
Royal launching and christening, 143-155
opportunity to make public speech,
154
Royal personages at launch, higher
expenditure permitted when
present, 143
Royal Prayer at christening of ships
and how it has evolved, 269
Royal yachts, launch of, 143
26 yachts built in Royal dockyards
1660-1688, 144
christening of royal yacht by reigning
monarch, RY *Britannia,* 148
rarely attended by members of Royal
family, 143-5; compare regular
attendance by Tsar or members
of his family at launch of Russian
Imperial yachts, 146
Rurik, battleship Russsian imperial
navy
launch 1906 Barrow in Furness, 192
blessing Orthodox priest, 192